Education Policy

Series Editors

Lance D. Fusarelli
North Carolina State University
Department of Education Leadership,
Policy & Human Development
Raleigh, North Carolina, USA

Frederick M. Hess
American Enterprise Institute
Washington, District of Columbia, USA

Martin West
Harvard University
Graduate School of Education
Cambridge, Massachusetts, USA

This series addresses a variety of topics in the area of education policy. Volumes are solicited primarily from social scientists with expertise on education, in addition to policymakers or practitioners with hands-on experience in the field. Topics of particular focus include state and national policy, teacher recruitment, retention, and compensation, urban school reform, test-based accountability, choice-based reform, school finance, higher education costs and access, the quality instruction in higher education, leadership and administration in K-12 and higher education, teacher colleges, the role of the courts in education policymaking, and the relationship between education research and practice. The series serves as a venue for presenting stimulating new research findings, serious contributions to ongoing policy debates, and accessible volumes that illuminate important questions or synthesize existing research.

More information about this series at
http://www.springer.com/series/14961

Ashley Rogers Berner

Pluralism and American Public Education

No One Way to School

Ashley Rogers Berner
School of Education
Johns Hopkins University
Baltimore, USA

Education Policy
ISBN 978-1-137-50223-0   ISBN 978-1-137-50224-7   (eBook)
ISBN 978-1-137-50226-1   (softcover)
DOI 10.1057/978-1-137-50224-7

Library of Congress Control Number: 2016957590

Cover image © urbanbuzz / Alamy Stock Photo

This Palgrave Macmillan imprint is published by Springer Nature
The registered company is Nature America Inc.
The registered company address is: 1 New York Plaza, New York, NY 10004, U.S.A.

For Abby and Hope

ACKNOWLEDGMENTS

I am indebted to many individuals and organizations for their generous support of this project. James Davison Hunter, founder and director of the Institute for Advanced Studies in Culture at the University of Virginia, introduced me to critical concepts in contemporary sociology and provided opportunities for me to work with some of our country's foremost scholars. It is a privilege to know and partner with John Witte, Jr., director of the Center for the Study of Law and Religion at Emory University, where I am a senior fellow. John provided counsel and encouragement throughout the writing process, and his *Religion and the American Constitutional Experiment*, now in its fourth edition, informed the legal background to this book. Rusty Reno at the Institute of Religion and Public Life offered not only a fellowship but also a serene place from where to work in Spring 2013. I owe particular thanks to David Steiner, with whom I have worked at the City University of New York (CUNY) Institute for Education Policy and now at the Johns Hopkins Institute for Education Policy; this book was made significantly stronger by his frank critique and by the myriad opportunities to engage with policymakers afforded through our work. I also wish to thank my colleagues at Hunter College's Roosevelt House Public Policy Institute and at the Johns Hopkins University School of Education. Their warm welcome has made all else possible.

Many others helped to shape this book. Mark Berner advised on nearly every chapter, pushed me toward clarity, and championed the merits of my argument as it developed. Frank Hanna, Bob Luddy, and Barbara Bryant generously underwrote the early stages of research and writing. Theresa Eileen Lynch, Anna Williams, Lauren Wilson, and John Patterson lent their talents to reviewing many of the chapters. Katherine Jo's expertise in educational philosophy led me to revise Chap. 2 completely; John Eckbert and Shanaysha Sauls played the same role with Chap. 3. I owe particular thanks to John Witte, Jr., Marc DeGirolami, and especially Mark Movsesian, for their patient explanations of constitutional law and for the important correctives they issued on Chap. 4.

All missteps, blind spots, and omissions are my own.

My deepest gratitude belongs with my two daughters, Abigail Rogers-Berner and Hopewell Rogers, without whose unstinting support and editorial assistance, this book would never have been completed. You make life worth-while. I love you.

CONTENTS

CHAPTER 1

Introduction

It is no secret that American education leaves many students behind intellectually, civically, and morally. Educational leaders disagree about *why* this is so. I argue in this book that much of the fault lies with two wrong turns that should be reversed: first, the nineteenth-century political decision to favor a uniform structure over a plural one; second, the early twentieth-century abandonment of a traditional, academic curriculum. We have been paying for these mistakes ever since. This book examines those mistakes in context and suggests a way to fix them.

The last 20 years have seen impressive movement in the right direction. Nevertheless, for most families, the structure of public education remains largely unchanged: the majority of American children still attend geographically determined, state-run schools. State-sponsored uniformity is problematic, not merely for the role it plays in lackluster educational results, but also for its incongruity with American principles of freedom.

Our students will continue to languish until we address the foundational problems that limit their future: a political arrangement that privileges the state above civil society, and a persistently entrenched pedagogy that unintentionally reinforces class divisions and disadvantages the neediest children.

Our state-operated system is held in place by three longstanding but mistaken beliefs: first, that only state schools can create good citizens; second, that only state schools can offer equal opportunities to all children; third, that any other arrangement is constitutionally suspect.

The evidence contradicts each of these claims. On citizenship: longstanding research suggests that private schools, particularly Catholic ones, often provide better civic preparation than public schools. On equity: non-public schools, and religious ones in particular, have met with success in closing the academic achievement gap. On constitutionality: in *Zelman v Simmons-Harris* (2002), the Supreme Court held that if funding for religious schools is the result of parental choice and not state action, it does not violate the US Constitution.

© The Author(s) 2017
A.R. Berner, *Pluralism and American Public Education*,
DOI 10.1057/978-1-137-50224-7_1

State laws and constitutions vary considerably, but many states have been able to enact tax credit or voucher programs that pass legal muster and support a more diverse array of educational options.

America's restrictive public education system stands in sharp contrast to the educational pluralism that other democratic nations take for granted. Most democracies have adopted what Charles Glenn calls a "civil-society" approach to education, not a "state control" one.[1] These countries assume that families should determine the atmosphere in which their children are educated, even while the government funds and regulates each school. For example, the Netherlands supports 35 different types of schools on equal footing; England, Belgium, Sweden, and most of the provinces of Canada also provide mechanisms for parental choice. The United States is the outlier among its democratic peers in financially supporting only state-operated schools.

These contrasts and this body of research are familiar to scholars who work in educational history, comparative education, and constitutional law. Many Americans, however, are unaware that other democracies fund religious schools and suspect that "the separation of church and state" would make such arrangements impossible here. Americans often associate traditional public schools with democratic citizenship, private schools with privilege. Few Americans know the story of our former pluralistic school systems and the religious prejudice that made them go away. I wrote this book to tell that story. *No One Way* represents less a new contribution than a translation. I hope it generates new conversations in boardrooms and school board meetings, around dining room tables, and on talk radio shows.

The problems of our public education system are not merely theoretical but urgent and material. A major restructuring of K-12 education is imminent, as the bills begin to come due on the massive municipal and state unfunded pension liabilities. Public education as it is currently structured is unsustainable. Now is the time to develop a new model that keeps faith with our democratic ideals, improves academic and civic outcomes, and uses financial resources responsibly.

Ultimately, the strongest argument for changing our definition of public schooling is neither financial nor academic, but rather philosophical: supporting diverse school types comports with American principles, with the American experience in every other field of public life, and indeed with our stated desire for educational equity and excellence. I will make this case more explicitly in chapters to come.

What Happened?

Our school system took its current form because of unfortunate political decisions that were made 150 years ago. My background is in history. One of the tasks of historians is imagining ourselves in a different time and place and, with as much compassion as possible, trying to understand why real people acted as they did, even if we ultimately criticize their decisions.

This task is difficult, not least because of the inescapable nature of culture, the taken-for-granted backdrop to our individual experiences and social encounters. Speaking in sociological terms, culture consists of the ideas and institutions in which we operate, the sea in which we swim. Cultures change, of course; a groundbreaking technology or powerful idea, translated into new systems and vocabularies, can alter the texture of our lives. But once the innovation becomes established, we cease to attend to it. In this sense, culture is both liberating and limiting: it liberates us from perpetual deliberation but limits our sense of what is possible.

An example: ask yourself how long it takes to get from New York to Boston. Three or four hours, right? Yes, if you live in the modern era of planes, trains, and automobiles—but not if you are traveling on foot or horseback. Or when was the last time you heard a vigorous argument for an American monarchy? Probably never. We no longer believe in the divine right of kings or use horses to transport ourselves, and our conceptual universe has adjusted accordingly. Constitutional democracy and automobiles are part of the texture of our lives, and we pay them no particular notice. We forget, of course, that neither was inevitable. Things could have developed quite differently.

In a similar way, our imaginations have adjusted to the current educational model, and we have forgotten how it evolved. It seems inevitable when in fact it is historically contingent. But to see this clearly, and to envision a different future, requires imagination and perspective, the twofold process of zooming in to examine core principles and then panning back to look at how other societies have addressed the same issues. That is what this book intends to do.

WHAT NOW?

This is what I mean by educational pluralism: changing the structure of public education so that state governments fund and hold accountable a wide variety of schools, including religious ones, but do not necessarily operate them. Such educational pluralism provides a better way to train an increasingly diverse generation of young people in the habits of academic excellence, moral clarity, and democratic citizenship. Educational pluralism offers a *different way of doing public education* by accommodating both individual belief and the common good. And it suggests a way out of the winner-takes-all mentality that characterizes so many educational debates today. Within this new framework, we must also continue to raise academic expectations by embracing a content-rich, subject-oriented liberal arts curriculum. Initiatives such as the Common Core State Standards (CCSS) are a necessary but insufficient step in this direction.

This book focuses more on the structure of education than on the content, mostly because the latter has been so well addressed by others. Diane Ravitch and E.D. Hirsch come to mind, but many scholars have demonstrated the benefits of a traditional curriculum for closing the achievement gap. Chapters 2 and 6 do touch on pedagogy, insofar as it pertains to educational philosophy and the limitations of a plural structure.

WHY NOW?

The case for educational pluralism would have been impossible to make even 20 years ago. It is possible now only because some districts and states are correcting both wrong turns, despite political obstacles and persistent cultural reflexes.

Recent reforms have changed the landscape, particularly in big cities. Accountability structures, tougher standards, online education, charter schools, vouchers, and tax credits, have changed the educational experience of hundreds of thousands of children and their families. This makes it possible to contemplate rewriting the rules all the way down. In sociological terms, the plausibility structure has changed: what was inconceivable 30 years ago is now conceivable, because we have seen, experienced, and studied it. The challenge lies in arguing, against vested interests and against our cultural imaginations, that what families in some urban charter schools experience should be the norm across the country and, moreover, should be expanded to include religious and pedagogically distinctive schools as well.

The knowledge basis of a strong education presents a different challenge. The liberal arts curriculum (a rich and chronological engagement with literature, history, political philosophy, advanced math and science, plus fluency in at least one foreign language) was dismantled over a hundred years ago. The chief consequence is a particular dilemma for those who would deepen the academic content of K-12 education: the number of Americans who have experienced the liberal arts ideal is now quite small. This means that, in contrast to their counterparts in Finland or Singapore, far too few American adults ever master that depth of learning, or even understand what they are missing.

In the cases of both structure and content, the cultural force of habit is strong. It is not unprecedented, even in our young country, to challenge entire institutions and the attitudes that sustain them: slavery is the most profound example, but not the only one. It is my hope that, in clarifying and then questioning our system's historical and philosophical foundations, this book will provide a grammar for change.

WHAT I AM NOT ARGUING

I am not proposing a libertarian, market-based approach to education. This is popular in some quarters and is compelling to some; see Terry Moe and John Chubb's classic book on bureaucracy or James Tooley's work on low-cost but high-achieving private education in developing nations.[2] Nor am I arguing for the "privatization of education," a term regularly used to describe (and decry) vouchers and tax credits. Educational pluralism does not mean casting common purpose to the wind; it does not mean leaving all decisions in the hands of individual parents or businesses. Rather, educational pluralism represents a middle path: it accepts that the education of the young is a community concern in which all of us have an interest—hence the government regulation and oversight—but also that, because education entails moral commitment (see Chap. 2), it should honor the beliefs of the nation's families (up to a point, of course). Because the "school choice" movement has an inevitably libertarian association, I avoid that term.

Second, I am not arguing that educational pluralism will, of itself, solve the spectrum of problems that plague our system; it cannot. Put differently, accommodation is not enough; it is necessary but not sufficient for educational excellence. A plural structure makes space for the best of what education can and should be. That space, however, must be carefully tended and wisely used (see Chap. 6).

Finally, I cannot claim that educational pluralism does not generate new problems, because, of course, it does. We will look at some of those problems throughout the book.

THE BOOK

The book begins with educational theory and ends with practice. Chapter 2 discusses the three primary questions that schooling inevitably answers (intentionally or not): What is the nature of the child? What is the purpose of education? What is the role of the teacher? In answering these questions, educational philosophies draw upon deeper commitments and assumptions about human beings and what a life well lived looks like. The chapter then describes ways these questions are answered in different school contexts. I will argue that different approaches to education have deep significance, and that it is inappropriate (and intellectually dishonest) to enforce a uniform design.

Chapter 3 explores the dilemma of managing diverse beliefs within liberal democracies. I examine theoretical contrasts that play out in democratic societies through various angles: between pluralism and secularism, republican and liberal secularism, and what citizenship requires of our schools. I argue that a plural educational system rests upon a more democratic view of the relationship between the individual, the state, and society.

The next two chapters address Americans' visceral objections to educational pluralism. Chapter 4 disputes the commonly held "separation of church and state" argument and sets out the nuanced trajectory of Supreme Court decisions. The chapter examines the historical context in which our country adapted a uniform public school system and in which states enacted constitutional amendments that shut down plural funding. Chapter 5 challenges the belief that non-public schools undermine democratic citizenship and fail to narrow the academic achievement gap. This chapter examines existing research on citizenship formation and academic outcomes, addresses concerns about public accountability, and concludes that, within certain constraints, plural institutions are more responsive to the public, not less.

Chapter 6 talks about what educational pluralism *cannot* do: of itself, it cannot automatically create strong academic outcomes, nor close the achievement gap, nor maintain the integrity of distinctive school cultures. This chapter explores academic content and educational distinctiveness, with a dual focus upon how other democracies negotiate core curricula and examinations (and to what effect), and how other nations' intentional schools maintain (or fail to maintain) a unique mission and atmosphere. This chapter also sets out a theory of appropriate limits to educational freedoms, as well as some of the thornier issues that will pertain, including creationism versus evolution and the way that schools respond to LGBTQIA (lesbian, gay, bisexual, transgender, queer, intersex, and asexual) lifestyles.

Chapter 7 provides examples of major changes in educational philosophies (England's educational psychology) and structures (Canada, Finland), and locates them within the Collins/Hunter/Smith theory of social change. The chapter then summarizes the argument and outlines how a new structure might develop, and what the barriers to change might be. The book concludes on an optimistic note: American education is already moving toward what other countries consider normative, and, with a political theory that affirms the importance of educational freedom and a vocabulary that honors both individual belief and the common good, structural change is very much possible for the first time in well over a hundred years.

A few caveats. While I have taught in a variety of contexts, I have never made education policy. My academic background is in modern history, specifically the history of modern social movements and what makes them successful—or not—in changing the world. Thus, my arguments in this book fly at 30,000 feet above the political realities that influence education in Memphis, San Diego, or Washington, D.C. My colleagues on the front lines of policy-making understand the difficulties of forging change in ways that I do not. My purpose is not to set out a coherent strategy by which to implement educational pluralism but, rather, to challenge the framework in which education policy is made in the first place.

Second, although I refer to research that suggests an empirical advantage to distinctive schools and plural systems, I am not, in the end, arguing for the superiority of every school of choice and every plural system. There are simply too many factors that influence educational outcomes—from student demographics to teacher preparation and school funding—to make that claim. My argument to an American audience is more modest and straightforward: we should stop sentimentalizing the traditional public school and open ourselves up to a different way of doing public education. There is nothing to fear and much to gain from doing so.

NOTES

1. Charles L. Glenn, *Contrasting Models of State and School: A Comparative Historical Study of Parental Choice and State Control*, 1st ed. (Continuum, 2011).
2. John E. Chubb and Terry M. Moe, *Politics, Markets & America's Schools* (Washington, DC: Brookings Institution, 1990), James Tooley, *The Beautiful Tree: A Personal Journey Into How the World's Poorest People Are Educating Themselves*, 1st ed. (Cato Institute, 2009).

CHAPTER 2

Educational Philosophies and Why They Matter

Education initiates and indoctrinates children into a particular view of the world and of their place in it. As Charles Glenn wrote in *The Myth of the Common School* (1988), "Formal education ... presents pictures or maps of reality that reflect, unavoidably, particular choices about what is certain and what in question, what is significant and what unworthy of notice. No aspect of schooling can be truly neutral."[1]

IN WHAT SENSE?

The school's atmosphere and priorities, its traditions, the management of student discipline, the curriculum and how it is taught, the way adults relate to one another—all of these guide students' experience with the world. High-poverty schools that set high academic standards are teaching children that they are intellectually capable and that they have a wide-open future. Schools in which teachers and administrators are in and out of one another's classrooms, critiquing and challenging one another to improve, persuade children that lifelong learning is not only possible but also desirable and that excellence is something to be taken seriously. Middle schools that insist upon foreign-language fluency are informing students that the world outside their home is worthy of attention. Independent schools that let the children of major donors get away with cheating are persuading students that integrity can be sacrificed for financial gain. Religious high schools that encourage classroom debate teach students that curiosity, attentiveness, and disagreement are important aspects of the moral life; those that condemn "the wrong answer" teach students to hide from doubt. Public schools that eschew conversations about religion are teaching students that the search for God is either unimportant or too private to discuss publicly. School systems that enable a variety of beliefs and pedagogies, such as those in the Netherlands, Sweden, or many Canadian provinces, inform students that deep differences can be honored in civil society. In short, every aspect of formal education is potentially instructive about the human person,

© The Author(s) 2017
A.R. Berner, *Pluralism and American Public Education*,
DOI 10.1057/978-1-137-50224-7_2

the good society, the nature of authority, and the purpose of life itself.[2] This is true, whether or not it is intended; indoctrination can be explicit or tacit.[3]

Schooling is not the only formative domain in modern society; family, region, socioeconomic class, and media engagement—to name a few—also play a role. But schooling counts for a lot. As one English educator remarked, "Education is the only universal activity in British society, along with shopping and watching television. Education occupies at least 11 full-time years—for many people, with nursery and university, 16 years."[4] This places the USA, as a country, in an uncomfortable position. Instead of examining the distinctions between educational philosophies, we enforce a public school system without routinely examining the truth claims that it makes and how these claims clash or comport with other truths we may hold dear. We have habituated ourselves against seeing schools for the meaning-making institutions that they are.[5] Making the case that education is morally rich and educational philosophies diverse and important is the purpose of this chapter.

What Are Educational Philosophies?

Educational philosophies answer the questions of *how we should educate the child and why*. These questions do not stand on their own, however. They automatically engage deeper understandings of human nature, the meaning of human life, the source of authority, moral responsibility, and the just society. In fact, it is impossible to say almost anything about what we want our schools to *do*—for example to make good citizens or to create a pathway to prosperity or to enable socio-emotional health—without immediately asking deeper questions about what a civically responsible person looks like and why political community is important, whether capitalism is just, or whose notion of socio-emotional health we should trust.

The structure of America's public school system makes such interrogations difficult. Why is that? Some 87 % of American K–12 students attend traditional public schools,[6] and for the vast majority, this means the zoned neighborhood school.[7] Of the rest, 4 % attend charter and 9 % private schools.[8] These numbers obscure the amount of switching between schools that goes on, since an increasing number of districts permit intra-district choice, and since parents who have the means can move their families to "better" school districts.[9] Parents want to exercise choices about their children's education and do so when given the opportunity,[10] but their criteria usually revolve around school safety and attendance first, academic attainment second.[11] Most American parents have neither the luxury nor the opportunity to explore philosophical criteria such as:

- What kind of person does this school aim to encourage and why?
- What values will my child be taught along with the mathematics table and world literature?

- How does this school make sense of success and failure?
- Am I comfortable with the school's rationale for patriotism or its framework for human sexuality?

Unlike their European counterparts, American families have become habituated not to ask.

Educational philosophies, however, are hiding in plain view. State constitutions, school district budgets, and the Supreme Court's rulings on education engage with normative (i.e., morally prescriptive) claims about human life and the just community. In *Pierce v. Society of Sisters* (1925), for example, the Court overturned an Oregon statute that required all parents to send their children to public schools under penalty of law. Aimed at outlawing Catholic education, the Oregon statute drew upon deeper beliefs about the superior "fit" of Protestantism with democratic life.[12] When the Supreme Court overturned Oregon's law, it did so not only on instrumental terms but also on philosophical ones: "The child is not the mere creature of the State; those who nurture him and direct his destiny have the right, coupled with the high duty, to recognize and prepare him for additional obligations."[13] In a later case, the Court supported the right of Jehovah's Witnesses *not* to perform the Pledge of Allegiance in schools, in equally strong language: "Freedom to differ is not limited to things that do not matter much. That would be a mere shadow of freedom. The test of its substance is the right to differ as to things that touch the heart of the existing order."[14] When the Court limited the purview of the government in *Pierce* and *Barnette*, it also asserted particular things about human beings and the good society: that our loyalties are complex, not monistic; that we can and do hold distinctive and even opposing views about ultimate reality; that democratic life requires us to honor these differences in practice as well as in theory.

The American conflict over school segregation also brought educational philosophies into relief. In the early twentieth century, fully half of the American states either required or permitted "separate but equal" schools for black and white children. These laws in turn reflected deeper beliefs about racial differences and the inherent superiority of whites. For instance, in 1879 the Kansas legislature allowed towns and cities to "organize and maintain separate schools for the education of its white and colored children, except for the high schools...."[15] Separate schools remained the norm when, in 1948, Topeka's Superintendent of Negro Schools claimed that, "Negroes are not ready for equality."[16] Such laws and comments are shot through with assumptions about racial capacities. When the Supreme Court overturned these laws (*Brown v. Board of Education*, 1954), it did so on philosophical grounds:

> To separate them from others of similar age and qualifications solely because of their race generates a feeling of inferiority as to their status in the community that may affect their hearts and minds in a way unlikely ever to be undone.

> Segregation of white and colored children in public schools has a detrimental effect upon the colored children. The impact is greater when it has the sanction of the law, for the policy of separating the races is usually interpreted as denoting the inferiority of the Negro group ... Any language in contrary to this finding is rejected. We conclude that in the field of public education the doctrine of "separate but equal" has no place. Separate educational facilities are inherently unequal.[17]

The battle over school integration was, first and foremost, a philosophical one that highlighted opposing views about the significance of race upon the value of human beings and their standing before the law.

Educational philosophies are also evident in school mission statements and policies, and when we look closely, we see that they differ. The website of a Muslim school in California, for instance, states: "The mission of Granada Islamic School is to provide quality academic and Islamic education in a community that nurtures a strong Muslim identity, fosters brotherhood, and strengthens moral character."[18] This mission statement conveys the Muslim belief in the unity of the human person and the inseparability of spiritual, intellectual, and community life. A parent looking at the school would expect to find, at a minimum, teachers who are religiously observant, instruction on the tenets and sacred texts of Islam, and an approach to learning that values faithfulness above ability. She would not expect to find a libertarian approach to sexuality or a winner-takes-all attitude about school sports.

PS 8, a magnet middle school in Brooklyn, also emphasizes the values it seeks to promote: "PS 8 is a learning community dedicated to creativity, academic excellence and intellectual curiosity, with the aim of developing life-long learners and engaged citizens. We are committed to the intellectual, artistic, moral, emotional, social and physical development of each child."[19] A visitor might expect to see a tight-knit community, lots of hands-on learning, a project-based curriculum, and teachers who care about children's social and emotional needs. The spiritual or religious needs of the children are neither mentioned nor, one expects, explored in the classroom. Unlike Granada Islamic School, PS 8 rests upon a secular foundation.

Boston's Pacific Rim Charter School offers still another ethos, drawn from very different philosophical reserves: "Our mission is to empower urban students of all racial and ethnic backgrounds to achieve their full intellectual and social potential by combining the best of the East—high standards, discipline and character education—with the best of the West—a commitment to individualism, creativity and diversity."[20] Pacific Rim has selected the values from both East and West that it wants to nurture; its public ceremonies, curricular offerings, and articulated vision reinforce both individual responsibility and commitment to community.[21]

These three schools are distinct from one another. In contrast to PS 8, Pacific Rim articulates the rationale behind the virtues it wants to enjoin; in contrast to Granada Islamic School, Pacific Rim welcomes—and affirms—

diverse viewpoints among its students and faculty. The extent to which any school fulfills its mission is a separate question. The point is that ideals differ.

Educational philosophies are also present in classroom routines. David T. Hansen's elegant piece, "From Role to Person: The Moral Layerdness of Classroom Teaching," explores the philosophical dimensions of how a teacher manages her students' turn-taking. The management of turn-taking is "moral" in the sense of *mores*, the Latin term for "custom," or "an encompassing customary way of regarding roles and their occupants," he writes. This "usually implicit, often invisible moral order" establishes the teacher's authority, his relationship with the students, and theirs with one another.[22] Such practices are "moral" in another sense: They reflect the teacher's personal qualities, regard for individual students, and reason for being in the classroom in the first place.[23] Whom the teacher calls on, how she corrects students who talk out of turn, and how attentive she is to the varying needs of individual students influence how her students experience the classroom and themselves. For example, Ms. Smythe is "alert" to a sixth grade girl who was not called on in a given class, "acknowledge[ing] publicly her hopes and expectations, even if she cannot, in the name of fairness, cede her the floor immediately." In *seeing* this student, writes Hansen, Ms. Smythe not only honors the individual student but also helps all of them "recognize ways in which their personal conduct and their opportunities for learning are bound up with one another."[24] Likewise, Father Maran's response to a student's snapping his fingers for attention not only instructed the student in considerate behavior but also illuminated Father Maran's sense of dignity and self-worth:

> During one of Father Maran's eleventh-grade math lessons a student eager to be called upon snapped his fingers loudly as he waved his hand. Father Maran cut his behavior short: "Uh-uh!" he declared while shaking his head, "'Father Maran the teacher' is here today, not 'Father Maran the puppy.' I don't respond to that." As classmates grinned and chortled, the rebuked student spontaneously straightened himself and raised his hand again, at which point the teacher nodded permission to speak.[25]

Hansen calls such interactions "moral threads," because they "illuminate ways in which feelings about rights and obligations lie just beneath the surface of the behavior."[26] Hansen writes elsewhere that, "Many classroom exchanges typically discussed in instrumental terms can be perceived as symbolically important."[27] Based upon years of classroom observations, he argues that, "It is impossible to teach a subject in a classroom without also teaching, or at least inviting, dispositions toward that subject and toward one's fellow human beings."[28]

Sociologists sometimes call the tacit moral messages of the classroom "the hidden curriculum," or the "routine, embedded practices of classroom life that shape children's orientations in ways that are consistent with the demands of adult life." This curriculum "directs students' attention through invisible means, rather than through overt and explicit instruction."[29] Steven Brint's research team studied 64 elementary school classrooms and found that everyday routines prepared children for "the fast-paced, multiple task environments that many middle-class adults face in their jobs."[30] "Token economies, group projects, activity centers and rotations" implicitly "reinforced the market economy and personal choice," even though such concepts were not discussed or necessarily desired.[31] Such studies of the hidden curriculum suggest that more is going on in the classroom than we may intend or recognize. They also reinforce my larger point, which is that education is inherently normative.

Classroom *omissions and evasions* also betray underlying philosophies. Many teachers, constrained by an increasingly prescribed curriculum and by a concern about bringing offense—particularly one that might result in First Amendment litigation—shy away from philosophically rich debates. One public school teacher described how he avoided a "potentially volatile" debate on human cloning:

> It was early in my high school teaching career, in the middle of a discussion about human cloning. Cheryl had been arguing for limits on scientific research, and her hand shot up again from the back of the classroom. "We shouldn't play God," she insisted.

> Maybe not, but can we talk about God? Or at least about the ways in which religious beliefs influence our lives in a diverse society? Cheryl made her comment in the midst of an eleventh-grade English class discussion of Aldous Huxley's *Brave New World*. The chilling images of the Hatchery, where embryos on conveyor belts were genetically modified, had struck a chord with my students.

The teacher, Robert Kunzman, "maneuvered around the comment" and refocused on Huxley. Kunzman noted, "If an administrator had been observing my class, she probably would have complimented my deft handling." For him, however, "it didn't feel like a fine pedagogical moment," because it indicated his unwillingness to grapple, with his students, with differing notions of the good—"and this grappling is the responsibility of informed, respectful citizenship."[32] Kunzman claims his experience is typical: "Versions of my English class 'pedagogical evasion' episode play out in classrooms throughout the country, and extend across the curriculum."[33]

Katherine Simon researched this and agrees, "Although moral and existential issues arise frequently, they are most often shut down immediately. If moral issues are not shut down completely, they are often relegated to assignments for individuals, rather than explored in public classroom discussion."[34] Simon studied literature, history, and biology classes in one public and two religious schools. She found that, despite the facts that, "moral and existential questions are at the core of the disciplines" and "most people find moral and existential questions fascinating," the classrooms she visited sidelined them. Fewer than

2 % of the classes she visited engaged in any depth on matters of life, death, meaning, and purpose.[35]

Lack of philosophical depth is not a necessary outcome of our uniform public school system. Public schools are allowed to teach *about* religion and philosophy, and many do. The deeper problem is our lack of attention to the normative claims that schools inevitably reinforce across all subjects, routines, and curricula.

Even asserting the normative nature of education can be done from diverse philosophical stances. Peter McLaren, taking a Marxist view, holds that human life is "political in the ideological sense,"[36] and that the existing school system "is premised upon generating the living commodity of labor-power" and is about "social reproduction" in its most pernicious sense: co-opting people into capitalism.[37] Instead of tinkering around with pedagogy or adding a new "social justice" component, McLaren wants to prepare students to "transform the larger social order."[38] The moral urgency and priority here are clear. McLaren's approach to schooling makes no sense apart from the economic structuralism upon which it is based.

The Catholic Church also claims that education is morally charged, but for a different reason: human beings are "made in the image of God" and thus education inevitably involves "man whole and entire, soul united to body in unity of nature, with all his faculties natural and supernatural." It is inadequate to separate religious instruction from the other subjects: "every other subject taught [must] be permeated with Christian piety. If this is wanting, if this sacred atmosphere does not pervade … little good can be expected from any kind of learning."[39] Thus, only a Catholic education can possibly capture the truth about human beings and thus prepare students to serve the world that God has made. Like the Marxist view above, this makes no sense apart from the traditions and sacred texts that inform Catholic beliefs.

Finally, our own beliefs and assumptions influence how we interpret schools. What does annual, standardized testing imply about the child and the purpose of education, for instance? To different people the testing regime seems to honor the dignity and equality of children, or to reinforce capitalist oppression, or to diminish the child's creative impulses. Or take the issue of school uniforms: to one side, they are oppressive and infringe on children's autonomy; to another, they liberate children from consumerist comparisons. It depends on prior assumptions about who children are and what they need.

Conversely, which *omissions* do we see in the educational system and how do we interpret them? Again, it depends on who does the looking. Not everyone will notice that schools require *three years*, but not *fluency*, in a foreign language. Not every researcher finds it worrying that few public schools teach about world religions. Few American parents know that Finland has an academically rigorous national curriculum and requires their teachers to have master's degrees in the subjects they teach, or that some Canadian provinces fund Catholic, Protestant, Jewish, Muslim, and Inuit schools as well as home schooling. What we notice in the first place, and how we interpret it, depends upon our point of view.

There are philosophical assumptions built into every school mission statement, research report, staffing protocol, disciplinary code, curriculum, district budget, and state education law. We may be tempted to elide the differences and focus on what seem to be consensus goals, such as "ensuring equity and excellence for all students." But such a strategy begs too many questions. Equity and excellence (to name only two common aims) are second-order concerns that we hope would pertain to *all* school systems, public or private, religious or secular, and to how we fund and regulate the entire educational ecosystem. The prior questions are why equity and excellence matter in the first place, and on what terms. What if "excellence" looks slightly different in schools that have different aims? What if "equity" means something different in a Waldorf and a Jesuit school or an activist versus a religious pedagogy? Our common commitments—such as those to equity and excellence—may be derived from different beliefs about the world and thus carry distinct if not opposing consequences for how we structure education.

Starting from First Principles

In reflecting normative claims, education is no different from other human institutions. As so many have argued—Polanyi of the natural sciences;[40] Gadamer of the human sciences;[41] Sandel of political life;[42] MacIntyre of philosophy,[43] to name a few—there is no neutral place from which to view the world. All of us "arrange the world of ideas, people, and authority along the lines of belief congruence."[44] As political philosopher William Galston put it, "Every way of life represents a selection and ordering of values from a much wider field of possibilities."[45] The question is how clearly we see this when it comes to education—or not.

For several years, I taught comparative religion and ethics to extremely bright high school students. Instead of jumping headlong into case studies of ethical dilemmas, we took our time getting to know different philosophies of life and how they played out in the real world. For instance, we studied the Hebrew Scriptures using the Talmudic Hevruta method, which pairs students to read out loud, re-read, consider, and discuss important passages. I read parts of Abraham Joshua Heschel's *The Sabbath* to them out loud. We explored Kabbalistic thought. Rabbis who represented different traditions within Judaism spent hours with our class, explaining the practices of the faith and what *being a good Jew* meant in different communities. We followed the same model with Christianity, Islam, Hinduism, and Buddhism before turning to non-religious philosophies from Plato to twentieth-century postmodernists.

In every case, we tried to place our texts within their historical contexts and to seek examples of practice. For instance, we explored Stoicism alongside of Vice Admiral James Stockdale's essay on how Stoic philosophy enabled him to cope with years as a prisoner of war in Vietnam.[46] We studied Jeremy Bentham and discussed Princeton professor Peter Singer's use of utilitarian philosophy in bioethics. We spent weeks with Marx, working through his economic structuralism, teasing out its implications for the present day, and tracing structuralist thought through other iterations such as Shulamith Firestone's *Dialectic of Sex* (1970). The class had a field day with Nietzsche, delighting to find his legacy represented—and misrepresented—in modern culture. And so on. By the time we discussed actual ethical problems, such as under what conditions abortion should be legal or whether capital punishment was ethical, my students could articulate the ways in which a libertarian, a Catholic, or a Marxist (to name a few) might begin to approach it. While not aiming for *the* correct interpretation, they could nevertheless outline the questions each follower would bring the table and what her ultimate concerns might be. They could work backward, too; they could read serious essays on the American invasion of Iraq or the growth of Walmart stores in Mexico and discern the perspective from which each author wrote. In the process, they developed a more finely honed understanding of their own core beliefs and where those beliefs cohered or clashed with those of others.

I recount this by way of illustrating that, when we are trained to look for them, we find the connection between philosophy and practice everywhere. Educational philosophies are no different. They emanate from richer, deeper philosophical explorations of life such as those that my students studied every year. Educational philosophies are generative, too; they yield distinctive school practices and atmospheres.

I am simplifying for illustration. But consider how a school founded by a religious community might differ in important ways from one founded by an expressivist, a materialist, or a structuralist.

Religious believers understand human life to be primarily about connection with the divine. Believers craft their lives from the resources of faith: their engagement with sacred texts, religious community, the sacred presence, and religious practices. For them, the physical world does not exhaust reality but, rather, points beyond itself. Human life is to be lived in faithfulness to the sacred encounter, from which it derives its ultimate meaning.

For religious educators, the child is multi-faceted—body, soul spirit, and mind—and education should nurture all of them. Every aspect is meant ultimately to serve the divine plan; it does not stand on its own. Religious schools therefore place a high premium on spiritual formation, which means (among other things) becoming attentive to a higher power and living one's life in response.

For example, Regis High School in New York City believes each (male) student "has unique worth" and should be "'a man for others,' a Christian humanist who would share with others the gifts he has been given and, above all, the gift of himself."[47] Theological training of students is extensive, as are the service requirements—for juniors, 25 visits to a single site, and for seniors, weekly service.[48] Regis's academic chops earn it a top place on national high school rankings, but this is not seen in instrumental terms within the community.

Rather, "the significance of [a student's] own life is largely determined by the difference he makes in the lives of other people." Religious schools generally expect teachers to exercise formational influence upon children. Regis High School, for instance, believes that adults are there to "assist," "exercise a positive and constructive influence," and "work to provide [the student] with the knowledge, training and challenges commensurate with his high level of ability."[49] Given the academic rigor and the spiritual and emotional goals of the school, this is no small task.

Put differently, for many believers, education aims to raise children who identify with the faith and who carry its principles into the world. The Modern Orthodox Ramaz School in New York City exemplifies this approach. The Ramaz mission statement notes a commitment to charity for all people, the building of character, love of Torah, support for democratic principles, and "a sense of responsibility for the Jewish people and all of mankind."[50] This responsibility comes from Scripture and extends to the whole world: "An informed love and reverence of *Torah* is critical to the observance of *mitzvot* relating to God and humanity, commitment to the Jewish people, and responsibility for all humankind and the physical world. We foster intellectual honesty, a spirit of objectivity, respect for diversity of views, as well as the equality and dignity of all people."[51] The school explicitly notes the intertwined nature of the religious and the secular and was created in the 1930s to challenge the norm of separating the two: "[the founders] envisioned a *yeshivah* day school in which a child would not experience an intellectual or emotional clash between being a Jew and an American."[52]

In contrast, an expressivist philosophy places paramount importance upon self-development. More often termed "Romanticism," this view of the world rejects any notion of discoverable truths that lie outside of the individual's unique experience.[53] Because there is no such thing as a universally understood "good life," a school's job is to help each student discover *her* good life. Authority exists, of course, but its source is the individual self, which is *made* instead of given.

The best-selling educational philosopher in England's inter-war period, Percy Nunn, summed it up this way:

> *There can be no universal aim of education* if that aim is to include the assertion of any particular ideal of life; for there are as many ideals as there are persons. Educational efforts must, it would seem, be limited to securing for everyone the conditions under which Individuality is most completely developed—that is, by enabling him to make his original contribution to the variegated whole of human life as full and as truly characteristic as his nature permits.[54]

Because this educational philosophy sees psychological wellbeing and self-expression as antecedent to intellectual growth, many adherents resist "received" knowledge that comes in the form of set texts or chronological history unless these sources serve as fodder for self-expression.[55]

Teachers play a less directive role in an expressivist than a religious class-room. The reflections of A.S. Neill, for example, were popular among teacher educators in the 1960s and 1970s. Neill's *Summerhill* was "a surprise best-seller and one of the most influential books of the era;" it was required reading in at least 600 university courses and sold 200,000 copies a year by 1970.[56] Neill rejected the directive role of teachers: "If adults try to force their values on children, there is bound to be some warping of child nature."[57] Another expressivist stated more quietly, "The first care of teachers and parents should be to get out of Nature's way and allow her free scope, and avoid excessive checks and inhibitions."[58]

The modern-day constructivist movement draws upon expressivist princi-ples. One constructivist textbook opens with the words, "The image of the child [is] a competent, creative, powerful force to learn from rather than to teach to."[59] Teacher and students form a community of active learners. The textbook continues, "the only thing that qualifies us as teachers is that we have a lot to offer," presumably because of age and experience.[60]

A materialist view of the world holds that there is nothing transcendent about life. Human beings are carbon-based organisms; human behavior expli-cable according to instincts, neurochemical reactions, or genetic make-up; and human life meaningful according to its fitness for survival, economic competi-tion, or heroic service. Materialist accounts of education assume that, as society industrializes and diversifies, religious beliefs will disappear as will the need for religious schools.[61]

Materialist philosophies come in many different guises, and some of them have influenced American education. Herbert Spencer's application of evolu-tionary theory to education was influential across the English-speaking world in the late nineteenth and early twentieth centuries.[62] His *Education: Intellectual, Moral, and Physical* (1859) gained broad readership in the USA.[63] Spencer sought to apply evolutionary doctrine to all spheres of life; he coined the term "survival of the fittest," which Charles Darwin adopted in later editions of *The Origin of Species*. Spencer thought that what mattered most about children was their need to survive a competitive world. "The competition of modern life" wrote Spencer, "is so keen that few can bear the required application with-out injury ... Hence it is becoming of especial importance that the training of children should ... fit them mentally for the struggle before them ... and make them physically fit to bear its excessive wear and tear."[64] Not surprisingly, the first order of life was "deliberate self-preservation."[65] Spencer supported schools that were vocational and "modern," not oriented toward explorations of meaning and purpose.

An alternative materialist view stresses the child's inherited capacities, not his capacity to survive evolutionary competition.[66] The child, in this view, consists of pre-determined capacities that educators judge and channel accordingly. IQ testing, tracking, and the eugenics and "mental hygiene" movements sprang from this belief. "Exact knowledge of the nature and amount of individual differences in intellect, character, and behavior is valuable to educational theory and practice," wrote psychologist Edward Thorndike, who spent his career at Teachers College, Columbia. Each student's traits could be measured:

> It is more scientific and more useful, to think of human individuals as all measured upon the same series of scales, each scale being for the amount of some one thing, there being scales for everything in human nature, and each person being recorded as zero in the case of things not appearing in his nature.[67]

Thorndike acknowledged that family culture and education shaped the expression of inherited traits, but he still maintained that children were amenable to testing to determine their individual differences and capacities. Thorndike's peer, Edward Titchener, wrote that bodies and minds were utterly reducible to quantitative data.[68] The new frontier, he wrote in 1909, was to quantify human emotion.[69]

We see materialist approaches to the child in the common practice of prescribing psychotropic medications to control student behavior. The benefits of psychiatric medications are not in dispute, but scholars note with some concern the widespread use of drugs to regulate the classroom behavior of low-SES children and, at the other extreme, to increase the performance of high-achieving college students.[70] The question to ask is: What other elements of a child's life influence behavior besides biology? Are we operating with a reductive view of the human person when we leave them out?

Despite the influence of materialist thought on education, schools reinforce it by omission instead of intention. Teaching human health from the standpoint of biology alone gives the impression that the most pertinent concerns are protection against disease or pregnancy, not the interplay between sexual behavior and emotional or spiritual health. Teacher preparation programs and public school leaders do not generally consider students' spiritual development alongside social and emotional development. This may change over time. See, for instance, Mona Abo-Zena's study of religious explorations in public kindergartens, or Lisa Miller's work on the value of preparing teachers to hold conversations with children about their religious lives.[71]

Finally, structuralist philosophies hold that the visible components of society—art, technology, social institutions, forms of government, even human psychology—are governed by a single underlying substructure. Structuralists identify the substructure differently: for Hegel, the substructure consisted of dominant ideas; for Marx, economic production; for feminists, gender relationships. However defined, the substructure acts as an oppressive force upon human society until we recognize and unmask its power.[72] While there are obvious overlaps with materialist views, structuralism is distinguished by its imperative to change the world. Its accounts of education anticipate radical change in every domain.[73] How does this play out in schools?

Economic structuralists believe that social class determines the visible aspects of culture. Peter McLaren writes that "all distinctions collapse into class."[74] Paolo Freire, author of the widely read *Pedagogy of the Oppressed* (1970), sees children as of two types: elite or oppressed.[75] Both types are alienated from their true humanity.[76] The radical teacher's job is to awaken them. Reading, writing, mathematics, are oppressive if not used in the service of revolution. Like a religious classroom but unlike an expressivist one, the structuralist classroom has a universal—not an individual—purpose. In 1932, George Counts published a popular volume called *Dare the Schools Build a New Social Order?* that wanted schools to be the vanguard of collectivism.[77] Although he was speaking about adult education, Freire thought its purpose was to unmask the false consciousness spawned by capitalism, guide students into liberation, and re-make society.[78] More recently, Peter McLaren writes, "The tradition of critical pedagogy … represents an approach to schooling that is committed to the imperatives of empowering students and transforming the larger social order in the interests of justice and equality."[79] This stance "is founded on the conviction that schooling for self and social empowerment by means of class struggle is *ethically prior* to a mastery of technical skills, which are primarily tied to the logic of the marketplace."[80] The curriculum is an oppressive tool to "prepare students for dominant or subordinate positions in the existing capitalist society," and that the purpose of education is to help students develop a class "voice," which is "the development of a consciousness of the necessity of class struggle against the rule of capital and not the formation of individual agency or bourgeois assertiveness."[81] An education that fails to radicalize students should be considered a failure.

As one might expect, such beliefs generate an activist role for the teacher.[82] She must not be above the student but rather engage in a dialogical relationship focused upon ending alienation.[83] Peter McLaren wants teachers to be "transformative intellectuals" who "shape schooling according to the logic of emancipatory interests." In addition to their emancipatory work in the classroom, teachers can "join together in a collective voice as part of a social movement dedicated to restructuring the ideological and material conditions both within and outside of schooling."[84]

The same imperative to revolution plays out in feminist and queer theory, but with the goal of changing gender relationships or heteronormative culture instead of economic production.

The activist role of the teacher seems to have particular resonance in schools of education. The President of the National Council on Teacher Quality wrote in 2013, commenting on an academic study of teacher training, that

[the activist vision] of a teacher is seen by a considerable fraction of teacher educators (although not all) as more important than preparing a teacher to be an effective instructor. This view of a teacher's role as transformational is not wrong, as teachers often serve as the means by which children overcome challenges inherent in their backgrounds. But it is one that is often taken to absurd extremes in practice. For example, a textbook used in a math course for elementary school teachers is entitled *Social Justice through Mathematics*, which explains why the view is so often disparaged.[85]

Religious, expressivist, materialist, and structuralist philosophies draw upon different sources and generate different educational priorities and practices. In practice, they are enacted not generally but specifically, within distinct traditions, such as Hasidic Judaism or Montessori. Each has its own sense of truth, authority, and meaning. Of course, no so-called worldview is hermetically sealed. In a plural society, beliefs interact and influence one another in ways that are not always obvious. Schools that operate out of strong principles sometimes employ tools from completely different philosophic systems.[86] Nor is pure idealism possible; philosophies do not float above economic, artistic, and social infrastructures but, rather, engage with and make sense of them. I explore this further in Chap. 7. Here, I have separated broad orientations for the sake of clarity and argument.[87] My point is that philosophical distinctions are not trivial; they matter for how we "do" schooling.

Educational philosophies matter profoundly for the way we do education, but the structure of American public schooling limits our capacity to see this, and worse: It encourages the hegemony of one view over the other. There is simply no way to honor a Catholic way of seeing the child in our current public education structure[88]; there is no way to create a publicly funded Inuit school or one that is based on socialist or Marxist principles. Indeed, the uniform public school system was designed precisely to limit conflict between competing ideals. And yet, of course, imposing uniformity does not avoid the problems of deep difference: It merely occludes them. This is a form of covert indoctrination, which an English educator put this way: "Indoctrination occurs when pupils are given one view of the world in such a way that they are unable to see any other."[89]

Absent the flexibility of a plural educational system, there is no space to consider the differences that exist in our educational philosophies. Recognizing the significance of distinctive and often incompatible approaches is the first step.

Toward Plural Education

A plural school system takes philosophical differences into account. It does not assume a neutral stance for any school. Rather, educational pluralism creates the conditions to support various kinds of schools within a common framework of accountability. Ideally, pluralism separates the fiscal from the operational aspects of schools. Counties with plural systems thus have a more expansive understanding of "public education," one that is not limited to a traditional neighborhood school but includes the vast array of schools (Catholic, Montessori, Cree, or otherwise) that receive support. Although some urban districts in the USA offer inter-district choice programs between schools that differ from one another in emphases and curricula, such an arrangement does not reflect the philosophical pluralism that I advocate here.

Most liberal democracies support educational pluralism through one of a number of funding mechanisms. The most common is for the government to provide a fixed percentage of the operations of non-state schools. Norway provides 85 %, Estonia 100 %, Denmark between 75 and 85 %, and Luxembourg 90 %. Any Israeli school that implements 75 % of the government's core curriculum is fully funded—whether religious, secular, Arab-language, or Hebrew-language. The Netherlands, the most educationally plural country in the world, gives block grants for staff, facilities, and operations to each of its 36 different types of schools. Half of Belgium's French-speaking students attend Catholic or independent schools that are fully funded by the state.[90] England funds all operations and 85 % of capital costs, a policy that enabled the percentage of Jewish children in Jewish day schools to increase from 20 % to more than 60 % between 1975 and 1990.[91] Still other democracies (among them Sweden and Romania) assign per-pupil funding, usually weighted according to special needs or economic disadvantage, to follow students to public or private schools.[92]

Such countries also constrain funded schools in important ways. As I explore in Chaps. 5 and 6, most educationally plural countries enforce a common curriculum and assessments, although they allow schools to teach the material according to their distinctive missions. Educationally plural systems often set the hiring and admissions standards for funded schools. Because creating a distinctive school culture requires faculty who support the school's ideals, most Canadian provinces, French-speaking Belgium, Ireland, and Italy allow schools to hire faculty on the basis of beliefs.[93] The Netherlands, Northern Ireland, and England (within constraints) also allow schools to hire on the basis of beliefs and fund belief-oriented teacher training programs.[94]

There is similar variety when it comes to admissions requirements. Norway and Slovenia require open admissions. The Netherlands and French-speaking Belgium allow religion- or philosophy-based admissions, but require that the school's beliefs have been clearly and publicly articulated in advance. France forbids admissions based on a student's religion or philosophy but requires all parents to agree to support the mission of the school.[95] England allows religious schools to give priority to students from the same religious faith, but they must not exclude non-congregants if open slots exist. These policies have been at various times contested.[96]

Americans often have visceral objections to educational pluralism, and this book explores the most important ones in Chaps. 4 and 5. In the present chapter, my argument is that plural school systems follow naturally from the understanding that educational philosophies differ in meaningful ways. Educational pluralism brings the inherent normativity of schooling into the open and implementing educational pluralism would bestow immediate intellectual and operational benefits to our school system.

Consider, for instance, the thickening of important concepts as "equity" and "excellence" when we begin with robust first principles instead of *assuming* both ideals are social goods without defending them on specific terms. Religious educators can champion equity because all humans are made in the image of God, and academic excellence because God calls us to good stewardship of our minds. Expressivist educators can champion equity because each individual's self-expression is valuable, and excellence because knowledge increases our creative capacities. Structuralists can rest their case upon the enmeshment of oppressors and oppressed and the need to free both simultaneously. Materialist educators can talk about *both* our common genetic heritage *and* our distinctive individual attributes.

We would also have more tools with which to challenge the *risks* to equity and excellence that inhere in all four approaches. There are resources from within each orientation and the specific traditions that enact them that can challenge and provoke. Religious believers may need to be reminded that intellectual cultivation is important to spiritual life, and expressivists that children need academic substance with which to work out their own identities. Structuralists who dislike systematic learning[97] may need to be reminded that the great activists of history (from Marx and Gandhi to Martin Luther King, Jr.) were exceptionally well educated and thus could articulate their arguments with intelligence and conviction. Materialist educators might explore other solutions to student behavior in addition to, or in lieu of, the neurochemical one.

Educational pluralism helps citizens maintain an awareness of the role that belief plays in education, which in turn creates space for discussion and compromise. The USA has not experienced such discussions and compromises in more than a hundred years. We have simply lost the habit. The expansion of tax credit and voucher programs makes such conversations possible again, but here, too, cultural biases are at work: opponents are quick to call such plans "the privatization of education" instead of considering the *public* benefits of diverse types of schools.[98] The far right is quick to champion "choice" on libertarian terms, instead of considering the *public* benefits of appropriate government oversight and accountability. Foregrounding the philosophical assumptions and the public nature of schooling would cut through both extremes and provide an important space for democratic formation and deliberation.

For comparison, consider the depth of discussion about education in England, which is one of many democracies that support pluralism. At issue in a Parliamentary debate in 2004: Should the government regulate the admissions policies of publicly funded religious schools?[99] Specifically, should the government require religious schools to hold open admissions instead of allowing the first seats to go to children of the same faith? I am agnostic on the substance of the debate. Of interest here are the terms and the framework of debate.

The lead Labour member who opposed regulations, Kevin McNamara, argued for the non-neutrality of education: every school must be free to create a culture that fulfilled its religious or philosophical mission. McNamara argued for the non-neutrality of secularism: the government should build a "pluralist, not a secular, society." McNamara finally argued that pluralism created space for institutional integrity *and* compromise. He mentioned, for instance, the novel way that educational leaders in Leeds had resolved the problem of three schools with uneven enrollment, two of which were Catholic:

> Instead of closing one school and leaving two schools fully subscribed with Catholics, the decision was taken to keep all three schools open, with each school taking a percentage of non-Catholic, usually Muslim, children. At the same time, there was a drive to develop an ethos to enable children of other faiths to feel at home. Prayer rooms were made available and provision was made to meet the need of Muslim girls for appropriate school uniforms. The idea of twinning Catholic schools with other schools with a significant Muslim intake was also proposed as part of this strategy.

Debates about belief and schooling are not confined to England's upper echelons of power. The number of students in Jewish, Catholic, Hindu, and Muslim schools has been rising for 20 years, and Anglican leaders are reinforcing the religious aspect of the Church of England's many schools (see pp. 126–127). The composition and emphases of these schools may change over time, but the flexible structure remains.[100]

In contrast, American families and educators live with the consequences of a uniform public school system. Teachers' professional judgments and moral autonomy are significantly diminished. Teachers' views about pedagogy, the child, and the whole project of education are overshadowed by the school in which they teach or the program in which they trained. Parents do not have the opportunity to exercise judgment about schools—unless, of course, they make enough money to move to a "better" school district or pay tuition for private schools. If their children remain in the public system, their voices are effectively muted; federal courts tend to honor the judgments of school districts above those of parents.[101] Administrators lose the chance to create intentional communities that go "all the way down." They cannot hire teachers based upon a shared commitment; they cannot refer to larger norms that might guide school culture. Most students, for their part, never encounter philosophical commitment or disagreement in a serious way. A healthy alternative would be to spend their school years within intentional communities in which adults made clear connections between beliefs and behavior. It is no use protesting that such communities would be "oppressive": *all* communities, including "neutral" public schools, exercise influence over children's formation. The question is not whether we can avoid this fact (we cannot), but rather how we can honor and regulate it in an effective way.

If education inevitably involves basic questions of human nature, meaning, and destiny, then why should one view be privileged above another? Why should progressive and traditionalist educators compete for hegemony, or secular and religious perspectives not coexist and cooperate? In a liberal democracy such as ours, why should there not be room for many different pedagogical approaches and school structures? The natural consequence of plural beliefs should be a structure that honors them. This is the subject of the next chapter.

NOTES

1. Charles Leslie Glenn, *The Myth of the Common School* (Amherst: University of Massachusetts Press, 1988), 11.
2. Ashley Berner, "Persuasion in Education," *Comment*, Spring 2013, 28–33, https://www.cardus.ca/comment/article/4609/persuasion-in-education/. A partial version of this chapter was published in the above publication.
3. Elmer John Thiessen, *Teaching for Commitment: Liberal Education, Indoctrination, and Christian Nurture* (McGill-Queen's University Press, 1993), 78.
4. Copley, Terence. 2005. *Indoctrination, Education and God: The Struggle for the Mind.* London: SPCK, vii.
5. Religious and philosophical minorities are an exception, as for example the Jehovah's Witnesses in the early twentieth century or Evangelical Protestants in the third quarter of the twentieth century.
6. United States Department of Education, "The Condition of Education at a Glance," *National Center for Education Statistics*, 2015, https://nces.ed.gov/programs/coe/ataglance.asp.
7. United States Department of Education, "The NCES Fast Facts Tool Provides Quick Answers to Many Education Questions (National Center for Education Statistics)," *National Center for Education Statistics*, 2009, https://nces.ed.gov/fastfacts/display.asp?id=6.
8. United States Department of Education, "The Condition of Education at a Glance."
9. United States Department of Education, "Public School Choice."
10. David S. Deming et al., "School Choice, School Quality and Post-Secondary Attainment" (National Bureau of Economic Research, 2011); Ashley Jochim et al., "How Parents Experience Public School Choice," Making School Choice Work Series (University of Washington Bothell: Center on Reinventing Public Education, December 2014); Ashley Jochim, "Lessons from the Trenches on Making School Choice Work," *The Brookings Institution*, August 12, 2015, http://www.brookings.edu/blogs/brown-center-chalkboard/posts/2015/08/12-school-choice-lessons-jochim.
11. Patrick J. Wolf and Thomas Stewart, "The Evolution of Parental School Choice," in *Customized Schooling: Beyond Whole-School Reform*, ed. Frederick Hess and Bruno V. Manno (Cambridge, MA: Harvard Education Press, 2011), 91–105, 93–102.
12. This is discussed in detail in Chap. 3.
13. Pierce v. Society of the Sisters of the Holy Names of Jesus and Mary, 268 United States Reports 510 (Supreme Court of the United States 1925).
14. West Virginia State Board of Education v. Barnette, 319 United States Reports 624 (Supreme Court of the United States 1943).
15. Legislature of Kansas, *An Act to Incorporate Cities of the First Class*, 5242, 1879.
16. "The People Fight Back" (Citizens Committee on Civil Rights, 1948), http://www.kansasmemory.org/item/213389/page/1.
17. Oliver Brown, Mrs. Richard Lawton, Mrs. Sadie Emmanuel et al. v. Board of Education of Topeka, 347 United States Reports 483 (Supreme Court of the United States 1954).
18. www.granadaschool.org, accessed July 29, 2013.
19. http://ps8brooklyn.org/about/mission/, accessed July 29, 2013.

20. www.pacrim.org, accessed July 29, 2013.
21. Scott Seider, *Character Compass: How Powerful School Culture Can Point Students Toward Success* (Harvard Education Press, 2012), 169–212.
22. David T. Hansen, "From Role to Person: The Moral Layeredness of Classroom Teaching," *American Educational Research Journal* 30, no. 4 (Winter 1993): 651–74, 656.
23. Ibid., 657.
24. Ibid., 659.
25. Ibid., 660.
26. Ibid., 660.
27. David T. Hansen, "The Emergence of a Shared Morality in a Classroom," *Curriculum Inquiry* 22, no. 4 (1992): 345–61, 346.
28. Ibid., 355.
29. Brint et al. 2001, 165.
30. Brint et al. 2001, 167.
31. Brint et al. 2001, 165.
32. Kunzman 2006, 1–2.
33. Kunzman 2006, 5.
34. Katherine G. Simon, *Moral Questions in the Classroom: How to Get Kids to Think Deeply about Real Life and Their Schoolwork* (New Haven: Yale University Press, 2001), 53–4.
35. Ibid., 2.
36. McLaren 1998, 2003, 2007, 31.
37. McLaren 1998, 2003, 2007, 29, 27.
38. McLaren 1998, 2003, 2007, xvii.
39. *On Christian Education: Rappresentanti in Terra.* Encyclical of Pope Pius XI December 31, 1929, sections 58, 80.
40. Michael Polanyi, *Personal Knowledge; towards a Post-Critical Philosophy.* (Chicago: University of Chicago Press, 1958).
41. Hans-Georg Gadamer, *Truth and Method* (New York: Continuum, 1998), http://site.ebrary.com/id/10727513.
42. Michael J. Sandel, *Liberalism and the Limits of Justice* (Cambridge [Cambridgeshire]; New York: Cambridge University Press, 1982).
43. Alasdair C. MacIntyre, *Three Rival Versions of Moral Inquiry: Encyclopaedia, Genealogy and Tradition : Being Gifford Lectures Delivered in the University of Edinburgh in 1988* (London: Duckworth, 1990).
44. Thiessen, *Teaching for Commitment*, 153.
45. William A. Galston, *Liberal Pluralism: The Implications of Value Pluralism for Political Theory and Practice* (Cambridge, UK; New York: Cambridge University Press, 2002), http://dx.doi.org/10.1017/CBO9780511613579, 53.
46. James B. Stockdale, "Master of My Fate: A Stoic Philosopher in a Hanoi Prison" (Essay, Center for the Study of Professional Military Ethics, 1995), http://www.usna.edu/Ethics/_files/documents/Stoicism2.pdf.
47. "Profile." http://www.regis-nyc.org/section/?ID=158, downloaded August 21, 2013.
48. "Christian Service." http://www.regis-nyc.org/section/?id=125, downloaded August 21, 2013.
49. http://www.regis-nyc.org/section/?id=158 and http://www.regis-nyc.org/section/?id=88, downloaded September 8, 2013.
50. http://www.ramaz.org/public/mission.cfm, downloaded September 7, 2013.

51. http://www.ramaz.org/public/corevalues.cfm, downloaded September 7, 2013.
52. http://www.ramaz.org/public/legacy.cfm, downloaded September 7, 2013.
53. I explore the expressivist strand and its importance in American educational philosophy in Chap. 5.
54. T. Percy Nunn, *Education: Its Data and First Principles* (London: Edward Arnold, 1920), 5.
55. Hirsch 2009, 24, 211.
56. Ravitch 387.
57. Ibid., 13.
58. Hall, *Aspects*, 1907, vi.
59. Chaille, 7.
60. Chaille, 45.
61. See, for instance, David Owen, *English Philanthropy, 1660–1960*. (Cambridge: Belknap Press, 1964); James Murphy, *Church, State and Schools in Britain, 1800–1970*. (London: Routledge & K. Paul, 1971); H. C Dent, *The Training of Teachers in England and Wales, 1800–1975* (London: Hodder and Stoughton, 1977); Adrian Wooldridge, *Measuring the Mind: Education and Psychology in England, C. 1860-C. 1990* (Cambridge [England]; New York: Cambridge University Press, 1994). The last two in particular recount the development of modern education without a reference to the role of religion or even of metaphysical claims.
62. See Ravitch 2001, 27–29, 81; Smith 2003, 55; Cremin 1961, 91–92; Chambliss 1968, 25–31. Spencer influenced education across the English-speaking world. In 1932, two educational historians wrote, "With the exception of Locke's *Thoughts*, it [*On Education*] is the most widely read treatise on education that England has produced. It is still read." Dover and Cavanagh, 1932, xv.
63. T.J. Jackson Lears, *No Place of Grace: Antimodernism and the Transformation of American Culture, 1880–1920* (Chicago: University of Chicago Press, 1981). Spencer's optimism and apparent scientific rigor catapulted him to trans-Atlantic fame. See page 22 for a discussion of a dinner held at Delmonico's in 1882 in Spencer's honor, at which were present "the honor role of educated bourgeoisie."
64. Spencer, 137.
65. Spencer, 8.
66. Wooldridge, 'Child Study and Educational Psychology in England, 1880–1950', p. 108. Francis Galton, cousin to Charles Darwin, sought to demonstrate the hereditary nature of intelligence by charting biological traits among populations. In 1884, he opened an anthropometric laboratory in London which investigated intelligence and heredity and which influenced the work of educational psychologists in England and the USA.
67. Thorndike 1903, 1910, 4–5.
68. Titchener, *A Text-Book of Psychology, Volume 1* (New York: Macmillan Company, 1909), 6.
69. Thorndike 1909, 240.
70. Joseph P. Davis, "Pathologies of the Achieving Self," *The Hedgehog Review* 9, no. 2 (Spring 2009); Nikolas Rose, "Neurochemical Selves," *Society* 41, no. 1 (2003): 46–59.

71. Mona M. Abo-Zena and Ben Mardell, "When the Children Asked to Study God, What Did the Parents Say: Building Family Engagement Around Sensitive Topics," *Religion & Education Religion & Education* 42, no. 3 (2014): 289–307; Ben Mardell and Mona M. Abo-Zena, "'The Fun Thing about Studying Different Beliefs Is That … They Are Different': Kindergartners Explore Spirituality," *Young Children* 65, no. 4 (2010): 12–17; Lisa Miller, *The Spiritual Child: The New Science on Parenting for Health and Lifelong Thriving,* 2015; Lisa Miller, "Religiosity and Substance Use and Abuse Among Adolescents in the National Comorbidity Survey," *Journal of the American Academy of Child & Adolescent Psychiatry* 39, no. 9 (2000): 1190–97.

72. Kenneth R. Minogue, *Alien Powers: The Pure Theory of Ideology* (New York: St. Martin's Press, 1985).

73. See, for instance, Detlef K. Müller, Fritz K. Ringer, and Brian Simon, *The Rise of the Modern Educational System: Structural Change and Social Reproduction* (Cambridge [etc.]; Paris: Cambridge university press ; Editions de la maison des sciences de l'homme, 1987); Phillip McCann, *Popular Education and Socialization in the Nineteenth Century* (London: Methuen, 1977).

74. McLaren, 175.

75. Freire 1970, 2011, 131.

76. Freire 1970, 2011, 44, 49, 56.

77. Ravitch, 215–17.

78. Freire 1970, 2011, 45, 48–49, 79, 106.

79. McLaren 1998, 2003, 2007, xvii.

80. McLaren 1998, 2003, 2007, 189.

81. McLaren 1998, 2003, 2007, 245.

82. Freire 1970, 2011, 39, 54.

83. Freire 1970, 2011, 68–9, 71–3, 76, 80.

84. McLaren 1998, 2003, 2007, 253, 245.

85. Walsh 2013, 21.

86. I think about the Mustard Seed School in Hoboken, New Jersey, a private Christian school that uses constructivist methods (http://www.mustardseed-school.org). A religious view of life is evident across the school policies. Teachers are believers. The admissions team balances the socioeconomic composition of each class, with 50 % on scholarship. There are daily worship services that rein-force the Biblical narrative. The use of (Romantic) constructivist pedagogy does not contravene the Christian view of the child. Rather, the staff's trips to Reggio Emilia, Italy, and its use of constructivist classroom practices, are viewed as important tools to achieve the ends of a religious education.

87. Interested readers can find excellent accounts of educational philosophy (and theory) here: Diane Ravitch, *Left Back: A Century of Battles over School Reform* (Simon & Schuster, 2001); E. D Hirsch, *The Knowledge Deficit: Closing the Shocking Education Gap for American Children* (Boston: Houghton Mifflin, 2006); E. D. Hirsch, *The Making of Americans: Democracy and Our Schools* (New Haven: Yale University Press, 2009); Steven M Cahn, *Classic and Contemporary Readings in the Philosophy of Education* (New York: McGraw-Hill, 1997); Randall R. Curren, *A Companion to the Philosophy of Education* (Malden, MA: Blackwell, 2003), http://public.eblib.com/choice/publicfull-record.aspx?p=214150.

88. Unless the state permits vouchers or tax credits.

89. Terence Copley, *Indoctrination, Education and God: The Struggle for the Mind* (London: Society for Promoting Christian Knowledge, 2005), 6.

90. See Ashley Berner, "School Systems and Finance," in *Balancing Freedom, Autonomy, and Accountability in Education* (Tilburg: Wolf Legal Publishers, 2012), for details.

91. Helena Miller, "Meeting the Challenge: The Jewish Schooling Phenomenon in the UK," *Oxford Review of Education* 27, no. 4 (2001): 501–13, http://www.tandfonline.com/doi/abs/10.1080/03054980120086202, 501.

92. Anders Böhlmark and Mikael Lindahl, *Independent Schools and Long-Run Educational Outcomes Evidence from Sweden's Large Scale Voucher Reform* (Munich: CESifo, 2012). Berner, "School Systems and Finance."

93. Lucy Vickers, "Religious Discrimination and Schools: The Employment of Teachers and the Public Sector Duty," in *Law, Religious Freedoms and Education in Europe*, ed. Myriam Hunter-Hénin (Farnham, Surrey, England; Burlington, VT: Ashgate Publication, 2011).

94. Christopher McCrudden, "Religion and Education in Northern Ireland: Voluntary Segregation Reflecting Historical Divisions," in *Law, Religious Freedoms and Education in Europe*, ed. Myriam Hunter-Hénin (Farnham, Surrey, England; Burlington, VT: Ashgate Pub., 2011).

95. Berner, "School Systems and Finance."

96. England allows religious schools to give admissions priority to students from the same religious faith, for which there is often a test of routine religious observance. Even where religious priority *is* allowed, however, a school with open spots may not *exclude* a child based on race or religion. For instance, a 2009 case before the UK's High Court concerned the admissions policies of a state-funded Jewish school, the Jewish Free School (JFS). JFS only admitted children whose mothers had been *born* Jewish or who had converted to Judaism in a ceremony recognized by the Orthodox Rabbinate. In the 2009 case, *E, R (on the application of) v Governing Body of JFS & Anor*, a boy ("M") had been refused admission because his mother had converted from Catholicism to Judaism under Reform, not Orthodox, practices. The High Court ruled, not that the school had been guilty of religious discrimination, but that it had unwittingly violated the 1976 Race Relations Act. The Majority Judgment did not accuse the school of overt racism. Rather, although "the grounds on which the rejection of M was made may well be considered perfectly reasonable in the religious context," it was nevertheless illegal because "the [grounds of rejection] amount to ethnic grounds under the legislation." E, R (on the application of) v Governing Body of JFS & Anor [2009] UKSC 15 (UKSC (2009) 2009), section 124.

97. Freire 1970, 2011, 71–3, 76.

98. Rob Reich, "Not Very Giving," *The New York Times*, September 4, 2013, sec. Opinion, http://www.nytimes.com/2013/09/05/opinion/not-very-giving.html.

99. House of Commons Hansard Debates for 20 July 2004 (pt 1), Denominational Schools. Available at https://www.publications.parliament.uk.

100. At least, for now. State support for religious schools is perennially in dispute.

101. Eric A. DeGroff, "Parental Rights and Public School Curricula: Revisiting Mozert after 20 Years," *Journal of Law & Education*. 38, no. 1 (2009): 83.

CHAPTER 3

Political Philosophies and Why They Matter

"What is the state afraid of?"[1] So begins a recent essay on democratic education. It is an important question for the United States, whose public school system is uniform and managed exclusively by the state. America's public schools are not "uniform" operationally; they vary in financial resources, teacher quality, neighborhood, student demographics, and even curricular emphases. They are, however, uniform conceptually. They were intended to provide a uniform experience: the common school was designed to "create in the entire youth of the nation common attitudes, loyalties, and values, and to do so under central direction by the state. In this agenda, 'moral education' and the shaping of a shared national identity were of considerably more importance than teaching basic academic skills."[2] I outline the historical origins of America's uniform system below.

The United States is an outlier among democratic nations in its commitment to a uniform, state-provided school system, standing with Brazil, Greece, Latvia, Mexico, and Uruguay.[3] Elsewhere, including in Germany, France, the Netherlands, Sweden, Hong Kong, Denmark, Israel, and most provinces in Canada, the state either operates a wide array of secular, religious, and pedagogical schools, or it funds all schools but operates only a portion of them. These systems are not designed to be uniform. They are intentionally pluralistic.

Structural differences between school systems arise naturally from differences in the political philosophies that undergird them.

Traditional political philosophy examines the relationship between the individual and the state.[4] It is concerned with the origin, scope, and legitimacy of state authority and power, and of the rights, duties, and obligations of individual citizens. I use "individual" to mean an independent and morally responsible human actor,[5] and the abstract "state" to indicate the realm of governmental power.

© The Author(s) 2017
A.R. Berner, *Pluralism and American Public Education,*
DOI 10.1057/978-1-137-50224-7_3

The notion of "civil society" as a distinctive sphere seems to have developed in the eighteenth century, "in reaction against the rationalistic universalism associated with the Enlightenment."[6]

The concept of "civil society" bears elaboration. Civil society is the family, the synagogue, the Elks Club, philanthropies that support after-school programs and cancer research, local baseball leagues, the YMCA (Young Men's Christian Association)—in short, the voluntary endeavors through which we engage with one another. Contemporary political philosopher William Galston describes civil society as the "network of intimate, expressive, and associational institutions that stand between the individual and the state."[7] "Between" is not precisely true; as Galston noted elsewhere, "The expansion of the modern state means that most civil associations are now entangled with it in one way or another."[8] But while individuals, government, and the associations of civil society are intertwined practically, they are distinct conceptually.

Why do these concepts matter? They matter to how we envision democratic life and how we organize schooling to fit that ideal. What kind of citizen do we want schools to cultivate? How do we affirm families' diverse commitments while also nurturing a common attachment to democracy, and to one particular democracy?[9] Who is in charge of education: the individual, the state, or civil society? In what combination? Why?

In this chapter, I argue that although it was put in place *via* democratic processes, the ideal of a uniform public school system serves our democracy poorly. I also argue that, while the state ought to fund and regulate public education, it should not serve as the majority operator of that system. Rather, as so many democratic systems present, and as our own used to reflect, the daily work of education belongs to the associations of civil society with their diverse, nimble, and responsive, cultures. Educational pluralism operates *here*, in the mediating space between the individual and the state, responsive to private belief and political power, and subject exclusively to neither.

First to political philosophy.[10] Governance exists on a spectrum. Anarchy stands on the one side and totalitarian dictatorship on the other; the first assigns all authority to individuals and the second to the state.[11] Democracies operate at one of the many points in between, with varying roles assigned to the individual, the state, and the institutions of civil society. Some political scientists go so far as to say that democracy simply cannot exist without civil society:

> Modern democracy, as well as the limited forms of representative government that preceded it, have only succeeded in conjunction with a civil society. It constitutes the sphere of autonomy from which political forces representing constellations of interests in society have contested state power. Civil society has been a necessary condition for the existence of representative government including democracy.[12]

The importance of civil society is not disputed in a democratic context, but the precise role that the associations of civil society should play, is. Who should administer social services, for instance: independent and even faith-based organizations, or the state alone? Should the railroads be privatized or the management of prisons subcontracted to for-profit companies? Should publicly funded health care be channeled through independent physicians or in government clinics alone? Or, as pertains here, should the state manage education completely, or rather share this provision with the voluntary sector? The balance between individuals, the state, and the voluntary sector is not answered once and for all but requires re-negotiation as the contours of modern democratic life shift.[13]

For instance, Canadian political theorists Charles Taylor and Jocelyn Maclure describe the current tension in their country between "republican" and "liberal-pluralist" philosophies.[14] Both philosophies assume a secular, democratic constitutional framework but differ in their construction of the public square: must participation in public life, too, require secular and democratic language and behavior? Or may those with non-secular viewpoints participate on their own terms? Neither version is morally neutral; both make claims about the ideal relationship between the individual, the state, and civil society.

Canada's republican secularism asks citizens to set aside non-secular beliefs when they engage in the public square. A private citizen may wear a Star of David, but a district judge may not. A Muslim may live out her faith freely in private and voluntary domains, but should not refer to the Koran in democratic debates. Public debate should be in secular terms that match the secular state.[15]

In the United States this has been called "civic republicanism."[16] Civic republicanism emphasizes unity over difference and national over private interest; its adherents "desire for differences to be 'healed'."[17] Civic republicanism often sees sectarian beliefs as threatening to civic unity and seeks to create an ideologically neutral public culture in which all citizens can participate.

Canada's liberal-pluralist secularism, in contrast, welcomes religious observance in the public square as long as it does not infringe upon the rights of others.[18] A district judge may wear a Star of David but must recuse himself from cases involving publicly sanctioned expressions of faith. A Muslim public school teacher may wear hijab but may not proselytize students. Individuals are free to use religious language in public debate, even though others may not understand.

This version of liberal-pluralist secularism focuses on *individual* conscience; it does not engage with associational rights, or the rights of institutions within civil society. Below, I summarize the liberal pluralism of William Galston, which emphasizes associational as well as individual rights. Galston's liberal pluralism enables us to ask, for instance, whether a Catholic hospital is free *not* to dispense birth control or whether a state-funded Jewish school may refuse to admit a non-Jewish student. The relevance of liberal pluralism for education is clear: educational pluralism depends upon a stable democratic government and individual rights, to be sure, but it also relies upon the associations that comprise civil society to provide schools.[19]

Democratic theorists do not contest the importance of a strong civil society to creating and sustaining democratic life. Alexis de Tocqueville was the first commentator on the texture and extent of American civil society and its leavening effect upon democratic culture (*Democracy in America*, 1835). Tocqueville compared the political and social equality of the American people favorably to the hierarchies of European nations. Tocqueville described in meticulous detail the administrative and political devolution of power that— for the moment, anyway—served as a hedge against a totalizing state. While Tocqueville much preferred democracy to aristocratic feudalism, he was not sanguine about the risks inherent in democratic culture. Rather, he saw greater danger from the withdrawal of the equal selves into "individualism," or "a calm and considered feeling which disposes each citizen to isolate himself from the mass of his fellows and withdraw into the circle of family and friends; with this little society formed to his taste, he gladly leaves the greater society to look after itself."[20] Absent the communities of class and continuity that marked aristocratic societies,[21] he asked what would prevent the new democracy from deteriorating into a random gathering of self-interested individuals.[22] This was one of Tocqueville's persistent concerns.

The first check on individualism he identified is "the free institutions of the United States and the political rights enjoyed there," which "provide a thousand continual reminders to every citizen that he lives in society."[23] Participatory democracy ensures that individuals are mindful of the public interest—even if they dispute what that entails.

The second check is the abundance of civic associations in America. In other countries, important endeavors would be undertaken by the state, but in the United States they fall within the domain of civil society. Tocqueville marveled at the capacity of Americans to engage in projects designed to solve social problems or advance various agenda:

> Americans of all ages, all stations in life, and all types of disposition are forever forming associations. There are not only commercial and industrial associations in which all take part, but others of a thousand different types—religious, moral, serious, futile, very general and very limited, immensely large and very minute. Americans combine to give fetes, found seminaries, build churches, distribute books, and send missionaries to the antipodes. Hospitals, prisons, and schools take shape in that way. Finally, if they want to proclaim a truth or propagate some feeling by the encouragement of a great example, they form an association.[24]

Tocqueville believed that these reciprocal, voluntary activities led to the mutual attachment and understanding that made democratic life possible.[25] They prevented the isolation of individuals into private interests and small loyalties, and they served as a protection against the growth of the state which was, in his view, inevitable if regrettable as society modernized. In sum, "If men are to remain civilized or to become civilized, the art of association must develop and improve among them at the same speed as equality of conditions spreads."[26]

For Tocqueville, then, the associations of civil society protected modern democratic life from the potentially isolating effects of liberty on the one hand, and the hegemonic power of the state, on the other.

Contemporary reflections on civil society abound. Some were inspired by the work of Robert Putnam, who argued in 1995 that American civil society was deteriorating. Putnam's *Bowling Alone: The Collapse and Revival of American Community* (1995) and *American Grace: How Religion Divides and Unites Us* (2012, with David Campbell) theorize that voluntary associations serve society in the forms of "bonding capital and bridging capital," or social relationships among members of a single group and between members of different groups, respectively.[27] *Bowling Alone* sparked an interest among scholars and activists to examine, debate, critique, and possibly renew this sector of national life, which Putnam saw as imperiled.[28]

At the same time, scholars began to discuss the deterioration and restoration of civil society in countries dominated by communist ideologies.[29] The totalizing states of the USSR (Union of Soviet Socialist Republics) and its client nations in Eastern Europe had left little room for the individual or for the associations of civil society. Civic engagement developed as state power deteriorated; throughout the 1970s, it was argued, activists in the satellite nations developed political, cultural, and religious associations that, while not recognized by the totalizing state, nevertheless constituted the beginnings of civil society. This nascent third sector exerted pressure upon the regimes and simultaneously prepared a generation of leaders for the post-Soviet era in Eastern Europe.[30] The extent to which the former USSR itself developed those associations is still disputed.[31] The scholarly consensus, however, is that the associations of civil society offer fertile training ground in democratic governance and serve as a vital check on an overweening state.

A still more recent commentary on civil society comes from Charles Murray's *Coming Apart: The State of White America, 1960–2010* (2012). Murray describes the white underclass whose members, bereft of the blue-collar jobs that used to insure a living wage, now have low levels of educational attainment and virtually no engagement in the voluntary sector at all.[32] Murray's findings echo those of the Institute for Advanced Studies in Culture's large-scale survey of parent culture (2011–2013). The Institute's survey found that 19 % of the 3000 parents in the study were essentially "detached" from education, from aspirations, and from the associations of civil society. The researchers described this group (of which 65 % are white) this way:

> They lack the vision, vitality, certainty, and self-confidence required to embrace any agenda, even a relativistic one. In this sense, they are more morally overwhelmed and unresolved than committed relativists. Theirs is a universe of low parental efficacy, where political, religious, and social programs are confounding, peer influence looms large, and people just try to get by. Given a choice between this plan or that strategy, their choice is to remain undecided, to stand aside, to watch what others do.[33]

Like Charles Murray's residents of the fictitious Fishtown, the Institute's "detached" are non-participants. Their withdrawal stands in marked contrast to the civic engagement of contemporary immigrants, for whom ethnic societies and religious communities serve as gateways into American society generally.[34] Political scientists view community participation as a key indicator of civic preparation, and thus its absence as something democracies should worry about.[35]

The importance of civil society to a flourishing democracy, then, is not contested among democratic theorists. The real question is what role civil society should play in providing public services generally and public schooling in particular. In a uniform school system, the answer is no role at all. In a pluralistic school system, in contrast, non-governmental organizations may, at government expense, create and deliver education that reflects families' beliefs and pedagogical preferences. The state regulates the scope of educational freedom in significant ways—which I explore in Chap. 6—but does not seek to homogenize the school experience.

Such different arrangements reflect different roles assigned to the individual, the state, and civil society. I explore this interplay below only insofar as it affects the structure of democratic educational systems.

DEMOCRATIC EDUCATIONAL THEORY

Political philosophers who agree about the independence and value of civil society often disagree about whether or not voluntary associations should play a role in public education. Two American scholars, Amy Gutmann and William Galston, exemplify such disagreement and carry it into their discussions of democratic education.[36] Their two views of democratic education are based upon two different views of the ideal democratic society. Gutmann's arguments cohere with civic republicanism as understood in this chapter; she supports a public square devoid of particularist beliefs and a public school that prepares students for it. Galston writes from the liberal-pluralist camp, which elevates the expressive liberties that exist within civil society and supports a school system that reflects them.[37]

Amy Gutmann believes that education belongs in the hands of the state and thus supports America's current school system. She begins *Democratic Education* (1987, 1999) with the important question, "Who should share the authority to influence the way that democratic citizens are educated?"[38] and concludes that while there are many participants, the structure, management, and philosophy of education properly remain in the hands of the state. Why?

First, only the state can create the space children need to become democratic citizens. This space is neutral with respect to the larger moral claims of human life, but non-neutral about educational purpose: its aim is democratic cultivation and, specifically, "democratic deliberation." As Gutmann puts it, "All citizens must be educated so as to have a chance to share in self-consciously shaping the structure of their society."[39] Non-governmental institutions such as the family or the synagogue are not organized democratically and, as such, cannot prepare children to become citizens.[40] In fact, the public schools are designed to provide an alternative to the non-democratic institutions that otherwise surround a child.[41] They are also designed to teach children how to use "public reason," or a discourse that is not dependent upon confessional or partisan commitments:[42]

> Public schools can avoid even indirect repression and still foster what one might call a democratic civil religion: a set of secular beliefs, habits, and ways of thinking that support democratic deliberation and are compatible with a wide variety of religious commitments.[43]

The public school thus initiates children into a form of bilingualism: at home, they may operate within the discourse and practices of Modern Orthodoxy, but at school, they learn to use secular or "public" vocabulary and argumentation. Reciprocity and cooperation result from this shared, secular engagement. Thus, the public schools uniquely offer a space in which children learn to put aside the particularities of their subcultures temporarily so as to engage in public life.

Second, the management of the public schools is democratic, whereas the management of non-public schools is not. The latter are responsive only to parental demands. Public schools, on the other hand, represent the varied interests of federal, state, and local governments; educators; parents; and students.[44] While governmental authority can become repressive, professional educators serve as a buffer between the tyrannies of state and family alike.[45] In the ideal public school students, also, are invited into the decision-making and thus practice their democratic skills.[46] The failures of the public school sector are attributable to lack of resources or to over-bureaucratization, both of which can be corrected without altering the governing structure.[47]

Finally, public education bestows social and moral capital to religious and ethnic minorities. Public schools change the texture of American life by enabling connections between students from diverse ethnicities, beliefs, and income levels. Even Catholic families, whose values were at odds with the Protestant common schools of a 100 years ago, can have confidence in the common ground that public schools offer now.[48]

For Gutmann, then, public schools occupy an important and unique space in American culture. They advance democratic cultivation and public reason across a diverse population; they are managed according to democratic principles; they provide additional goods such as social and moral capital that make American society more generous and tolerant. The voluntary associations that comprise civil society may be important to individuals, but the loyalties they engender may work against citizenship formation.

William Galston views state education through a different lens. In *Liberal Pluralism* (2002), he argues for the "parsimonious" use of state power in defining and cultivating citizenship in young students.[49] Why?

First, Galston does not view Gutmann's "public reason" as neutral with respect to ultimate meaning and purpose. Rather, it reflects a distinctive Enlightenment rationalism and preference for individualist autonomy over other systems of belief.[50] The outcomes and values Gutmann seeks (deliberative democracy, individual autonomy) are worthy goals, but they represent one view among many for how human life ought to be lived and democracy to be organized.[51] Thus, when the state agrees only to fund schools of this kind, it "side[s] with the ultimate claims of one group and not others."[52] Instead of promoting one view of the world and preparing children for it, "the value-pluralist liberal state will respect self-aware, autonomous lives but will not insist on promoting Socratic or Millian ideals (or any others) as valid for all citizens."[53] Rather, it will accommodate the beliefs of Catholics, Jews, and Evangelical Christians (for instance) in public institutions.

Nor, says Galston, is the goal of bilingualism, in which students learn the language of belief at home and public reason for at school, fitting for a democracy. Far better to enable cultural and religious minorities to offer the "fact" of their beliefs to the public square, an interaction in which "the secular interlocutor is being asked to experience that clash imaginatively as part of a process that could create a wider shared understanding—even if the particulars of faith are not easily[54] communicable."[55]

Finally, a uniform education simply cannot exhaust the civic goods that we want our schools to promote. The civic good of tolerance, which is "a principled refusal to use coercive state power to impose one's views on others, and therefore a commitment to moral competition through recruitment and persuasion alone,"[56] comes more readily from encountering, instead of occluding, the differences in why and how citizens construct their lives. This entails allowing "individuals and groups to live in ways that others would regard as unfree."[57] The Amish, the fundamentalists, and the Hasidim might not endorse an Enlightenment version of democratic deliberation, but their communities and schools might nurture other civic virtues—such as "law-abidingness, personal and family responsibility, and tolerance of social diversity"[58]—goods that a secular public school is not designed to cultivate. There are absolute limits to what a democracy should allow to be cultivated in schools, of course, and there are limits to what kinds of education a democracy should support financially (I distinguish and outline these various limits in Chap. 6).

From Galston's liberal-pluralist perspective, then, the capacity of state-controlled education to enhance democratic culture is questionable from the beginning. Galston is also skeptical about the public schools' unique capacity to bestow social and moral capital—a question I address empirically in Chap. 5.

There is another possible configuration, one that emphasizes the educational autonomy of individuals and families and resists external authority in the educative process. This point of view, associated with classical political liberalism, was largely put to rest with the development of universal, state-funded schooling that, in Europe and the United States, dates back to the early nineteenth century. The contemporary libertarian impulse by and large does not deny the role of civil society or the state in schooling.[59] When economist Milton Friedman introduced the idea of school vouchers in 1955, he did not argue against state regulation or even, in certain circumstances, state provision of education. Rather, he placed his pitch for portable, per-capita funding for school children within the "neighborhood effect," to wit, the fact that a "stable and democratic society is impossible without widespread acceptance of some common set of values and without a minimum degree of literacy and knowledge on the part of most citizens." Thus, even within Friedman's theoretical construct that privileged "school choice," the state had to ensure minimum academic proficiencies and standards.[60] Some of Friedman's progeny no doubt disagree.[61] I touch on their potential to impede the development of educational pluralism in Chap. 7.[62]

Liberal pluralism is different from both the state-orientation of totalitarian countries and the individualism of classical political liberalism. Liberal pluralism recognizes that "human responsibility is diversified, requiring different kinds of effort and various types of organizations for its achievement;"[63] we have responsibilities as citizens, parents, children, workers, religious adherents, and so on, but our responsibility is not reducible to any of these domains. Liberal pluralism does not require that ultimate loyalty be bestowed upon any one entity, whether nation or creed. Rather, it recognizes that human loyalty is divided and organizes society so as to honor these loyalties as far as possible. Galston calls this "maximal feasible accommodation."[64]

James Skillen, who identifies as a Christian Democrat, put it this way in his analysis of principled pluralism:

> One of the aims of the normative framework we are seeking ... is to avoid or to overcome the absolutization of the family, the state, the market, and the individual in order to promote societal differentiation and integration in a well balanced and just fashion ... a healthy society needs both undemocratic families and a democratic government, both disciplined schools and profit-making enterprises, both strongly encumbered selves and free-choice consumers.[65]

Such is the imperfect balance between individual, state, and society sought by a liberal-pluralist political philosophy. Liberal pluralism neither places ideology in the hands of the state nor abandons individuals to their own private worlds. It honors the point made in Chap. 2: institutions are not morally neutral but, rather, normative all the way down.

This is not to say that the uniform public school system was put in place by non-democratic means; it was not—as I discuss below. Rather, the uniform public school system reflects the concerns of the nineteenth-century's Protestant majority about the disruptive effects of Catholic immigrants on American democracy. In their minds and with their votes, the majority chose to remove education from the hands of civil society and to place it exclusively within the realm of the state. This response may be explicable on historical grounds, but it has not served democratic cultivation as hoped.

To return to David Steiner's question, quoted at the beginning of this chapter: what is the state afraid of? Civic republicans fear the potential of diverse belief systems to undermine democratic life. Thus, while they do not restrict the activities of civil society in any way, they view a state-controlled school system as an important mediator of diversity and the primary source of a common political attachment. Liberal pluralists, in contrast, fear the state's power to determine orthodoxy for a plural population, and they enjoin a diversified school system. These political philosophies are in tension with one another and yield quite different forms of public education.

The next section recounts specific ways in which divergent political philosophies influenced the structure of schools systems in Prussia, the Netherlands, and the United States.[66] I do so to highlight that school systems are historically and philosophically contingent. The US uniform school system, for instance, was created to mediate the Catholic loyalties held by thousands of immigrants; it relied and still relies upon state instrumentality to forge civic unity. The Netherlands' system, in contrast, became increasingly pluralistic and oriented toward civil society instead of the state. The development of public education in all three nations illustrates both the importance of political philosophy and the possibility of negotiation, even reversal, in how school systems are configured—important lessons to remember as we evaluate and possibly challenge the status quo.

From Political Philosophy to Educational Practice

The early 1800s found Europe emerging from centuries of war. Although the causes of the wars had been multiple (religious, political, and financial), the political question the wars inspired was singular: how could Europe's modern leaders create unity and stability, *without recourse to violence*, among populations that differed in substantial ways? This was no mean task.

Elites in Prussia, the most powerful of the Germanic states, drew upon the Romantic notion of the nation-state as an antidote to diverse and potentially disruptive beliefs. Under this ideal, the people's identity would come, first and foremost, from commitment to the German *Volk*—rather than to creed. Following its leading philosophers and theologians, Prussia's political leadership elevated the ideal Germanic community above other loyalties.[67] State schooling became the mechanism through which to cultivate a new kind of German, whose scattered passions would be transformed into a "new identity and a common will," based upon a "common fatherland."[68]

Education existed as part of the state, not independent from it. Teachers were civil servants. Because the Catholic and Protestant churches remained strong, the tactic of strong leaders such as Otto van Bismarck was to co-opt rather than supplant them.[69] Religious schools still existed, but the central government appointed the provincial boards that managed them, and teacher preparation occurred in state seminaries designed to inculcate Germanic loyalty.[70] Prussia's system was superficially plural, but it was oriented toward, and controlled by, the state. When Bismarck unified the German states in 1870, he extended Prussia's educational model to new territories.[71]

The risks of this strategy became clear by the 1930s. The education system and, in particular, the teacher training institutions, had become the conduit for attachment to the German *Volk*.[72] By the time the National Socialists came to power in 1933, "Educators were more likely than other public employees to join the Nazi Party," and teachers and professors made up a full quarter of Nazi Party membership.[73] In 1933, the state fired a third of all school superintendents; in 1936, it required all school children to join the Hitler Youth; in 1936, the Party closed all Catholic schools outright.[74]

The Prussian educational model had elevated the state above other attachments. Thus, while the state supported religious schools, it also disabled their independence. This raises the question of the optimal relationship between state and schools; even within a plural system, the state can exert different degrees of control. A school system that gives meaningful authority to non-state providers may serve to inhibit the state from exercising ideological hegemony. Indeed, in the post-war period, the newly constituted Western German government restored authority to independent schools as a corrective to the state-orientation and prohibited the central government from guiding the values of the school system.[75]

Elites in the Netherlands also sought to unify the diverse population through state schools, but they relied upon a common philosophy (Enlightenment deism) rather than a common loyalty to do so. Parliament passed laws in 1801 and 1806 that brought local schools under the pedagogical and curricular oversight of the national government. All public schools were to promote a "general Christianity" that resembled the Enlightenment deism of the nation's political class rather than the Catholic or Protestant creeds of the general populace.[76] In the southern provinces, these laws led to revolution so extensive that, in 1830, these provinces broke away and formed their own country: Belgium.[77] Belgium's new constitution specified the right to educational freedom, which meant a plurality of schools, funded by the state. Today, half of the children in the French-speaking section of Belgium attend religious schools that are fully funded by the state.[78]

In the Netherlands' remaining provinces, the struggle between the state and religious communities continued for decades. The Parliamentary majority viewed the state's governing role in education as a hedge against social division and civil war.[79] The liberalizers in Parliament wanted to pluralize education for precisely the same reason: to avoid the kind of rebellion that had created the nation of Belgium.[80] The Catholic leadership continued to resist non-sectarian education. In the late nineteenth century, a Protestant leader articulated the social theory known as sphere sovereignty which, when joined with the historical Catholic resistance to homogenization, came to shape the school system.

It was Abraham Kuyper (1837–1920), a Dutch Reformed minister, Parliamentarian, and Prime Minister (1901–1905), who brought "sphere sovereignty" into public discourse. Sphere sovereignty, he explained, asserts that the voluntary associations of society, whether the press, the church, the family, or the arts, possess inherent dignity that derives from their own (not the state's) purpose, and should be honored with meaningful responsibility. The state's proper role is minimal and consists solely of "mediat[ing] among these 'spheres,' ensuring that justice is done, the rights of individuals are protected, and that tasks that can only be undertaken by the whole society are carried out."[81] The state should prevent abuse and exercise appropriate, if limited, regulations. However, the state should not intervene in the texture of familial life, the conduct of business, or the relationship between a pupil and a teacher.[82] It follows that the state should not be the exclusive operator of publicly funded schools but should, rather, support the voluntary sector's provision of schools as well.

Sphere sovereignty resembles the Catholic notion of "subsidiarity," or the "ethical principle that a larger and higher ranking body should not exercise functions which could be efficiently carried out by a smaller and lesser body; rather the former should support the latter by aiding it in the coordination of its activities with those of the greater community."[83] That is, the smallest unit capable of executing a social function should do so. In its modern incarnation, subsidiarity is the hallmark of a Papal encyclical on the just society (*Rerum Novarum*, 1891),[84] and subsidiarity has subsequently become a cornerstone of European human rights law[85] and a justification for the US federalism.[86]

It is important to note that, despite his pastoral vocation, Kuyper did not argue for a theocracy or for state funding of religious schools per se. Rather, he supported a radical pluralism designed to enable Catholic, Protestant, Jewish, atheist, and socialist institutions to exist on their own terms, as assets rather than burdens within democratic society. Kuyper's philosophy, which he preached in the pulpit and in Parliament, appealed to the growing electorate. As the right to vote expanded, individuals of creedal rather than deistic beliefs joined the political conversation and gradually pluralized the school system. By the 1920s, the Netherlands' government supported all schools on equal footing.

Today, the Netherlands funds more than 30 different kinds of schools, of which only 30 % are operated by the state; religious and civic associations operate the overwhelming majority. Charles Glenn wrote recently, "Among the world's nations with universal schooling, the Dutch can justly claim to provide the most freedom to parents to choose schools which correspond to their convictions ... Dutch laws and policies sustain the most pluralistic school system in the world, with dozens of models of education enjoying full public financing."[87] The Dutch may have the most generous pluralism, but they are not alone either in principle or in practice, as I describe elsewhere.

What of the American school system? The nineteenth century opened with educational uniformity in the Netherlands and pluralism in America's states; it closed with pluralism in the Netherlands and uniformity in the United States. Why did the United States move in the opposite direction? The short answer is that, in the United States, civic republicanism trumped liberal pluralism.[88]

In the early days of the Republic, education was organized and funded at the local level. Some towns, particularly in the Northeast, were diverse enough to support educational pluralism; Jewish and Catholic schools were funded alongside Congregationalist or Presbyterian ones. In small towns and the western frontier, non-sectarian schools developed out of necessity, since there were simply too few Baptists, Methodists, or Presbyterians to create their own schools. This was the origin of the "common school": Protestant but non-sectarian.

A movement to create uniform instead of plural education systems began in the 1830s. Its most important defender was Horace Mann, the chairman of the Massachusetts Board of Education (1837–1848). Mann's chief concern, like that of his compatriots in the Netherlands, was that religious divisions would disrupt the new republic; he viewed rural Calvinists and urban Catholics alike with suspicion.[89] Mann argued that America needed uniform, standardized schooling to create civic homogeneity. This required common instead of confessional schools and state, rather than local, regulation.[90] It is important to note that neither Mann nor any of his contemporaries referenced "the separation of church and state" as grounds for the common school. Indeed, Mann expected schools to inculcate a general, although not a creedal, religious belief. The separationist phrase, which originated in a letter written by President Thomas Jefferson in 1802, did not come into use until mid-century as discussed below and in Chap. 4.

Mann's ideas shaped the public education we know today, but initially his vision was seen as an unwelcome innovation that undermined religious identities and local cultures. It almost died on the vine as an affront to associational liberty.[91] The resistance to Mann's vision of uniformity, however, dissipated when waves of Catholic immigrants arrived on America's shores. Between 1845 and 1854, 3 million immigrants—many of them Catholic—were added to the 14 million Whites and 3 million African Americans already in this country. By mid-century, the Catholic population had grown to 17.6 % of the population. In some areas, it was higher; in New Hampshire, the Catholic population grew from 1370 to 85,000 (or 22 % of the population) between 1844 and 1894.[92] Many towns and cities began to support Catholic education alongside of Baptist, Congregationalist, and Jewish schools. Educational pluralism was what the immigrants had experienced in Europe and what they found in the United States.

For many Protestant Americans, such large numbers of Catholic immigrants posed an existential threat. After all, so the reasoning went, European Catholicism demanded obedience to religious community, not to individual conscience. The Protestant message had become, in America, even more individualistic than that in Europe.[93] Consequently, mid-century American Protestants viewed Catholicism and Catholic schools as inimical to democratic life. From 1840 until well after the Civil War, Protestant sermons and tracts betrayed a heightened concern about the effects of Catholicism upon American society. Catholicism was called "a foe of mental liberty," a "substitution of authority for conscience," and, in the words of one Yale-educated Protestant, "the most complete slavery of which the world furnishes any example."[94]

This antipathy animated new political forces: the Know-Nothing party organized on behalf of native-born Americans and by 1850 controlled many of the New England legislatures, nor did nativism abate after the Civil War. The (Protestant) Ku Klux Klan preached anti-Catholicism, burned crosses in Catholic neighborhoods, and firebombed Catholic churches well into the twentieth century.[95] The "risks" of accommodation were evident: in 1869, New York's Catholic population had become so politically influential that 20 % of New York City's excise taxes were allocated to Catholic schools.[96] In 1870, the California state legislature appointed funds for Catholic education.[97] Other cities allowed Catholic nuns and priests to teach in majority-Catholic public schools.[98]

Anti-Catholicism was not the only force behind the movement to de-fund religious schools. Some Protestant sects, particularly Baptists and Methodists, had long argued that government aid corrupted religious purity.[99] These groups called upon Jefferson's "wall of separation" to make their case against Catholic schools.[100] Secularist organizations, for their part, used separationist language to protest any type of religion in any state-funded school.[101]

These diverse strands (nativism, anti-Catholicism, secularism, pietism) together created the atmosphere in which Congress considered amending the Constitution. James G. Blaine of Maine, who was in turn Speaker of the House of Representatives, US Senator, Secretary of State and serial presidential candidate, represented the movement to "separate church and state."[102] In 1875, Blaine proposed a Constitutional amendment that would have prohibited the states from funding religious schools.[103] The so-called Blaine Amendment passed the House but narrowly failed in the Senate; the federal Constitution remained as it was.

The same could not be said for the state constitutions; the separationist impulse did not die in Congress. Rather, three-dozen states added "Blaine Amendments" to their constitutions between 1870 and 1900. These amendments vary but have been the primary impediment to state funding of non-public, and particularly religious, schools. New York's Blaine Amendment allows some state funding for non-public schools in the form of transportation, technology, utilities, and security. Florida's Blaine Amendment is stricter. It forbids direct *and* indirect aid to religious schools and includes the term "uniform schooling" for emphasis. On this basis, in 2004, the Florida District Court of Appeals struck down a statewide voucher program.[104] Ohio's Blaine Amendment forbids religious groups to control any part of public school funds.[105]

The states' Blaine Amendments have had both immediate and long-term consequences. State funding for non-public schools withered. So did public debate about which types of schools to fund. Methodists, Presbyterians, Catholics, and Jews had negotiated for a share of public school funds in 1850, but by 1900, the Blaine Amendments foreclosed these deliberations. Common schools, which promoted assimilation and stressed uniformity, became the dominant educational model.

Protestant hegemony in the schools, meanwhile, strengthened in the wake of the Blaine Amendments. State after state passed laws requiring that the Protestant Bible be read in public schools: Pennsylvania in 1913, Delaware and Tennessee in 1916, Alabama in 1919, Georgia in 1921, Maine in 1923, Kentucky in 1924, Florida and Ohio in 1925, and Arkansas in 1930.[106] It is supremely ironic that America's uniform schools were uniform *Protestant* schools for many decades.

As the educational landscape shrank, American parents became habituated to the state's control over their children's education. To be sure, the wealthy could always send their children to a private school or move to a neighborhood with "good" schools. The vast majority of Americans, however, have sent their children to the zoned district school. One concern with educational pluralism is that low-income parents might not know how to select schools for their children.[107] This argument is akin to saying that manumitted slaves should not be allowed to vote because their political inexperience has reduced their decision-making capacities. While some low-income parents may require help in navigating different educational options—particularly at first,[108] there is no evidence that they cannot learn to do so wisely. I address this issue in Chap. 6.

Many Americans are unaware that religious prejudice was a causal factor behind the common school movement our twenty-first century has inherited. It is a narrative of loss: Americans in the nineteenth and early twentieth centuries lost the experience of, and therefore the capacity to imagine, the benefits of diverse public education. This lack of imagination is still with us, and we have too readily believed that our schools are somehow ideologically neutral and democratically beneficial.[109] It would benefit us to re-examine the current configuration of public education in light of the first principles of political philosophy, the experience of other nations, and the empirical record of our public schools' accomplishments. It might be that we determine, as have citizens in the Netherlands and so many other countries, that yielding the provision, if not the regulation, of education to the voluntary sector comports with our ideals and advances democratic cultivation.

Summary

Political philosophy considers the possible configurations that can exist between the state, the individual, and civil society. In the nineteenth century, American democracy assigned control over education to the state, while most other democracies created space for non-state schools to be publicly funded and for non-state associations to manage them. Charles Glenn calls these two alternatives the "state-control" and the "civil society" models.[110]

Some contemporary scholars point to major international covenants as further evidence of civil society's importance to education elsewhere. Emory University School of Law's John Witte Jr., for instance, points to the

International Covenant on Economic, Social, and Cultural Rights' (1966) robust defense of non-governmental associations.[111]

In a similar vein, Charles Glenn argues that the Treaty of Maastricht, which created the European Union, embraces the civil society model for education.[112] The United States is not a signatory to these agreements, but we can take note of the value assigned to non-government education in democracies around the world and in international documents.

In a column for the *New York Times*, David Brooks argues that a healthy society requires a "thick ecosystem" in which diverse organizations create a rich "spiritual, economic and social ecology." He contrasted this with an abstract, rule-based "one-size-fits-all" approach favored by government technocrats. He wrote, "Technocratic organizations take diverse institutions and make them more alike by imposing the same rules. Technocracies do not defer to local knowledge. They dislike individual discretion. They like consistency, codification and uniformity."[113] Brooks's contrast aptly applies to public education: America has favored technocratic uniformity, while most other liberal democracies prefer a diverse ecosystem.

The civic republican argument that education belongs in the hands of the state is spurious. It claims that the state can create an ideologically neutral public space. This, it cannot do. As Lawrence Weinberg put it, "by choosing a singular worldview, whether it is the nondenominational Protestantism of the nineteenth century, or the supposed secular humanism of the late twentieth century, public education is defining orthodoxy."[114] Civic republicanism claims that uniformity prepares students for democratic participation. Uniformity, however, potentially breeds indoctrination of the worst kind, because it is implicit, unacknowledged, and occluded. As Canadian philosopher Elmer John Thiessen argued, "The best guarantee against institutional indoctrination is that there be a pluralism of institutions."[115] Civic republicanism claims that the state uniquely bestows social capital and civic preparation, but the empirical record casts doubts on this, as I explore in Chap. 5.[116]

The drive to create a uniform civic experience based upon one set of normative claims does not fit well with democratic principles. We do not expect adults to bracket their commitments when it comes to voting, or to allocating philanthropic dollars, or to buying a car, yet when it comes to educating young citizens, our system is designed to foreclose moral judgment about what matters and why. In contrast, educational pluralism rests on the assumption, with Tocqueville, that individualism and statism pose equal risks to democratic life, and that a plurality of schools serves as protection against both. Educational pluralism is also Constitutional, as I explore in the next chapter.

Indeed, the Supreme Court has acknowledged the manifold loyalties that we hope our children will sustain. In the words of *Pierce v. Society of Sisters* (1925), "The child is not the mere creature of the State; those who nurture him and direct his destiny have the right, coupled with the high duty, to recognize and prepare him for additional obligations."[117] Or, as a contemporary theologian asks, "How should government do justice to citizens (political creatures) who are always more than citizens and who are not, in fact, autonomous individuals but thoroughly interdependent social creatures?"[118] Educational pluralism has a greater chance of serving democratic citizens than uniformity—and we should engage this possibility in our democratic deliberations.

NOTES

1. David M. Steiner, review of *Review of Moral and Political Education, Making Good Citizens: Education and Civil Society*, by Stephen Macedo et al., *The Journal of Education* 183, no. 1 (2002): 101–6, http://www.jstor.org/stable/42742464, 101.
2. Charles Leslie Glenn, *The Myth of the Common School* (Amherst: University of Massachusetts Press, 1988), 4.
3. Also Bulgaria, Jordan, Lithuania, the Philippines, and Ukraine.
4. In this chapter, I use the term "state" generally, meaning any level of governmental authority.
5. This is a general term that is not intended to diminish those circumstances in which particular individuals, for mental or cognitive reasons, are deemed not to be morally responsible for their behavior.
6. Boris deWiel, "A Conceptual History of Civil Society: From Greek Beginnings to the End of Marx," *Past Imperfect* 6 (1997): 3–42, 5.
7. William A. Galston, *Liberal Pluralism: The Implications of Value Pluralism for Political Theory and Practice* (Cambridge, UK; New York: Cambridge University Press, 2002), http://dx.doi.org/10.1017/CBO9780511613579, 110.
8. Ibid., 114.
9. There are many scholars who have written thoughtfully on this matter. See in particular the essays in Robert K Fullinwider, *Public Education in a Multicultural Society: Policy, Theory, Critique* (Cambridge [England]; New York: Cambridge University Press, 1996).
10. Dr. Shanaysha Sauls rightly called my attention to the distinction within political philosophy between the nation-state and the representative democracy, both modern concepts which may have informed the school systems under discussion.
11. I have limited this discussion to democratic theory.
12. Michael Bernhard, "Civil Society and Democratic Transition in East Central Europe," *Political Science Quarterly* 108, no. 2 (1993): 307–26, 307.
13. Aristotle wrote about civil society on quite different terms than did Tocqueville.
14. Jocelyn Maclure and Charles Taylor, *Secularism and Freedom of Conscience*, trans. Jane Marie Todd (Harvard University Press, 2011).
15. I explore this tension in Chap. 6, in the context of religious schools and Quebec's provincial curriculum.
16. This is not to be confused with the civic republicanism (or civic humanism) described and debated by J.G.A. Pocock and Thomas L. Pangle: J.G.A. Pocock, *Politics, Language, and Time: Essays on Political Thought and History* (Chicago: University of Chicago Press, 1989), https://catalyst.library.jhu.edu/catalog/bib_1205109.; Thomas L. Pangle, *The Spirit of Modern Republicanism: The Moral Vision of the American Founders and the Philosophy of Locke* (Chicago: University of Chicago Press, 1988), https://catalyst.library.jhu.edu/catalog/

bib_1092578. It is rather the civic republicanism promoted by Benjamin Rush and George Washington—a common and nondenominational piety that sought public virtue, as described in John Witte Jr. and Joel A. Nichols, *Religion and the American Constitutional Experiment*, Fourth (Oxford: Oxford University Press, 2016). esp. 36–42.

17. Kathleen Knight Abowitz and Jason Harnish, "Contemporary Discourses of Citizenship," *Review of Educational Research* 76, no. 4 (December 1, 2006): 653–90, doi:10.2307/4124417, 657–659.

18. Or, less importantly here, does not place an undue burden upon public institutions.

19. I explore the limits of associational freedom in Chap. 6.

20. Alexis de Tocqueville, *Democracy in America*, ed. J.P. Mayer, trans. George Lawrence (New York: Harper Collins, 1988), 506.

21. Ibid., 507.

22. Ibid., 510.

23. Ibid., 512.

24. Ibid., 513.

25. Ibid., 515.

26. Ibid., 517.

27. Robert D. Putnam and David E. Campbell, *American Grace: How Religion Divides and Unites Us* (Simon & Schuster, 2012), 256–7.

28. National Commission on Civic Renewal, "A Nation of Spectators: How Civic Disengagement Weakens America and What We Can Do about It. Final Report of the National Commission on Civic Renewal." (College Park, MD: National Commission on Civic Renewal, 1997), http://eric.ed.gov/?id=ED424174.; Council on Civil Society, "A Call to Civil Society: Why Democracy Needs Moral Truths" (New York, NY: Institute for American Values and the University of Chicago School of Divinity, 1998). For a summary of disagreements see: James E. Fleming and Linda C. McClain, "Foreword: Legal and Constitutional Implications of the Calls to Revive Civil Society," *Chicago-Kent Law Review* 75, no. 2 (April 2000), http://scholarship.kentlaw.iit.edu/cgi/viewcontent. cgi?article=3193&context=cklawreview. Other scholars weighed in on the space between the market and the state; see as an example Claire Gaudiani, *The Greater Good: How Philanthropy Drives the American Economy and Can Save Capitalism* (New York: Times Books/Henry Holt, 2003). For a particularly trenchant commentary on the debate, see Alan Wolfe, "Is Civil Society Obsolete?: Revisiting Predictions of the Decline of Civil Society in Whose Keeper?," *The Brookings Institution*, Fall 1997, http://www.brookings.edu/ research/articles/1997/09/fall-civilsociety-wolfe.

29. Marcia A. Weigle and Jim Butterfield, "Civil Society in Reforming Communist Regimes: The Logic of Emergence," *Comparative Politics* 25, no. 1 (1992): 1–23, doi:10.2307/422094.

30. See, in particular, Bernhard, "Civil Society and Democratic Transition in East Central Europe."

31. James L. Gibson, "Social Networks, Civil Society, and the Prospects for Consolidating Russia's Democratic Transition," *American Journal of Political Science* 45, no. 1 (2001): 51–68, doi:10.2307/2669359.; Sergej Ljubownikow, Jo Crotty, and Peter W. Rodgers, "The State and Civil Society in Post-Soviet Russia: The Development of a Russian-Style Civil Society," *Progress in Development Studies* 13, no. 2 (April 1, 2013): 153–66, doi:10.1177/ 1464993412466507.

32. Charles A. Murray, *Coming Apart: The State of White America, 1960–2010* (New York, NY: Crown Forum, 2012).

33. Karl Desportes Bowman et al., "Culture of American Families Executive Report" (Charlottesville, VA: Institute for Advanced Studies in Culture, 2012), 26.

34. See, for instance, Vivian Louie's account of the networks within Chinese American communities or Tony Lin's work on the acclimating role played by Latino Pentecostal churches: Vivian S Louie, *Keeping the Immigrant Bargain: The Costs and Rewards of Success in America* (New York: Russell Sage Foundation, 2012). Rosin, Hanna. "Did Christianity Cause the Crash?" The Atlantic, December 2009. http://www.theatlantic.com/magazine/archive/2009/12/did-christianity-cause-the-crash/307764/.

35. I discuss this fully in Chap. 5. We might ask, then, whether civil society is essentially political. Two factors suggest otherwise. First, the associations of civil society are voluntary, whereas politics is ultimately about coercion. Groups within civil society—from the family to the synagogue to the Rotary Club—certainly carry authority, even oppressive authority, as do all institutions. However, they do not possess the power to incarcerate, fine, or put to death those who violate their codes. Second, to elide the civil and the political requires either a structuralist view of culture (here, that all human activity comes down to power relationships) or a definition of "political" so broad as to be meaningless. Shanaysha Sauls rightly pointed out to me that democratic theorists might also consider civil society part of individual, private life, and thus beyond the reach of government. Exchange with the author, March 2016.

36. The list of scholars who have recently addressed American civil society is extensive and includes Amitai Etzioni, Adam Seligman, Stephen Macedo, and Jean Bethke Elshtain. I focus on Gutmann and Galston because they are the most prominent (and, in my view, cogent) interlocutors in education.

37. I hesitate to use the more familiar "political liberalism," the usual contra point to civic republicanism; the former draws upon libertarian thinking and thus comes into conflict with principled pluralism. In education, the libertarian impulse often rejects state oversight of publicly funded private schools, for instance, whereas pluralism acknowledges the public nature of schooling and accepts the importance of governmental requirements such as academic proficiency. I explore this balance in Chap. 6.

38. Amy Gutmann, *Democratic Education* (Princeton, N.J.: Princeton University Press, 1987), 3.

39. Ibid., 47.

40. Ibid., 30–32.

41. Ibid., 48.

42. Gutmann follows John Rawls in seeking out a universally accessible public discourse. Rawls's work on this subject (see especially John Rawls, "The Idea of an Overlapping Consensus," *Oxford Journal of Legal Studies* 7, no. 1 (1987): 1–25, http://www.jstor.org/stable/764257, and John Rawls, "The Idea of Public Reason," in *Deliberative Democracy: Essays on Reason and Politics*, ed. James Bohman and William Rehg (Cambridge, MA: MIT Press, 1997), 93–145.), led to a rich discussion among political theorists about whether his ideals were attainable or desirable. See, for example, Mark Button, "Arendt, Rawls, and Public Reason," *Social Theory and Practice* 31, no. 2 (2005): 257–80, http://www.jstor.org/stable/23558465, and Marc Stears and

Mathew Humphrey, "Public Reason and Political Action: Justifying Citizen Behavior in Actually Existing Democracies," *The Review of Politics* 74, no. 2 (2012): 285–306, http://www.jstor.org/stable/23263303, and Jurgen Habermas, "Reconciliation Through the Public Use of Reason: Remarks on John Rawls's Political Liberalism," *The Journal of Philosophy* 92, no. 3 (1995): 109–31, doi:10.2307/2940842, on Rawls's broader liberal framework.

43. Gutmann, *Democratic Education*, 104.
44. Ibid., 70, 74, 297.
45. Ibid., 75.
46. Ibid., 89.
47. Ibid., 70, 302.
48. Ibid., 30–32.
49. Galston, *Liberal Pluralism: The Implications of Value Pluralism for Political Theory and Practice*, 20.
50. Ibid., 21, 107.
51. Ibid., 95.
52. Ibid., 20.
53. Ibid., 62.
54. Ibid., 101.
55. Ibid., 115.
56. Ibid., 126.
57. Ibid., 101, 111.
58. Ibid., 107.
59. The exception may be certain elements within the home schooling movement.
60. Milton Friedman, "The Role of Government in Education," in *Economics and the Public Interest*, ed. Robert A. Solo (New Brunswick, NJ: Rutgers University Press, 1955), 123–44, 125.
61. For a brief description of the debate within the "school choice" movement, see Michael J. Petrilli, "The School Choice Moveement's Schisms, Explained," *The Flypaper*, January 27, 2016, http://edexcellence.net/articles/the-school-choice-movements-schisms-explained.
62. There is a risk that these groups will fight the states' imposition of norms and standards, as they have the Common Core. I discuss this in Chap. 7.
63. James W. Skillen, *In Pursuit of Justice: Christian-Democratic Explorations* (Rowman & Littlefield Publishers, 2004), 7–8.
64. Galston, *Liberal Pluralism: The Implications of Value Pluralism for Political Theory and Practice*, 20.
65. Skillen, *In Pursuit of Justice*, 30.
66. These accounts are drawn largely from Charles Glenn's *The Myth of the Common School* (1988) and *Contrasting Models of State and School* (2011); I am, like so many others, deeply in his debt.
67. Such as Johann Gottlieb Fichte and Friedrich Schleiermacher. See Charles L. Glenn, *Contrasting Models of State and School: A Comparative Historical Study of Parental Choice and State Control*, 1st ed. (Continuum, 2011), 40–49.
68. Ibid., 41–43.
69. Ibid., 104–106.
70. Ibid., 56–59.

71. The story is more complicated; Bismarck tried to enforce interreligious schooling and to end Catholic schools—at one point, he incarcerated half of the Catholic clergy—but in neither was he successful. His Kulturkampf ended in a stalemate in which he allowed religious education to continue but under the auspices of the state. See Ibid., 104–106.
72. Ibid., 56.
73. Ibid., 156.
74. Ibid., 156–165.
75. Ibid., 177–184. The German leaders insisted upon a plural educational system over the objections of the Americans, who wanted a uniform system.
76. Ibid., 59–68.
77. Ibid., 73.
78. Ashley Berner, "School Systems and Finance," in *Balancing Freedom, Autonomy, and Accountability in Education* (Tilburg: Wolf Legal Publishers, 2012), find page.
79. Glenn, *Contrasting Models of State and School*, 123, 124. Only 6.4 % of the population could vote in 1848.
80. Ibid., 123–4.
81. Ibid., 130, 131.
82. Ibid., 131.
83. Domènec Melé, "Exploring the Principle of Subsidiarity in Organisational Forms," *Journal of Business Ethics* 60, no. 3 (2005): 293–305, http://www. jstor.org/stable/25123581, 293.
84. Pope Leo XIII, "Rerum Novarum: On Capital and Labor" (Papal Encyclical, Vatican City, Italy, May 15, 1891), http://www.papalencyclicals.net/Leo13/l13rerum.htm. See sections 49–59 on associations.
85. Paolo Wright-Carozza, "Subsidiarity as a Structural Principle of International Human Rights Law," *American Journal of International Law*. 971, no. 2003 (2003): 38–79.
86. George A. Bermann, "Taking Subsidiarity Seriously: Federalism in the European Community and the United States," *Columbia Law Review* 94, no. 2 (1994): 331–456, doi:10.2307/1123200.
87. Glenn, *Contrasting Models of State and School*, xviii.
88. Shanaysha Sauls raises the question of whether the theoretical underpinnings of the state shifted, from the constitutional democracy so prized by Tocqueville to the nation-state chosen by Otto von Bismarck. This is a fair question and one that future work might explore to good effect. Exchange with the author, March 2016.
89. Glenn, *The Myth of the Common School*, 8.
90. Ibid., 9.
91. Ibid., 120–135.
92. Charles L. Glenn, "The Discriminatory Origins of New Hampshire's 'Blaine' Amendment, Unpublished Testimony," April 2013.
93. Philip Hamburger, *Separation of Church and State* (Cambridge, MA: Harvard University Press, 2002), 193–201.
94. Ibid., 211–213.
95. Ibid., 216–217.
96. Glenn, "The Discriminatory Origins of New Hampshire's 'Blaine' Amendment, Unpublished Testimony", 14.
97. Ibid., 33.

98. Ibid., 26.
99. Witte and Nichols, Religion and the American Constitutional Experiment, 52–3.
100. Hamburger, *Separation of Church and State*, 275–283.
101. Ibid., esp. 331, 332.
102. I discuss the influence of "separationism" upon the Supreme Court in Chap. 4.
103. The text of the proposed amendment read, "No State shall make any law respecting an establishment of religion, or prohibiting the free exercise thereof, and no money raised by taxation in any State, for the support of the public schools or derived from any public fund therefore, shall ever be under the control of any religious sect, nor shall any money so raised ever be divided between religious sects or denominations."
104. John Ellis "Jeb" Bush, etc., et al., v. Ruth D. Holmes, et al.; Charles J. Crist, Jr., etc., v. Ruth D. Holmes, et al.; Brenda McShane, etc., et al., v. Ruth D. Holmes, et al. (Supreme Court of Florida 2006).
105. For a complete list of state constitutional prohibitions, see Witte and Nichols, *Religion and the American Constitutional Experiment*, 300–302.
106. Glenn, "The Discriminatory Origins of New Hampshire's 'Blaine' Amendment, Unpublished Testimony", 29.
107. Kimberly A. Goyette and Annette Lareau, *Choosing Homes, Choosing Schools* (New York, 2014).
108. See Thomas Stewart and Patrick J Wolf, *The School Choice Journey: School Vouchers and the Empowerment of Urban Families* (New York, NY: Palgrave Macmillan, 2014).
109. Glenn, *The Myth of the Common School*, 84–5.
110. Glenn, *Contrasting Models of State and School*. Terminologies used throughout.
111. United Nations, "International Covenant on Economic, Social and Cultural Rights" (Human Rights Office of the High Commissioner, December 16, 1966), http://www.ohchr.org/EN/ProfessionalInterest/Pages/CESCR. aspx, Article 13. And Witte and Nichols, *Religion and the American Constitutional Experiment*, 252–3.
112. Charles Glenn, "Religious Freedom in Education?" December 2012, 7. Shared privately with the author.
113. David Brooks, "Flood the Zone," *The New York Times*, February 6, 2012, http://www.nytimes.com/2012/02/07/opinion/brooks-flood-the-zone. html.
114. Lawrence D. Weinberg, *Religious Charter Schools: Legalities and Practicalities (PB)* (Information Age Publishing, 2007), 85.
115. Elmer John Thiessen, *Teaching for Commitment: Liberal Education, Indoctrination, and Christian Nurture* (McGill-Queen's University Press, 1993), 89.
116. I discuss this further in Chap. 5.
117. Pierce v. Society of the Sisters of the Holy Names of Jesus and Mary, 268 United States Reports 510 (Supreme Court of the United States 1925), 535.
118. Skillen, *In Pursuit of Justice*, 48.

CHAPTER 4

American Constitutions and Religious Schools

Educational pluralism inevitably involves government funding for religious schools. When Americans hear that other democracies fund Jewish, Catholic, and Muslim schools, they usually respond, "But *we* have separation of church and state." Such a statement can have, at its back, the view that only countries with official, or "established," religions fund religious schools. This is not accurate. Some educationally plural countries do have established churches; England and Denmark are in this category. Other countries, such as Australia and France, do not have official religions but still fund religious schools. The Netherlands, which is the most educationally plural country in the world and funds 36 different types of schools, many of them religious, has not had an established church since 1796.[1]

More often, however, the worry expressed by "we have separation of church and state" is that America's constitution forbids the funding of religious schools. This is not entirely accurate, either. Direct government funding of religious schools is unconstitutional, but other mechanisms pass constitutional muster. While the Constitution is secular and the Supreme Court's rulings prohibit religious endorsement by public schools, Congress's budget funds low-income students who attend religious schools, and the Supreme Court has upheld programs that allow state vouchers for students to attend religious schools. The relationship between government and religion in America is certainly complex and contested.[2] This chapter aims to illustrate that the Supreme Court has not erected an impenetrable wall between public funding and non-public schools—even religious ones.

The constitutional questions do not pertain to public school choice models such as intra-district choice, in which families select from among public schools. Charlotte-Mecklenburg County adopted this model for all high school students in 2001.[3] In New York City, parents select their children's high schools from a menu of school types that vary in emphasis and size. Some districts and states facilitate online learning, so that students have access to academic subjects that

© The Author(s) 2017
A.R. Berner, *Pluralism and American Public Education*,
DOI 10.1057/978-1-137-50224-7_4

their neighborhood schools may not provide. Florida Virtual School, whose courses are offered in schools across the country, was a pioneer.[4] Rural school districts offer online and college credit courses in increasing number.[5] Home schooling is constitutionally legal in every state. In 2011, nearly 2 million students, or 3.4 % of the school-age population, were so educated.[6]

Rather, constitutional questions become necessarily engaged when the government directly or indirectly supports students in philosophically distinctive schools. Here, the issues become whether a particular program amounts to government endorsement of religion, aims to benefit religion, or produces inappropriate entanglement between government and religious institutions. There are educationally plural systems and programs for which the Supreme Court has signaled support under particular circumstances. Each of the following mechanisms has been declared federally constitutional, with one exception: Education Savings Accounts have not been evaluated by the Supreme Court at the time of writing.

- *Charter schools* are public schools that differ from traditional public schools in pedagogical mission, cultural focus, and governance. In 2015, 42 states plus Washington, D.C., allowed them, though the number in many states is capped. In 2013, 4 % of American schoolchildren (2.3 million out of 55.5 million) attended charter schools.[7] In September 2015, Washington became the first state in the country to declare charters unconstitutional; a challenge is pending. Charter schools are distinctive in terms of governance and mission, and as such I include them in the mechanisms of pluralism. They are allowed to differ in terms of pedagogical mission; Scott Seider's book *Character Compass* (2012) describes charter schools in Boston that have created very different school cultures based on virtue ethics, Pacific Rim ethics, and performance ethics.[8] Charter schools may focus on an ethnic culture (such as the Hebrew culture) and may be affiliated with religious institutions that often provide before- and after-school religious activities. Charter schools are not allowed to promote religious doctrines,[9] although some legal scholars argue that they should be.[10] At the time of writing, there are religious charter school cases in the lower courts.[11] There is no federal prohibition on charters.

- *Pedagogical mission:* Some states fund schools with distinctive pedagogical missions. At least 30 charter schools across the country operate according to the Waldorf method, a pedagogy focused on imagination and the stages of development.[12] According to the American Montessori Society, more than 400 traditional public schools use Montessori methods.[13] South Carolina funds Montessori teacher preparation programs.[14] Such schools differ from the traditional neighborhood school in mission and culture, but as long as they are not religious, they do not raise constitutional concerns.[15]

- *Education tax credits* allow individuals or corporations to reduce their tax liability by giving a set amount of money to state-approved scholarship funds for (mostly low-income) children to attend private schools.[16] The credit may not be used to fund a school attended by the donor's children. Tax credit money is not considered "public" because it never goes through state treasuries; it is a credit, not a tax rebate. States with education tax credit programs are evenly distributed across the country: Arizona pioneered its program in 1997, and 12 other states in the Southeast, Midwest, and Northeast followed suit. The Supreme Court declared educational tax credits constitutional in 2011.[17] Legal challenges occur more frequently at the state level and involve both statutory and constitutional questions.[18]

- *Vouchers* are public school funds that can be used to send students to private schools. At the end of 2013, there were 16 voucher programs in nine states and the District of Columbia, plus one school district in Colorado. Most are means- or school-tested, that is, only students whose families fall below a certain income level or who have attended "failing" schools are allowed to use them.[19] Vouchers are the most problematic method of achieving educational pluralism because of state, not the federal, constitutions. In 2002, the Supreme Court declared Cleveland's voucher program to be constitutional, but many state constitutions forbid both direct and indirect public funding of religious schools, which precludes their use in religious schools. Still other state constitutions require public education to be "uniform," a provision that the Florida Supreme Court used to strike down a statewide voucher program in 2006.

- *Education savings accounts* (ESAs) are the newest path to pluralism. States with ESAs allow families to withdraw a per capita amount of money from the school district and use it for other academic pursuits, including private school tuition, early college, and online courses. Arizona, Florida, Mississippi, and Tennessee allow ESAs for special education students, but Nevada passed a universal ESA law that is currently contested as of writing.[20]

None of these mechanisms uses block grants from the government to religious schools—a practice that is common in other countries but would no doubt be deemed unconstitutional in the United States. Rather, the mechanisms are the consequence of secular laws, whose primary effect is not to advance religion, in which the religious schools benefit because of private choice, and in which there is not excessive entanglement between public and religious authorities. It is unclear whether this nascent pluralism will continue to grow, or whether the Supreme Court's present stance on tax credits and vouchers will hold. For now, mechanisms exist by which families can select state-funded (vouchers and charters) or state-sanctioned (tax credits and ESAs) schools that differ in important and distinctive ways.

But is not state support for religious schools a *prima facie* violation of the constitutional doctrine of the separation of church and state? As discussed in Chap. 3, "the wall of separation" is a totemic phrase drawn from an 1802 letter from Thomas Jefferson to a group of Connecticut Baptists.[21] The phrase left no discernible trace upon public discourse until the middle of the nineteenth century, when it became the calling card of various anti-immigrant and anti-Catholic groups. One Klansman, Hugo Black, became a US Senator and then a US Supreme Court Justice. Justice Black used Jefferson's phrase in one of the first education cases heard by the Court (*Everson v. Board of Education*, 1947). In today's world, "the separation of church and state" has become a common, if misleading, metaphor for what is a complex, nuanced, and evolving understanding of the relationship between government and religion. In fact, the Supreme Court's decisions do not support what many Americans mean by the phrase.

But interpreting the federal Constitution is not straightforward. For one thing, it involves wrestling with inherent tensions between principles. The Supreme Court has interpreted the First Amendment (1791) inconsistently and with considerable nuance. It reads as follows:

> Congress shall make no law respecting an establishment of religion, or prohibiting the free exercise thereof; or abridging the freedom of speech, or of the press; or the right of the people peaceably to assemble, and to petition the Government for a redress of grievances.

Among other things, this Amendment prohibits the federal government from establishing an official religion and also from curtailing religious freedoms. But what does this mean in practice? It depends on the facts of the case, and as a result, under some circumstances, the Court allows support for religious institutions and under others, not. This is further complicated by the fact that some cases involve both establishment and also free exercise concerns. Resolving this tension is difficult, since a strong anti-establishment ruling may violate free exercise, and vice versa. As legal scholar John Witte, Jr., put it,

> Too zealous an interpretation of the principle of separation of church and state … runs afoul of other constitutive principles of the disestablishment clause—particularly the principles of liberty of conscience and religious equality. The Court must be at least as zealous in protecting religious conscience from secular coercion as protecting secular conscience from religious coercion.[22]

Another way to put it is a tension between strict separationism and religious accommodation. John Witte, Jr., again:

Separationists forbid any government aid to religion; accommodationist allow aid that is equally or non-preferentially distributed among religions. Separationists forbid any government participation in religious worship, education, or charity. Accommodationists allow such participation so long as citizens are not coerced into participation. Separationists forbid religious and political institutions from cooperating; accomodationists allow for such cooperation in the delivery of charity, education, and other services.[23]

But why does the federal Amendment apply to the states, which have their own constitutions? Because in the early twentieth century, the Court began to use the Fourteenth Amendment's Due Process Clause as a vehicle to apply the First Amendment to state law. The Fourteenth Amendment (1868) reads,

> All persons born or naturalized in the United States, and subject to the jurisdiction thereof, are citizens of the United States and of the state wherein they reside. No state shall make or enforce any law which shall abridge the privileges or immunities of citizens of the United States; nor shall any state deprive any person of life, liberty, or property, without due process of law; nor deny to any person within its jurisdiction the equal protection of the laws (Section 1).

The Fourteenth Amendment was ratified in 1868 to give *federal* protection to freed slaves in the former Confederate states; it allows federal courts to judge the actions of the states, a process called incorporation.[24] In the landmark cases of *Cantwell v. Connecticut* (1940) and *Everson v. Board of Education* (1947), the Court "created a uniform national law of religious liberty" by "read[ing] the First Amendment guarantees of religious liberty into the general liberty guarantee of the Fourteenth Amendment."[25] The Supreme Court cases discussed below invoke the First Amendment and its incorporation via the Due Process Clause of the Fourteenth.

Interpreting the federal Constitution and predicting the Court's rulings are difficult for another reason: the Court's decisions are inevitably shaped by the cultural conflicts and imperatives of the times. We need look no further than the Court's ruling in 1857 that African Americans were not citizens (*Dred Scott v. Sanford*, 1857). *Dred Scott* cannot be understood apart from the heated contemporary debates over slavery and abolitionism, the Missouri Compromise, President Buchanan's inauguration, and the looming specter of civil war. Both legislation and also legal judgment vacated this decision when it became morally, culturally, and politically untenable.[26]

The Court may stand against the cultural momentum: early-twentieth-century rulings protected educational freedoms against anti-Catholic and anti-immigrant animus. For instance, in the 1925 *Pierce v. Society of the Sisters of the Holy Names of Jesus and Mary*, the Court struck down a nativist law in Oregon that required public school attendance.[27] *Pierce* established the right of families to educate their children outside of public schools, although it had no bearing on government funding for these options.[28]

Rigid, tension-free Court doctrines simply do not exist. Legal scholar Marc DeGirolami made this point in testimony before the US Commission on Civil Rights (2013):

> Conflicts can occur not only among different types of values, as when a religious organization's autonomy conflicts with the state's interest in a certain conception of equality, public welfare, or health, but also among different values of the same type, as when a religious organization's conception of equality conflicts with the conception of equality contained in, for example, the Americans with Disabilities Act ... or Title VII of the Civil Rights Act.

> It is not the burden of constitutional law conclusively to resolve these conflicts. That is because the state of being in conflict—the condition of experiencing and living within these kinds of conflicts—is often the best approximation of justice of which we are capable. Conflicts are not great evils to be hidden from or dodged.[29]

The Court's decisions, then, should be read in light of the principled tensions that pertain and of the cultural backdrop in which they are made.

MAJOR THEMES IN EDUCATION AND RELIGION CASES

The Supreme Court did not evaluate the constitutionality of *state* education laws until the twentieth century, when it began to use the incorporation doctrine to do so.[30] Since World War II, the Supreme Court has evaluated education laws that engage with civil rights and integration, property tax formulae, special education, race- and gender-based admissions—all important and consequential. My focus is on the Court's rulings on religion and education. When we turn to this theme, we find that Court's rulings have been more generous toward pluralism than many Americans imagine. What are the conditions that enable government funds to flow to private and, especially, religious schools?

The two cases most relevant to educational pluralism are *Lemon v. Kurtzman* (1971) and *Zelman v. Simmons-Harris* (2002). Why these two? *Lemon* established a rigorous constitutional test that the Court still uses; *Zelman* deployed *Lemon* to support Cleveland's voucher program.

THE LEMON TEST

Before 1971, many states provide textbooks, teachers' salaries, and tuition reimbursements, to private and religious schools. The Court had looked favorably upon these practices, as long as the underlying law did not *set out* to advantage religious schools but, rather, to support education generally (*Board of Education v. Allen*, 1968).

In 1971, however, the Court issued *Lemon v. Kurtzman* (1971). *Lemon* struck down programs in Pennsylvania and Rhode Island that reimbursed private schools for textbooks, materials, and teachers' salaries.

Lemon is what most Americans think of when they hear "separation," for it set out a specific test for constitutionality that still resonates with the Court. Under the "Lemon test," a constitutionally sound statute "must have a secular purpose, must have a primary effect that neither advances nor inhibits religion, and cannot create an excessive entanglement between church and state."[31] These criteria—secular purpose, primary effect, no excessive entanglement— are the basis on which the Court has judged state support for non-public schools ever since. The Court's use of *Lemon* has not been fully consistent, however; at times, its rulings have nuanced or even reversed previous decisions reached under *Lemon's* guidelines.

For instance, between 1971 and 1977, the Court struck down state programs that gave tuition subsidies to religious schools; that reimbursed religious schools for the costs associated with state-mandated exams; that provided block grants to religious schools serving low-income students; and that supported field trips for religious school students.[32] However in 1983, the Court upheld a Minnesota law that gave parents tax deductions for tuition, transportation, and textbooks if their children attended private schools, and for tutoring or educational supplies if public schools (*Mueller v. Allen*, 1983).

Why was Minnesota's law constitutional when Pennsylvania's had not been? The Court reasoned that Minnesota's law had universal application (i.e., to public as well as to non-public educational expenditures); had excluded religious materials from the textbook deductions; and had been "secular in purpose," since it affected all, not just some, of the state's students; and had not involved excessive entanglement between public and private sectors. Importantly, the Court did not accept the argument that this law advantaged religion, even though 96 % of the private schools involved were religious. Rather, the Court said, any benefit to students at religious schools was the result of private, not governmental, decisions and could not be considered "entanglement." The Court's language reflects this: "One fixed principle in this field is our consistent rejection of the argument that 'any program which in some manner aids an institution with a religious affiliation' violates the Establishment Clause."[33] In other words, a law may not have a primary effect of advancing religion (*Lemon's* language), but it may have a downstream effect of doing so.[34]

Former Justice Thomas Scalia commented that *Lemon* was like a "ghoul in a late-night horror movie that repeatedly sits up in its grave and shuffles abroad after being repeatedly killed and buried."[35] It is unpredictably, partially, even contrarily, applied. *Lemon* may be "proverbial among law and religion scholars as demonstrating the indeterminacy of the Court's case law."[36] Nevertheless, its three-pronged test remains important in the Court's rulings.

ZELMAN V. SIMMONS-HARRIS (2002)

Lemon set out the Court's criteria for evaluating educationally plural programs. *Zelman* reflects its use in support of educational pluralism. The facts of the case: in 1995, Cleveland's school district piloted a voucher program for students in failing schools. The students could apply the dollars toward tuition at private schools or private tutoring if they stayed in the public schools.[37] Forty-six out of the original 56 participating private schools were religious in nature. The challengers mounted a "range of choice" argument, arguing that the program did not provide sufficient non-religious choices and favored religious schools, thus constituting a breach of the Constitution. The Supreme Court heard the case in 2002.

The Court ruled 5-4 in favor of Cleveland's program. The majority claimed the program passed the *Lemon* test: the enabling law reflected a secular purpose and a neutral framework; religious schooling resulted from private, not governmental, choice; the program involved no endorsement of religion by the state. The Court rejected the "range of choice" argument, noting that the options available to Cleveland's students included 23 magnet schools and numerous charters—all of which were funded at much higher per capita rates than the voucher program.

Justice O'Connor concurred, noting that all levels of government collaborate with non-public and even religious institutions in numerous domains of American life without breaching the Establishment Clause. Justice Thomas commented on the civil rights implications of the case, pointing out that, "failing urban public schools disproportionately affect minority children most in need of educational opportunity."[38] Education scholar Joseph Viteritti put it this way in a summary of *Zelman*: "Applying the Establishment Clause to curtail the educational choices available to disadvantaged people would serve to constrain the liberty interest of poor families who would choose to send their children to nonpublic schools."[39]

Two of the dissenters, Justices Souter and Breyer, held that educational choice itself corroded civil society. They worried in particular about sustaining democratic culture in a system that reinforced religious divisions. Justice Souter's dissent additionally objected that *Mitchell* and *Mueller* were not appropriate precedents but, rather, had supported "supplementary, not substantial, aid" to religious schools. The voucher program, on the other hand, he considered "substantial." In their dissent, Justices Souter and Breyer drew upon the civic republican narrative: public schools create civic unity, and religious schools undermine it. *Zelman*, however, affirms the federal constitutionality of one form of educational pluralism when it meets the neutrality, private choice, and "no entanglement" criteria.[40]

Lemon and *Zelman* remain the most conspicuous cases on educational pluralism. The Court has set additional guardrails, however, when it comes to religion and public schools. What else do the Court's decisions suggest about government funds, religious schools, and religion in public schools?

When Funding Is Mandated by Congress: Yes

Title I is shorthand for Congress's allocation for economically disadvantaged children in public and private schools. Title I funding is substantial: in fiscal year 2015, Title I constituted $14.4 billion out of the US Department of Education's total discretionary budget of $68.6 billion (including Pell grants).[41] The federal funding flows to children in high-poverty public schools and children from impoverished families who attend non-public schools. It is administered by the district or state. Title I funding does not (and cannot) support religious schools as such, but it *must* support low-income children who may be in those schools. How does this work constitutionally?

The Court's first case on Title I funding was *Wheeler v. Barrera* (1974). *Wheeler* originated in Missouri, whose constitution prohibits state aid to religious schools. Fearful of trespassing the state constitution, school districts routinely withheld Title I services from students at non-public schools.[42] In *Wheeler*, the Court ruled against Missouri and insisted that it must provide comparable services to children in non-public schools without abrogating (or rewriting) its own constitution.[43]

The next two cases resulted in opposite rulings from the Court, thus illustrating the unpredictability of rulings on the First Amendment. In *Aguilar v. Felton* (1985), the Court struck down New York City's Title I program, which had involved sending public school teachers into religious schools to tutor Title I children enrolled there. Using the *Lemon* test, the Court's majority ruled that the administrative oversight amounted to "excessive entanglement." As a result of the ruling, New York City spent more than $100 million to provide Title I remediation and counseling, which it did by parking large vans near religious school properties. Children walked to the vans (outside of school property), thus avoiding "entanglement," while fulfilling the federal mandate to serve low-income children.

A decade later, New York City litigated to overturn *Aguilar*—and succeeded (*Agonisti v. Felton*, 1997). The Court acknowledged its changing interpretation of entanglement; it no longer felt that a public employee's presence equaled religious indoctrination or represented a symbolic union between church and state.[44]

Despite the Court's early interpretation of *Lemon* in *Wheeler* and *Aguilar*, when Congress appropriates funding for low-income students, it has to reach them, wherever they go to school.

When Equal Access Is at Stake: Yes

The Court's rulings suggest that state and district programs may not discriminate against students in religious institutions simply because they are religious institutions, as its decisions in *Witters* (1986) and *Zobrest* (1993) indicate.

Witters was a visually impaired student in the state of Washington who attended a Christian college. The state of Washington had decided that its general aid to visually impaired students could not be extended to Witters because his college was religious. In *Witters v. Washington Department of Services to the Blind* (1986), the Court held for Witters, stating in a unanimous ruling:

> A State may issue a paycheck to one of its employees, who may then donate all or part of that paycheck to a religious institution, all without constitutional barrier, and the State may do so even knowing that the employee so intends to dispose of his salary ... Any aid provided under Washington's program that ultimately flows to religious institutions does so only as a result of the genuinely independent and private choices of aid recipients.[45]

Witters' attendance at a religious college, the Court found, did not undermine Washington State's duty to extend disability support to him as a member of a protected class. Witters had been funded under neutral disability laws, and his choice of a college was therefore irrelevant. Witters received his stipend.

The Court reached a similar conclusion in *Zobrest v. Catalina Foothills School District* (1993). Zobrest was a young man who had been deaf from birth. He had attended public school through eighth grade with a district-funded interpreter present at all times. When Zobrest switched to a Catholic high school, the district refused to fund the interpreter, although they would have done so at a *non-religious* private school. As in *Witters*, the Court ruled for Zobrest, noting that the district's funding was provided neutrally to an entire class of people (individuals with disabilities), that its aim was not to advance religion, and that not to fund Zobrest would have constituted anti-religious discrimination.

While *Witters* and *Zobrest* serve as reminders that the Supreme Court's rulings have not erected an impenetrable wall between religious institutions and public funding, important qualifications remain. In another Washington state case (*Locke v. Davey*, 2004), the Supreme Court held for the state against a scholarship student who chose to major in "devotional theology." State support could go to students at accredited religious institutions (*Witters*), but not if these students were preparing for religious vocation (*Locke*).

WHEN PUBLIC SCHOOLS ENDORSE RELIGIOUS BELIEF: NO

As Chap. 3 outlined, America's school system shifted from pluralism to uniformity in the late nineteenth and early twentieth centuries. For decades, this meant Protestant uniformity. After World War II, the Supreme Court began to dismantle the Protestant atmosphere on establishment grounds. For public schools to allow prayers, devotional Bible reading, or the teaching of creationism, amounted to government endorsement of religious belief and thus violated the First Amendment.

The first time the Court evaluated a state's education policy for establishment violations was in 1947, in *Everson v. Board of Education*. The program: New Jersey's Board of Education reimbursed families for the costs of transporting their children to private schools. The plaintiff, a New Jersey taxpayer, claimed that this policy coerced him into supporting religion, because 96 % of the schools attended by these students were Catholic. Although the Court used separationist language, and even cited Jefferson's "wall of separation,"[46] the Supreme Court ruled that the law did *not* violate the Establishment Clause. Why not? Because the reimbursements went to families, not to religious schools, and thus support for religion was indirect. (This is a prelude to *Lemon's* private choice test.)

Everson reflected the nativist impulse; Justice Black had belonged to the Ku Klux Klan[47] and served as the "Kladd of his Klaven," the officer who initiated new members under an oath of allegiance to white supremacy and "the separation of church and state."[48]

The nativists could not have envisioned, however, what happened next: the Court began to use *Everson's* framework to dismantle the Protestant uniformity which nativism had stood for. In case after case, the Court struck down the vestiges of the majority culture such as "release time," school prayer and public display, and the teaching of creationism, as violating the Establishment Clause.

"Release time" is the policy that lets students break from school for religious instruction, which is provided by religious leaders on behalf of the families' belief system. Release time is no longer familiar to most of us, but at the time of *Everson*, some 2200 school districts participated.

The first release time case came before the Court one year after *Everson* (*McCollum v. Board of Education*, 1948). In *McCollum*, the Court found that Champaign, Illinois's release time program involved too tight a link between district administration and religious communities. How so? The school administrators were involved in managing the program, and its occurrence on school property constituted an "inherent social pressure" upon students who did not participate. As such, the program violated "the basic Constitutional principle of absolute separation." The ruling cited Jefferson's metaphor of the wall as "not a fine line easily overstepped."[49] Not all release time programs were struck down, as is explained below.

On the same grounds, the Court also struck down school prayers, Scripture readings, and religious displays that had been required by law in many states.[50] There could be neither public prayer (*Engel v. Vitale*, 1962) nor a moment of silence (*Wallace v. Jaffree*, 1985). Religious leaders could not offer prayers at high school graduation ceremonies (*Lee v. Weisman*, 1992), nor could athletes pray before sports events (*Santa Fe School District v. Doe*, 2003). There could be no Bible reading if it were for moral and religious instruction (*Abington School District v. Schempp*, 1963, and *Chamberlin v. Dade County Public Instruction Board*, 1964). Public schools could not post the Ten Commandments (*Stone v. Graham*, 1980).

The Court also struck down laws enjoining the teaching of creationism, which it deemed a religious instead of a scientific theory (*Epperson v. Arkansas*, 1968). *Epperson* prompted some states to require *both* evolution *and* creationism to be taught, but the Court put a stop to this, too (*Edwards v. Aguillard*, 1983).

Thus, the Supreme Court stripped away the vaguely Protestant uniformity of the public schools and replaced it with a secular uniformity. Evangelical Protestants experienced this as a profound loss; as one fairly typical essay put it in 1988, "Banning prayer in public schools has led to America's demise."[51] The deep truth, however, is that the more significant loss had occurred decades before, when school uniformity replaced pluralism. It is pure historical irony that the forebears of the Moral Majority had demanded this.

One unusual case bears mentioning: *Kiryas Joel Village School District v. Grumet* (1994). *Kiryas Joel* originated in upstate New York, in a community established by Hasidic Jews from the Satmar sect. The Satmars incorporated the Village of Kiryas Joel and created private schools that reflected the community's beliefs and practices. Children with special educational needs, however, had to attend the public schools (outside the Village) in the Monroe Woodbury Central School District so as to receive federal- and state-mandated support.[52] The Satmars argued that their children faced routine discrimination and incurred "emotional trauma" in the public school setting.[53]

The state legislature took the unprecedented step of creating a public school district that followed the boundaries of Kiryas Joel exactly, giving it "all the powers and duties of a union free school district."[54] Thenceforth, Kiryas Joel's special needs students were educated in a public school district that mapped onto their religious community precisely. The New York State School Boards Association and two taxpayers sued to overturn the state statute.

In 1994, the Supreme Court struck down New York's statute, because the legislature had failed to act in a "religiously neutral way."[55] It was not clear that the legislature would "provide equally to other religious (and non religious) groups,"[56] and therefore the statute violated the Establishment Clause. This anomalous case leaves open the question: if the statute had offered school district status to a variety of groups, not respecting their religious affiliation, would it have been constitutional?

WHEN THE STATE IMPEDES FREE EXERCISE: NO

The Court's rulings indicate that establishment concerns may not be used to constrain free exercise. Thus, while the Court has secularized public schools (and universities), it has simultaneously prevented them from penalizing religious belief.

The free exercise cases came about because, unsurprisingly, in the wake of *Everson* and *McCollum*, public schools and universities worried about violating the Establishment Clause. Some public schools and universities withdrew funding and space from religious groups altogether. The Court has deemed such exclusionary policies unconstitutional. The Court has extended its protection of free exercise in its evaluation of off-campus release time programs, equal access policies on high school and university campuses, and federal and state construction grants.

We know that *McCollum* struck down Illinois's release time program because of its tight link between district and religious leaders. However, the Court upheld New York's release time program four years later (*Zorach v. Clauson*, 1952). Why? Unlike those in Illinois, New York's programs occurred off campus and did not involve public school administrators. The Court majority argued in this new release time case that there was "no constitutional requirement which makes it necessary for government to be hostile to religion and to throw its weight against efforts to widen the effective scope of religious influence."[57] There are still more than 200 release time programs operating in New York City alone.

The Court also disallowed "viewpoint discrimination" against religious groups and insisted that they receive equal access to campus facilities, forums, and even funds that are made available to their non-religious peers. The first case on point was *Widmar v. Vincent* (1981), which held that if universities allow student-led groups to convene on campus, they must not exclude religious ones.

The facts of *Widmar* illustrate the confusion that existed (and still exists) about separation of church and state. The University of Missouri at Kansas City had allowed registered student groups to use campus buildings. In 1981, it singled out religious groups and revoked their privileges, citing establishment concerns. A student group sued on free exercise and free speech grounds. The Supreme Court found for the students, holding that "the University's exclusionary policy violates the fundamental principle that a state regulation of speech should be content-neutral."[58]

The Court's reasoning in *Widmar* illustrates the distinction between neutral, secular laws that happen to benefit religious groups among all others, and laws that inherently privilege religious groups. The university's open forum policy, said the Court, had a demonstrably secular purpose, was neutral with respect to religion (neither advancing nor inhibiting religious belief or practice), and did not foster "an excessive government entanglement with religion" since the group was student-led. Having created an open public forum, the university could not discriminate on the basis of viewpoint unless it could demonstrate a "compelling state reason" for doing so.

Congress liked *Widmar* so much that it passed an Equal Access Law (1984) to extend the principle to high schools. The Equal Access Law was tested and upheld by the Court in 1990 (*Board of Education v. Mergens*).

Several years later, the Court held for a religious group at the University of Virginia that had been denied funding (*Rosenberger v. University of Virginia*, 1995). Specifically, the Court ruled that, "the State's actions are properly interpreted as unconstitutional viewpoint discrimination rather than permissible line drawing based on content."[59] Even more pointedly, "The violation following from the University's denial of [Student Activities Fund] support to petitioners is not excused by the necessity of complying with the Establishment Clause."[60] In 2001, the Court extended this logic to religious after-school programs, arguing that the evangelical Good News Club posed no threat to the public school's neutrality (*Good News Club v. Milford Central School District*, 2001).

Rosenberger, in particular, illustrates the widespread confusion about what the constitution requires and what "separation" means. Schools and universities had become so fearful of violating the Establishment Clause that they had violated the free exercise and free speech rights of religious students and student groups. The Court has been clear that, while public institutions may not endorse religious beliefs, neither may they discriminate against them.[61]

Finally, the Court generally supports construction programs at religious colleges. In 1971, it upheld a federal building program that included religious colleges, as long as the new buildings, such as libraries and performing arts centers, remained perpetually secular in nature as opposed to being used for religious instruction or worship (*Tilton v. Richardson*, 1971). In 1974, it ruled that South Carolina could float revenue bonds for all of its colleges and universities, including religious ones (*Hunt v. McNair*, 1973). In 1976, the Court upheld Maryland's policy of providing public services to religious colleges and universities alongside secular ones (*Roemer v. Maryland Public Works Board*, 1976). Here, too, the Court prevented establishment concerns from overriding everything else. In the previous two sections, then, we see that the Court secularized the public schools under the Establishment Clause while prohibiting viewpoint discrimination under the Free Exercise Clause.

In summary, the Supreme Court's rulings suggest that states may not give block grants to religious schools, fund teacher salaries at private schools, or reimburse parents for religious school tuitions; the Supreme Court has struck down these practices. However, other kinds of support are possible and, in many states, used to good effect. Many Americans may be surprised to learn that New York, for instance, helps non-public schools pay for utilities, transportation, security, and technology. The larger, well-organized religious communities, such as the Jewish Orthodox and Roman Catholics, have become savvy at accessing the statutory funding streams, but theoretically any non-public school could do so. Other states subsidize secular subjects in non-public schools, grant tax deductions for families whose children attend them, or pay the administrative costs of state-required testing and reporting. The most capacious support comes in the form of tax credits and vouchers, which the Court has held constitutional as long as the enabling laws pass the *Lemon* test.

CONSTITUTIONALITY: CONCLUSIONS

This survey of the constitutional parameters of public education is by no means exhaustive. It has left many vital educational issues, such as the Supreme Court's rulings on school segregation, property-based school funding mechanisms, special education, and race-based admissions, entirely unexplored, as it has the rulings of lower courts. The chapter has instead sought to explore what "separation" has come to mean and to highlight the circumstances under which plural structures of education are constitutionally viable.

As its interpretations currently stand, the Supreme Court has not erected an impenetrable wall between public funding and religious schools. Some of my colleagues would say, "For now." The split nature of Supreme Court rulings on education may be seen in a case that upheld Arizona's education tax credit program (*Arizona v. Winn*, 2011). The majority dismissed the case on technical terms: the plaintiffs, a group of taxpayers, did not have standing to challenge the federal constitutionality of a tax credit program. Four Justices dissented, claiming that the harm to taxpayers was significant and that taxpayer standing should have been granted. The 5-4 split in *Arizona* is a reminder that the next few appointees to the Court will matter for how wide or narrow the opening is for pluralistic education. Others point to cases such as *Christian Legal Society v. Martinez* (2010), which allows universities and colleges to have policies that require all-comers policy for organizations at publicly funded universities, as a worrying sign for religious accommodation.[62] As of writing, however, none of the mechanisms for plural education is at immediate risk in the highest court.

The most significant barrier to educational pluralism occurs in the states, some three dozen of which operate with nineteenth century Blaine Amendments as discussed in Chap. 3. The Blaine Amendments forbid direct and, in some cases, indirect funding of religious schools.

There are two ways to remove the barriers established by Blaine Amendments: amend state constitutions by referendum or legislative act, or persuade the Supreme Court to rule such amendments unconstitutional. Both avenues to repealing Blaine Amendments are possible, if not likely. When Florida's legislature passed a voucher program for low-income students, the program foundered upon the state constitution's mandate for "*uniform* public education." Activists subsequently organized to overturn the state's Blaine Amendment, but they have not been successful at the time of writing. Political will is driven, as we have seen, by cultural forces that are pre-political.

The second scenario is also possible, as a recent petition from Colorado makes clear. The history of the case: in 2011, the Douglas County School District created a voucher program for low-income students to attend private schools, some of which are religious. The district alleged that the program was constitutional according to federal criteria because the district's financial support was "neutral," and private schools were funded only as a result of private choice. In roller coaster fashion, the district court struck down the program (2011); the Colorado Court of Appeals court upheld it (2013); and the Supreme Court of Colorado reversed the ruling and struck down the program.[63]

On October 28, 2015, the Douglas County School District appealed to the Supreme Court, asking it to overturn the Blaine Amendment itself as unconstitutional. Here are the words from the petition:

The question presented is: Can Colorado's Blaine Amendment, which the unrebutted record plainly demonstrates was born of religious bigotry, be used to force state and local governments to discriminate against religious institutions without violating the Religion Clauses of the First Amendment and the Equal Protection Clause of the Fourteenth Amendment?[64]

These certainly are the questions we must ask of the Blaine Amendments: are they inherently discriminatory and thus in violation of the Free Exercise Clause? Does their lineage of anti-Catholicism matter today? It is unclear as of writing whether the Supreme Court will hear the case, but if it does, the federal constitutionality of the Blaine Amendments will be held up to scrutiny.

There is an additional source of support for educational pluralism in the Supreme Court's rulings: the Court's articulation of the positive role that cultural diversity plays in democratic life. The year before *Lemon*, the Court upheld tax-exempt status for places of worship with the words, "The government grants exemptions to religious organizations because they uniquely contribute to the pluralism of American society by their religious activities."[65] The Court had made the same point early, in an education case in which Jehovah's Witnesses won the right for their children not to salute the American flag:

We can have intellectual individualism and the rich cultural diversities that we owe to exceptional minds only at the price of occasional eccentricity and abnormal attitudes. When they are so harmless to others or to the State as those we deal with here, the price is not too great. But freedom to differ is not limited to things that do not matter much. That would be a mere shadow of freedom. The test of its substance is the right to differ as to things that touch the heart of the existing order.[66]

If we have the "right to differ as to things that touch the heart of the existing order," why does this not extend to parents' rights over their children's education? Such language gestures toward the greatest intellectual challenge to our public school system: the goal of uniformity itself. As Lawrence Weinberg put it in his book on charter schools, "By choosing a singular worldview, whether it is the nondenominational Protestantism of the nineteenth century, or the supposed secular humanism of the late twentieth century, public education is defining orthodoxy."[67] Uniformity breeds indoctrination of the worst kind, because it is implicit, unacknowledged, and occluded. As another educator wrote, "The best guarantee against institutional indoctrination is that there be a pluralism of institutions."[68]

The point of this chapter, however, is to set out the high court's support for, and constraints upon, educational pluralism. To the question of whether the US Constitution allows educational pluralism, the federal courts have given a qualified "yes." With the federal judiciary's present support for the mechanisms of pluralism, and with movements afoot to circumnavigate the Blaine Amendments, America's education system seems to be returning to the pluralism that Americans in the early- and mid-nineteenth century took for granted and that our partner nations around the world accept as a right. Having established its constitutionality, the next question is whether pluralism is up to the tasks we set out for our school system.

NOTES

1. Charles L. Glenn, *Contrasting Models of State and School: A Comparative Historical Study of Parental Choice and State Control*, 1st ed. (Continuum, 2011), 86.
2. The most thoughtful exploration may be found in John Witte Jr. and Joel A. Nichols, *Religion and the American Constitutional Experiment*, Fourth (Oxford: Oxford University Press, 2016).
3. David S. Deming et al., "School Choice, School Quality and Post-Secondary Attainment" (National Bureau of Economic Research, 2011).
4. http://www.flvs.net/Pages/default.aspx, accessed April 16, 2014.
5. Michael McShane and Brittany Wagner, "Course Access for Missouri Students" (St. Louis, MO: Show-Me Institute, January 20, 2016), http://showmeinstitute. org/blog/school-choice/course-access-missouri-students.
6. "Statistics About Non-Public Education in the United States," Information Analyses (Washington, DC: United States Department of Education, June 9, 2015), http://www2.ed.gov/about/offices/list/oii/nonpublic/statistics.html.
7. "A Growing Movement: America's Largest Charter School Communities" (Washington, DC: National Alliance for Public Charter Schools, December 2013).
8. Scott Seider, *Character Compass: How Powerful School Culture Can Point Students Toward Success* (Harvard Education Press, 2012).
9. Janet Decker and Kari A. Carr, "Church-State Entanglement at Religiously Affiliated Charter Schools," *Brigham Young University Education and Law Journal* 2015, no. 1 (March 1, 2015): 77–107.
10. Benjamin Siracusa Hillman, "Is There a Place for Religious Charter Schools?," *Yale Law School Review* 118, no. 554 (2008): 814–48, http://www. yalelawjournal.org/note/is-there-a-place-for-religious-charter-schools.
11. John Witte and Joel A. Nichols, *Religion and the American Constitutional Experiment*, Fourth (New York, NY: Oxford University Press, 2016), 203.
12. https://amshq.org/School-Resources/Public.aspx, accessed April 5, 2014.
13. https://amshq.org/School-Resources/Public.aspx, accessed April 5, 2014.
14. http://ed.sc.gov/agency/se/school-transformation/MontessoriPrograms.cfm, accessed April 5, 2014.
15. Some disagree, of course. From time to time, former students call out the religious aspects of Waldorf schooling, e.g., http://www.quackwatch. org/04ConsumerEducation/waldorf.html, accessed April 5, 2014.
16. Not all tax credit programs focus upon private school scholarships exclusively; many allow funds to flow to public schools as well.
17. Arizona Christian School Tuition Organiza-Tion v. Winn et al., 563 United States Reports 125 (Supreme Court of the United States 2011).
18. "Florida School Choice," *Institute for Justice*, accessed December 6, 2015, https://ij.org/case/florida-school-choice/.

19. "School Choice Now: The Power of Educational Choice," School Choice Yearbook (Washington, DC: Alliance for School Choice, 2013), http://s3. amazonaws.com/assets.allianceforschoolchoice.com/admin_assets/ uploads/167/School%20Choice%20Yearbook%202012-13.pdf, 11.

20. Arianna Prothero, "School Vouchers for All? Nevada Law Breaks New Ground," Education Week—Charters & Choice, June 4, 2015, http://blogs.edweek.org/ edweek/charterschoice/2015/06/school_vouchers_nevada_law_breaks_new_ ground.html?cmp=SOC-SHR-FB.

21. Philip Hamburger's Separation of Church and State details this history, and it is not necessary to rehearse it here. In summary, Jefferson may have intended to champion a no-go zone between the government and religious institutions (although that is doubtful, since he supported partnership between religion and state in Virginia), but the recipients of the letter did not take it as such. Their complaint had been against the privileges that Connecticut granted to Congregationalists but not to Baptists. The Baptists wanted what other minorities wanted, which was not the end of contact, but rather a level playing field.

22. Witte and Nichols, Religion and the American Constitutional Experiment, 2016, 227.

23. John Witte, Religion and The American Constitutional Experiment, Second Edition (Westview Press, 2005), 192.

24. For an interesting debate on incorporation, see Philip Hamburger, "Privileges or Immunities," Northwestern University Law Review 105, no. 1 (2011): 61–147; Frederick Gedicks, "Incorporation of the Establishment Clause Against the States: A Logical, Textual, and Historical Account," SSRN Scholarly Paper (Rochester, NY: Social Science Research Network, February 5, 2012), http:// papers.ssrn.com/abstract=1997807.

25. Witte and Nichols, Religion and the American Constitutional Experiment, 2016, 196.

26. The Civil Rights Act of 1866 and the Thirteenth and Fourteenth Amendments to the Constitution vacated Dred Scott by defining a federal citizen as anyone born in the United States who is not the subject of a foreign power, and by making all persons (i.e., blacks), and not just those who were citizens before the amendments (i.e., whites), equal before the law.

27. Quick Bear v. Leupp (1908), a federal establishment case, reflects the cultural tension over the provision of sectarian schools. At issue was whether members of the Sioux tribe in South Dakota could spend tribal funds on Catholic schools. The Court ruled it could. Meyer v. Nebraska (1923) was the first state education law the Court considered: Nebraska's prohibitions against foreign language instruction and instruction in a foreign language. The Court ruled that the law violated teachers' Fourteenth Amendment rights. The third early education ruling was Pierce v. Society of Sisters (1925). Oregon had passed a law requiring all students to attend public schools—in effect, outlawing Catholic education and other forms of private religious education. The Court struck down the law for violating students' due process and free exercise rights—engaging both First and Fourteenth Amendment rights.

28. The Court still refers to Pierce, as when it ruled that Amish families could withdraw children from school at age 14, in accordance with community custom (Wisconsin v. Yoder, 1972).

29. Marc DeGirolami, "Testimony before the United States Commission on Civil Rights." March 1, 2013, https://centerforlawandreligion.files.wordpress.com/2013/03/us-commission-on-civil-rights-testimony-degirolami-1.pdf. Used with permission of the author.

30. Furthermore, the federal government's operational role in education is modest. Each state sets its own education policies, and the federal contribution is merely 8–10 % of state education budgets.

31. Lemon v. Kurtzman, 403 United States Reports 602 (Supreme Court of the United States 1971), 613.

32. *Sloan v. Lemon*, 413 United States Reports 825 (Supreme Court of the United States 1973). Levitt v. Committee for Public Education, 413 United States Reports 472 (Supreme Court of the United States 1973). Wolman v. Walters 433 U.S. 229 (1977), 433 United States Reports 229 (Supreme Court of the United States 1977).

33. Mueller v. Allen, 463 United States Reports 388 (Supreme Court of the United States 1983), 393.

34. The Court's tone here is reminiscent of the *Zorach* decision (1952), in which it found "no constitutional requirement which makes it necessary for government to be hostile to religion and to throw its weight against efforts to widen the effective scope of religious influence (Zorach v. Clauson, 343 United States Reports 306 (Supreme Court of the United States 1952), 314.)" *Mueller* also presages the favorable ruling the Court gave to the Ohio voucher program in *Zelman v. Simmons* (2002), which is discussed below.

35. Lamb's Chapel v. Ctr. Moriches Union Free School District, 508 United States Reports 384 (Supreme Court of the United States 1993).

36. Mark Movsesian, Frederick A. Whitney Professor of Contract Law and Director, Center for Law and Religion, St. Johns University School of Law, on March 29, 2016, in conversation with the author.

37. The program set the voucher amount at $2250 per year, with priority given to low-income students. Children who stayed in failing public schools received $360 for additional tutoring.

38. Zelman v. Simmons-Harris, 536 United States Reports 639 (Supreme Court of the United States 2002), 676–7.

39. J. P. Viteritti, "Reading Zelman: The Triumph of Pluralism, and Its Effects on Liberty, Equality, and Choice," *Southern California Law Review* 76 (2003): 1105–88, 1110–1.

40. Since the use of *Lemon* varies with the composition of the Court and case at hand, it is always possible that *Zelman* could be challenged and reversed.

41. "Fiscal Year 2015 Budget: Summary and Background Information" (United States Department of Education, March 4, 2014), http://www2.ed.gov/about/overview/budget/budget15/summary/15summary.pdf, 2, 27.

42. Betsy Levin, "Between Scylla and Charybdis: Title I's 'Comparable Services' Requirement and State and Federal Establishment Clauses," *Duke Law Journal* 1976, no. 39 (1976): 39–67, 41–42. In 1974's dollar amounts, "Expenditures ranged from about $10 to $85 for the disadvantaged nonpublic school student to about $210 to $275 for the disadvantaged public school student." 43.

43. Ibid., 47. In the interim, Congress enacted a bypass amendment to Title I that allowed federal funds to flow directly to needy students in non-public schools.

44. In a follow-up case (*Mitchell v. Helms*, 2000), the Court upheld Louisiana's distribution of federal funds to all schools, 30 % of which happened to be Catholic in some parishes.

45. Witters v. Washington Department of Services for the Blind, 474 United States Reports 481 (Supreme Court of the United States 1986).

46. Arch R. Everson v. Board of Education of the Township of Ewing, 330 United States Reports 1 (Supreme Court of the United States 1947), 15–16. "Neither a state nor the Federal Government can set up a church. Neither can pass laws which aid one religion, aid all religions or prefer one religion over another. Neither can force nor influence a person to go to or to remain away from church against his will or force him to profess a belief or disbelief in any religion ... In the words of Jefferson, the clause against establishment of religion by law was intended to erect '*a wall of separation between Church and State* [emphasis added].'"

47. Philip Hamburger, *Separation of Church and State* (Cambridge, MA: Harvard University Press, 2002), 426.

48. The Klan had funded Black's successful Senate bid and publicly celebrated his appointment to the Court. Ibid., 433. http://history.hanover.edu/courses/excerpts/227kkkmanual.html, downloaded 10/23/2014.

49. Illinois ex rel. Vashti McCollum v. Board of Ed. of School Dist. No. 71, Champaign County, Illinois, 333 United States Reports 203 (Supreme Court of the United States 1948), 231.

50. A typical prayer: "Almighty God, we acknowledge our dependence on Thee and beg Thy blessing over us, our parents, our teachers and our nation" (New York State, 1962).

51. http://www.forerunner.com/forerunner/X0098_Ban_on_school_prayer.html, downloaded October 30, 2014.

52. These events occurred during the high water mark of separationism, that is, after *Aguilar v. Felton* (1985) but before *Agonisti v. Felton* (1997).

53. Board of Education of Kiryas Joel Village School District v. Grumet, 512 United States Reports 687 (United States Supreme Court 1994), at 693.

54. Ibid.

55. Ibid., 703.

56. Ibid., 702.

57. Zorach v. Clauson, 343 United States Reports 306 (Supreme Court of the United States 1952), 314.

58. Widmar v. Vincent, 454 US 263 United States Report (Supreme Court of the United States 1981), 267–77.

59. Rosenberger v. Rector and Visitors of the University of Virginia, 515 United States Report 819 (Supreme Court of the United States 1995), 269.

60. Ibid.

61. The court's rulings on equal access are extensive and extend to the broad use of public facilities—not merely educational ones (*Lamb's Chapel v. Ctr. Moriches Union Free School District, 508 United States Reports 384 (Supreme Court of the United States 1993*).

    Good News Club v. Milford Central School, 533 United States Reports 98. Accessed October 12, 2016.

62. See in particular Witte and Nichols, *Religion and the American Constitutional Experiment*, 2016, discussion of *Martinez*, pages tbd, and Jon Inazu's defense of

"strong pluralism," in John D. Inazu, "The Four Freedoms and the Future of Religious Liberty," SSRN Scholarly Paper (Rochester, NY: Social Science Research Network, October 8, 2012), http://papers.ssrn.com/abstract=2158861, for his skepticism about the all comers' policies.

63. "Douglas County School District v. Larue," *Becket Fund*, October 28, 2015, http://www.becketfund.org/douglas-county-school-district-v-larue-2011-present/.

64. Petition: Douglas County School District, et al., v. Taxpayers for Public Education, et al. (Supreme Court of the United States 2015).

65. Walz v. Tax Commission of the City of New York, 397 United States Reports 664 (Supreme Court of the United States 1970), 689.

66. West Virginia State Board of Education v. Barnette, 319 United States Reports 624 (Supreme Court of the United States 1943), 641.

67. Lawrence D. Weinberg, *Religious Charter Schools: Legalities and Practicalities (PB)* (Information Age Publishing, 2007), 85.

68. Elmer John Thiessen, *Teaching for Commitment: Liberal Education, Indoctrination, and Christian Nurture* (McGill Queen's University Press, 1993), 89.

CHAPTER 5

Citizenship, Achievement, and Accountability

What do we want our education system to accomplish, and can a plural educational system deliver it? American public education has had two longstanding aims: to form democratic citizens and to provide the academic and social capacities necessary for productive adulthood. These aims have held over time, despite significant changes in how we understand citizenship, vocation, and equal access to both.[1]

In 1779, then-Governor Thomas Jefferson argued that Virginia's townships should fund schools for all students. He explained that a common education would enable the next generation to protect democracy and rise above the circumstances of birth.[2]

In 1954, the Supreme Court reflected these themes when it declared *de jure* segregation to be unconstitutional in *Brown v. Board of Education*:

> Education is perhaps the most important function of state and local governments … It is the very foundation of good citizenship [and] the principal instrument in awakening the child to cultural values, in preparing him for later professional training, and in helping him to adjust normally to his environments.[3]

The Court's assumption was the same as Jefferson's: public education exists to create equal access to academic preparation and citizenship training.

In 2012, the Council on Foreign Relations' education report sounded an alarm based on the same goals.[4] "The United States' most foundational strengths are its liberty, democracy, capitalism, equality of opportunity, and unique ability to generate innovation," wrote the authors. "Without a wide base of educated and capable citizens, these strengths will fade, and the United States will lose its leading standing in the world."[5] While not everyone agrees that American education is in such dire shape,[6] it is hard to imagine a leader from Left or from Right who would disagree that "[t]he United States cannot be two countries—one educated and one not, one employable and one not."[7]

© The Author(s) 2017
A.R. Berner, *Pluralism and American Public Education*,
DOI 10.1057/978-1-137-50224-7_5

Is a uniform school system the best way to prepare students for citizenship and adult life? These were certainly its aims. As Charles Glenn put it, "The common school was intended ... above all as the instrumentality by which the particularities of localism and religious tradition and ... of national origin would be integrated into a single, sustaining whole."[8] Was this confidence warranted in the 1840s, and should it be warranted today?

Abundant scholarship suggests that, in fact, a uniform structure provides no *inherent* advantage over a plural one. Rather, studies from the United States and abroad indicate that well-constructed plural systems can help nations realize their academic and civic goals, and that non-public schools often narrow the achievement gaps between rich and poor.[9] This chapter explores such research with an eye to strong civic and academic outcomes.

DEFINITIONS

American educators have argued about academic content and civic formation for a long time. In this book, I use minimalist definitions that resonate across many countries and contexts.

Academic preparation: *"The ability to apply important knowledge effectively to twenty-first-century work environments."*[10]

Democratically engaged: *"Helping students develop relevant knowledge and understanding, and form positive attitudes toward being a citizen [of the nation] and participating in activities related to civic and citizenship education."*[11]

These definitions come from two international organizations: the Organisation for Economic Co-operation and Development (OECD) and the International Association for the Evaluation of Educational Achievement (IEA). Because the use of OECD and IEA research is contested, I want to touch on the limitations of their data sets and on how I use them here.

The OECD administers the famous (or infamous) Programme for International Student Assessment (PISA) tests to 15-year-old students in 65 countries every three years. Its 2012, exam surveyed 510,000 students in reading, math, and science.[12] The IEA, for its part, assesses the civic knowledge and civic attachment of adolescents in its member countries. In 2009, it surveyed 140,000 eighth-grade students and 62,000 teachers and principals in more than 5000 schools in 38 countries—the largest such survey ever conducted.[13]

Using international definitions and data is imperfect and controversial. This is particularly true in the case of PISA results, which are regularly used to bludgeon the American school system for its inadequacies. It is true that comparing national test scores begs a lot of questions. The many incommensurable components between (and even within) countries make direct comparisons tenuous.[14] Test scores are an incomplete measure of students' abilities.[15] The assessment questions may be culturally biased and thus yield spurious results.[16] Countries can boost performance unfairly by excluding certain student populations; Vietnam's "stunning" performance on PISA 2012 can be attributed, at least in part, to significant school drop-out rates among disadvantaged students.[17] Some left-leaning educational leaders consider the OECD's agenda to be capitalistic and thus its findings suspect.[18]

These and other cautions remind us to hold our comparisons lightly. The inherent limitations of international assessments, however, do not preclude our learning something from them. The PISA data offer general indices of academic achievement within and between countries; they explore the effect of education systems upon narrowing gaps between wealthy and poor, native and non-native, students. It is not demonstrable that the tacit motives behind the test are to reinforce existing class structures—in fact, the opposite can and has been argued.[19] The PISA scores are thus imperfect and blunt but nevertheless serviceable instruments.

Just to be clear, I use PISA here not to compare national rankings per se, but rather to allay concerns about plural education. I am thus comfortable using the OECD's understanding of "academic preparation" and making broad-brush observations about uniform and plural systems.

What we mean by "citizenship formation" is also contested, but not to the same degree or for the same reasons. The two most common approaches to citizenship in American schools, civic republicanism and political liberalism, are more similar than not. Civic republicanism emphasizes the unifying aspects of democratic life.[20] Political liberalism emphasizes the individual differences that have a right to flourish within democratic life.[21] Despite the philosophical distinctions between them, both approaches value political knowledge and civic skills. Religious schools often place the same content within a theological framework. See, for instance, the discussion of Alberta, Canada's, Catholic framing of the state-mandated social studies curriculum (p. 149).

So-called critical views of citizenship exist in universities but scarcely touch elementary and secondary schools. Feminist, cultural, reconstructionist/ Marxist, and queer versions of citizenship focus on power structures within society that need to be overturned.[22] Critical citizenship guides students to resist patriarchal, Anglo/White, capitalist, or heteronormative institutions within American society.[23] Yet another approach, "transnational citizenship," emphasizes the complicated, overlapping nature of loyalty and aims to inspire "citizens of the world" rather than of the nation.[24] Critical and transnational citizenship movements are not (or perhaps, not yet) influential in public school classrooms.[25]

Instead, recent research indicates that transmitting political knowledge and civic skills (important to both civic republican and liberal traditions) occupy the lion's share of "citizenship preparation" in American classrooms[26] and seem to be in other Western democracies.[27] This may change over time, but for now, I am comfortable using the IEA's understanding of citizenship.

America's interest in promoting citizenship fluctuates. It declined during the 1970s in the wake of the Vietnam War and amidst a growing conviction among political theorists that explicit civic education did not influence adult democratic behavior. (This view is no longer accepted.) Political interest in civics grew in the 1990s, after a spate of national surveys showed widespread civic illiteracy. In response, activists created new organizations, more robust curricula, online resources, and research projects—all designed to cultivate citizenship in schools.[28]

Other democracies have also experienced "civic turns" in the last decade.[29] A key driver has been the perception, particularly in Europe, that recent immigrants have not integrated well into civil society. Many governments have instituted policies designed to boost civic integration, such as requiring linguistic proficiency and civic understanding *prior* to naturalization.[30] These plans have naturally affected schools. Citizenship "has been introduced in the curriculum of almost every European country, the United States, Canada, and Australia."[31] Studying the role of schools in aiding civic integration has become a "preoccupation" in political theory from Europe[32] to Asia.[33] In contrast to government reports from earlier decades,[34] all but three governments surveyed by IEA in 2009 reported that citizenship education was a "medium" or "high priority."[35]

But how do we measure citizenship? At the very least, we have to include political knowledge and civic skills—which are both aspects of academic preparation—as well as civic behaviors and attitudes. Political scientist David Campbell talks about four key measures of civic formation:

- Participation in public-spirited collective action (community service);
- The capacity to be involved in the political process (civic skills);
- An understanding of the nation's political system (political knowledge);
- Respect for the civil liberties of others (political tolerance).[36]

I refer to these measures throughout the chapter. The IEA assesses these domains and more,[37] and those results are discussed below. Based on the measures surveyed, the IEA's description of what it means to prepare "democratically engaged" students is reasonable: "*Helping them develop relevant knowledge and understanding, and form positive attitudes toward being a citizen and participating in activities related to civic and citizenship education.*"

SUMMARY OF DEFINITIONS

Academic preparation and civic engagement involve knowledge, skill, and attachment, which overlap significantly. An immigrant's son cannot become a lawyer if he does not write well; a lawyer cannot vote intelligently if he does not know his country's history; a social studies teacher will struggle to help her students critique society if she does not value society in the first place. If we have no conception of our legal rights, they are "mere parchment pronouncements."[38] These are the standards we must bring to our examination of uniform and plural schooling. The question is, to what extent does uniform education abet or plural education impair academic and civic preparation?

INTERNATIONAL RESEARCH

There is no evidence from international studies that uniform school systems are superior or that plural school systems harm students. A simple look at the 2012 PISA test results reveals that plural systems often outperform uniform ones.[39] A "simple look" is insufficient to make the case needed here, however; as discussed above, direct international comparisons are problematic for a variety of reasons. What we need, at a minimum, is research that controls for socioeconomic status (SES). This is eminently possible, because PISA gathers information about social background through a 30-minute student questionnaire about family structure, parental educational levels, and the educational environment at home.[40] School principals fill out a similar survey and, in some countries, so do parents.

Two recent projects attempt to connect social background with PISA scores. In their 2014 study, Eric Hanushek, Paul Peterson, and Ludger Woessmann used parental education as a proxy for general socioeconomic standing. They then compared students from low-, middle-, and upper-class standing in different countries to one another. The results show that plural systems can produce top results. On math scores, for instance, seven of the ten countries with the highest scores among students from the most disadvantaged homes have plural systems.[41] Seven of the ten countries with the highest scores among students whose parents have had a *moderate* level of education have plural systems.[42] Seven of the ten countries with the highest scores among students from educationally *elite* homes have plural systems.[43] This analysis also indicates that some countries with uniform school systems, such as Japan and Korea, score at the top of the PISA charts and hold their advantage across all socioeconomic levels.

Hanushek's team correlated the National Assessment of Educational Progress (NAEP) to PISA scores (not a straightforward task)[44] and used parental education alone as a proxy for socioeconomic standing.[45] We can draw a modest conclusion from this study: many countries with plural education systems are academically successful, not only for the wealthiest students but also for the most disadvantaged.

Another report comes from the OECD, which analyzed the 2012 PISA data through the lens of excellence and equity. The OECD defines equity as "providing all students, regardless of gender, family background, or socio-economic status, with opportunities to benefit from education."[46]

Instead of using a single measure (such as parental education) as a proxy for social background, this project creates an index that reflects cultural, social, financial, and educational factors—"indicators such as parental education and occupation, the number and type of home possessions that are considered proxies for wealth, and the educational resources available at home," as well as immigration status and native language capability.[47] The OECD therefore takes more factors into account than did Hanushek, et al.

The OECD's results are ambiguous. On the one hand, many plural systems (such as Australia, Canada, Finland, Hong Kong-China, Liechtenstein, and the Netherlands) are above average on both excellence and equity. On the other hand, some plural systems (such as Chile, Israel, and Luxembourg) are *below* average on excellence and equity. The United States hovers just below the average on both measures.[48]

Which countries do best by immigrant students? It depends who those immigrants are. America can no longer claim pride of place as the "nation of immigrants," as Patrick Wolf and Stephen Macedo describe in their study of European school systems. The United States has a lower percentage of English language learners now than a 100 years ago, and "[m]any European countries—not to mention Canada—are far more deeply divided than the US by language and ethnic and national culture."[49]

To be specific: 21 % of K-12 students in the United States are immigrants, but it is 29 % in Canada, 26 % in New Zealand, and 23 % in Australia.[50] All three outperform us—and they all have plural systems. These countries, however, prioritize highly skilled immigrants, not family members—as ours does—so the comparison is not exact.[51]

A better comparison is with Switzerland, Lichtenstein, Hong Kong, and Luxembourg. These countries also have higher percentages of immigrant students (24 %, 33 %, 35 %, and 46 %, respectively) than the United States does (21 %), and like us, they accept immigrants without discriminating by profession. Singapore is not far behind (18 %). None of these countries sacrifices strong academic outcomes[52] or equity.[53] All of them have plural educational systems.

In sum, when we look at scores on internationally normed tests, we find no discernible patterns to suggest that plural systems do worse by their students. In fact, the opposite case could be made.

But let us move away from international test scores and turn to research in particular countries, which often shows that plural systems can be advantageous for underprivileged students.[54] One of the more surprising findings in the last decade comes from James Tooley, Professor of Education Policy at Newcastle upon Tyne. Tooley's work with the financial arm of the World Bank led him into schools and neighborhoods around the world. In Hyderabad, India, he encountered something unexpected: in the highest-poverty area of the city, many children attended unregulated, ramshackle, yet intellectually challenging private schools—which their families preferred to the attractive but education-ally lacking public schools. Fascinated, Tooley quit the World Bank and began to study unregulated private schools in India and elsewhere.

His research team's findings in China, Ghana, Nigeria, Kenya, and India confirmed what Tooley had seen in Hyderabad: in urban and peri-urban areas, a majority of economically deprived children attended under-the-radar, unreg-ulated schools. Astonishingly, these schools often outperformed public schools and came close to catching the private, state-recognized schools of the middle classes.[55] They did so at a fraction of the cost of state schools.[56] Tooley became convinced that the colonial emphasis on state-operated education had been, on balance, misguided—and that the desperately poor knew it.[57]

Expanding access to private schools has become a priority in more developed countries. When the Australian national government discovered that its private schools closed achievement gaps more effectively than did state schools, it provided vouchers for low-income students to move to the independent sector. As a result, nearly half of the students in elite independent schools come from economically disadvantaged homes.[58] Countries with longstanding educational freedom, such as the Netherlands, resist comparing schools across sectors; the point of having diverse schools is not that they are *better* but that they are *different*.[59] Nevertheless, in seven European countries with plural systems, after controlling for family background, students in religious schools outperformed those in state schools, and with less funding.[60] There are many more such examples.

The analyses above do not demonstrate that plural systems *automatically* generate excellence and equity. Other factors besides structure are at play, such as financial resources, teacher quality, disciplinary atmosphere, and curricular rigor.[61] Although there is no straight line between structure and performance, my claim holds: plural systems are manifestly capable of nurturing academic excellence, and of doing so equitably.

But what about democratic formation? It is possible that plural systems produce reasonably well-educated, but civically isolated, young adults. We may wonder whether the center can hold in the Netherlands, with its 36 different school types, or in Alberta, which now includes Inuit and homeschooling in its mosaic of funded options. Do such countries help students prepare for democratic life?

The most basic measurement of democratic engagement is whether adults vote or not. Across OECD countries, 72 % of registered voters cast a ballot in their latest national election cycle.[62] Denmark, Sweden, New Zealand, and the Netherlands, among others, have plural education systems and above-average voter participation; Israel, Canada, and the United Kingdom are a few of the countries that have plural systems and below-average voter participation. In the United States, 67 % of voters came out in the 2012 national election.

The voting data, however, offer us no causal connection between educational structure and voter participation. They merely suggest, minimally, that countries with plural educational systems do not appear to produce democratically indifferent populations.

More detailed analysis leads to the same conclusion. The IEA's 2009 survey, described above, examined civic knowledge by posing 79 questions, 73 of which were multiple-choice, and 6 of which were "constructed-response" that were coded by each country's research team. The survey explored civic society and systems, civic principles, civic participation, and civic identity. It assessed students' specific knowledge and capacity to reason with and from the knowledge.[63] The results were scored on three levels indicating general to advanced understanding of the facts and theories of governance.[64]

It is clear from this data set that students from educationally plural countries do just fine on civic knowledge: six of the top-scoring ten countries have plural systems.[65] As with academic performance (of which civic knowledge is a subset), multiple factors influence these results. The IEA's analysis takes into account the variations in policy environment, recent history, curricula, demographic composition, and economic standing of each country. As with the literacy and numeracy assessed by PISA, there is no straight line between educational structures and outcomes.

What about with civic attachment and participatory behaviors? There are no discernible differences between uniform and plural systems when it comes to students' attitudes toward equal rights for men and women, ethnic and racial minorities, and immigrants; their trust in civic institutions; or their interest in political issues.[66]

In sum, international research suggests that plural educational systems do not impair, and often seem to enhance, students' academic outcomes and civic formation.

RESEARCH ON AMERICAN SCHOOL SECTORS

What do we find when we turn to the United States? We find an academic and civic advantage to private and charter schools—particularly for minority and low-income children.[67] These research findings have been validated many times and reflect a general consensus in the field. While we cannot assume that radically pluralizing our system would yield these results writ large—such research represents a small percentage of our students—we can at least claim that our fear of plural systems is unwarranted and should be reconsidered.

Two important caveats when examining school sector research. First, school sector research must try to separate the "school effect" from family background, and can never entirely do so. The difficulty is this: because children with well-educated and/or affluent parents enter school with clear educational advantages, their high performance is not surprising. It does no good to compare the results of students from private and public schools without discounting, or "controlling" for, family background. The important questions are whether different school settings elicit different outcomes from the same student, and whether there is any predictability about which school setting does a better job. Researchers are developing increasingly sophisticated mechanisms to control for family background and thus answer the key questions. A good example, complete with diagrams, may be found in Bryk, Lee, and Holland's *Catholic Schools and the Common Good* (1993).[68]

Second, school sector research has to contend with "selection bias." Here, the question is whether students whose parents *selected* a school are already so different from those whose parents did not that any supposed "school effect" is spurious. How can we get around this problem? The lottery mechanism for charter school admissions offers what is considered the gold-standard opportunity, as the families who entered the lottery were of the same "selection" category. Scholars can thus compare the academic outcomes of students who won a charter seat with those who went by default to the traditional district school. This method has its limitations, though, and newer methods are now being used. Some of them are discussed below.

ACADEMIC PREPARATION

First and most importantly, there is no evidence that America's public schools, as a category, provide superior academic preparation to other schools. The crucial question is not whether some public schools are outstanding (they certainly are),[69] but whether public schools are *inherently* better than non-public schools at narrowing the academic achievement gap. Such a stance cannot be supported by research that compares the effect of traditional public, charter, and non-public schools on student outcomes.

School sector research, or comparisons between public, Catholic, Protestant, Jewish, and independent schools (as examples), began in earnest with the work of James Coleman. In 1964, Coleman, then a young sociologist at Johns Hopkins University, was given oversight of the federal government's largest study of schooling outcomes to date. The purpose of the project was to assess whether the Civil Rights legislation was making a difference in educational opportunity. Before *Equality of Educational Opportunity* (1966), known simply as *The Coleman Report*, school quality was judged by inputs such as per-student funding, number of books, number of teachers, extra-curricular activities, and so on. Coleman's report changed this. He focused on outcomes.

Assuming that minority and low-income children entered the school system with disadvantages, the "fundamental question" of the 1966 survey was how well the schools mediated those disadvantages. Did the schools enable young people to thrive despite having uneducated parents, underemployed parents, non-English-speaking homes, impoverished neighborhoods, or racially prejudiced surroundings?[70]

Coleman's team pursued this question through numerous lenses. The team analyzed data from 4000 schools. All the teachers, principals, and superintendents in these schools participated, as did students in third, sixth, ninth, and twelfth grades—a total of 645,000 students.[71] Students completed extensive surveys and took achievement tests in core academic subjects. In contrast to the current Partnership for Assessment of Readiness for College and Careers (PARCC) or Smarter Balanced assessments, which attempt to avoid subject matter that might be tied to SES,[72] Coleman's measured specific knowledge and skills that all students should have learned—regardless of background.[73]

Coleman's team controlled for family background.[74] They examined school climate. They compared the achievement test scores. They assessed the influence of classmates' motivations and teachers' backgrounds upon student achievement and attitudes. Again, the question they asked was not whether some students did well or whether some schools produced generally good results, but whether the public schools were able to mitigate the disadvantages with which some children entered them.

The research team concluded that America's public schools *did not change the outcomes that were predicted by a child's background.* The schools therefore failed to provide equality of educational opportunity.[75] Children born in disadvantage stayed in disadvantage.

Seventeen years later, Coleman published the results of another study, this one examining not only public but also Catholic and non-Catholic private schools. In *High School Achievement: Public, Catholic, and Private Schools Compared* (1982), Coleman concluded that the achievement gaps within public high schools actually *increased* with every passing year of high school.[76] He wrote: "The data serve as a reminder that the public schools of the United States constitute a rather highly stratified and differentiated set of schools, not the common school envisioned by Horace Mann."[77]

Non-Catholic private schools elevated student performance across all income groups. However, helping all students to the same degree did nothing to address the achievement gaps, which persisted across all four high school years—an only partially successful outcome.[78]

Catholic high schools, in contrast, simultaneously raised performance and narrowed the gap between advantaged and disadvantaged children—and narrowed it year after year until the results, by the end of high school, were nearly "homogeneous."[79] That is, in a Catholic high school, a disadvantaged child would graduate on par with her more advantaged peers. In Coleman's words, "Catholic schools come closer to the American ideal of the 'common school,' educating all alike, than do the public schools."[80] Coleman's conclusions were stunning and controversial, and they sparked an increased interest in school sector comparisons.

Have Coleman's conclusions held over time? Yes, although with important qualifications and via different methodologies. Subsequent studies confirm an academic advantage to private, and particularly Catholic, high schools, although with greater nuance than Coleman's initial research. William Jeynes's meta-analysis (2007) suggested that religious schools raised academic attainment across the board—even after factoring out the social and family effects—and began to close the achievement gap.[81] Bryk, Lee, and Holland reached the same conclusion.[82] Two separate analyses of public and private high school graduates (2011 and 2014) showed that America's private high schools—particularly Catholic and non-religious independent schools—generated academic attainment above and beyond family culture.[83] A study in Los Angeles (2010) concluded that minority students who won need-based scholarships to attend Catholic middle schools surpassed their peers who did not, across a variety of academic measures.[84] Vivian Louie's research on immigrant students (2012) suggests that Catholic schools do a particularly good job of providing the social capital necessary for social and educational advancement.[85] A 2012 Brookings study showed that a scholarship program that allowed underprivileged kids in New York City to attend a private elementary school for three years substantially increased college enrollment among African Americans.[86] Note that the matter at hand is how these schools change the life trajectory of disadvantaged students, not whether the schools are objectively better for *all* students.

Where do public charter schools fit into a pluralistic picture, and how do their outcomes differ from traditional public schools? Charters are publicly funded and publicly accountable, but not publicly operated, schools. They are allowed to craft distinctive albeit non-religious missions and, in most states, build school cultures that follow. Because they differ from traditional district schools in these important ways, charters represent an important move toward pluralism. As to outcomes, the answer seems to be that it depends on which group of students we are talking about, and where the charters are located geographically.

The most prominent charter research comes from CREDO, Stanford University's Center for Research on Educational Outcomes. CREDO's latest raft of data compares the outcomes of charter students in 27 states with matched peers in the neighboring traditional public schools.[87] In aggregate, charter school students' reading test scores are equivalent to an additional seven days of reading instruction over their traditional school peers, and their math scores are comparable. This is hardly headline news.

The story becomes more interesting by demographic subgroup. The students who benefited most clearly from attending a charter school were among the most educationally vulnerable: Black and Hispanic students living in poverty, and all English language learners. The effect size is particularly striking for Black students living in poverty, for whom attending a charter school was the equivalent of gaining 29 extra days in reading and 36 in math over their traditional public school peers.[88] For Black *non*-poverty students, charter school results were no different than traditional public schools. For Whites, Asians, and not-in-poverty Hispanics, charters produced a *negative* effect.[89]

The results also differ according to location. In the aggregate, urban charters give students the equivalent of 40 additional days in math and 28 additional days in reading per year. As above, these gains are particularly significant for Black, Hispanic, low-income, and special education students.[90] Some cities are hyper-performers: charter students in Boston, Newark, and Memphis (to name a few) perform at a level so high that they will "erase the learning deficits" that exist in their region between advantaged and disadvantaged students.[91] Other cities (although far fewer)—Austin, Ft. Myers, and Las Vegas among them— produce negative learning effects.[92]

What makes the difference? The president of CREDO, Dr. Margaret Raymond, believes it is attributable to the state's charter accountability laws. Some of the first charter states, such as Arizona and Ohio, passed weak accountability laws and consequently allow low-performing charters to stay open. In other states, such as Massachusetts and New York, the bar to opening and renewing a charter is high, and the schools superior.[93] Teacher recruitment also matters; charters thrive when it is possible to attract well-educated, enthusiastic teachers. The top five cities (Boston, Newark, San Francisco, New York City, and Washington, DC) "[s]erve as hothouses of young talent for charter operators," as does the "second tier" (Memphis, New Orleans, Detroit, Milwaukee). Others (Ft. Myers, Phoenix, Las Vegas) are not so lucky.[94]

As a sector, therefore, charters moderately improve academic outcomes in reading but not in math. In states with very high quality standards, on the other hand, charters prove academically transformative for the most educationally vulnerable students. As a sector, the trajectory of charter schools is in the right direction: the aggregate learning gains of charter school students improved between 2009 and 2013.[95] Other research also shows compelling gains.[96]

The conclusion reached above—that the academic advantage belongs to charter and private rather than to traditional public schools—holds despite the fluidity of the school sectors themselves. How are the sectors changing? Catholic schools, at their zenith during Coleman's work, have declined in number— although new and nimble structures may reverse that trend.[97] The number of charter schools continues to expand, and their academic standards are becoming higher.[98] The number of homeschooling students, virtually nonexistent 50 years ago, is equal to that of charter students. Some public school districts have meanwhile become more innovative and have increased performance. As an example, during the Bloomberg years, New York City created 150 small high schools that are yielding fruit for disadvantaged students.[99] Other low-performing districts are now under charter or state control, although academic outcomes have been mixed.[100] Thus, over time, we should expect to see shifts in the academic performance of all sectors—one hopes, for the better.

Some of the findings will no doubt become more specific as new research (explores the important distinctions that exist *within* each school sector charter schools being the exception). For instance, the intellectual heft of Protestant schools varies greatly: church-based fundamentalist schools may take an anti-intellectual stance,[101] while classical Christian schools seek academic coherence and rigor.[102] Hasidic schools often resist the study of secular material, whereas independent Jewish day schools offer tremendous access to intellectual debate.[103] It is not possible to claim that a given student will *always* perform better academically in a non-public than in a public school; there are simply too many variations and variables. Major research projects are underway to probe these questions,[104] but much more work remains to be done.

Finally, the findings will sharpen as the methodology used to compare school effects becomes more sophisticated. Coleman's work relied upon regression analyses, which hold background characteristics (such as parental education and income) constant, in an effort to assess the "outcome of interest" (such as the "Catholic school effect"). Regression analysis is methodologically rigorous but also inflexible: it cannot look at the interaction of factors across time. Propensity analysis is a new approach that matches similar students in different environments and studies the effects across time.[105] One recent use of propensity analysis indicated no statistically significant advantage to Catholic elementary schools; this study found that the Catholic school advantage disappeared when family characteristics were taken into account.[106] This single study is striking, but it has not been replicated (yet) nor does it contravene the research cited above, which explored middle schools and high schools, not elementary schools. Structural equation modeling allows researchers to evaluate more than one outcome variable at the same time. This approach recently allowed researchers to determine the effect of two pre-K programs (Montessori and HighScope) upon two different types of children over multiple points of time, simultaneously.[107] Structural equation modeling has not, as of this writing, been applied to school sectors in the higher grades.

An emerging area of research looks at how schools within a high-choice system affect one another. As more and more states adopt tax credit and voucher policies, it is becoming possible to assess the impact of such policies on an educational ecosystem. A 2010 study of the impact of Florida's tax credit program on a large school district indicated that academic outcomes improved not only for those students who left the public schools, but also for those who remained in them.[108] The reasons for the public school improvement are not clear. It might have been the result of increased competition for students and Title 1 funding, or it might simply have been the fact that the scholarships went to the lowest-performing students,[109] leaving the public schools with a less challenging student body.

The results from Florida echo research from abroad. Sweden allowed districts to pluralize through a per-capita funding mechanism in 1992; in some districts, as many as 45 % of the students attend non-public schools. Twenty years on, these reforms seem to have boosted the performance of all schools within a heavily plural district without raising educational costs.[110] In the Netherlands, "the educational performance of all schools is enhanced in areas where they coexist in a 'balance of power' and no single type of school dominates the others."[111]

Despite the evolving nature of school sector research, the changing methodological approaches, and the difficulty of importing lessons from abroad or even from one district to another, however, it seems clear that traditional public schools do not have an inherent academic advantage. The empirical record shows, rather, that private and charter schools provide at least as good, and sometimes better, academic preparation for students—particularly minority and low-SES students. This research record has never been successfully challenged.[112]

DEMOCRATIC FORMATION

But what about citizenship? Surely in this domain, America's public schools have an inherent advantage.[113] The record suggests otherwise: private schools often do a better job. I find this particularly striking, since the original rationale for a uniform system was that it *uniquely* prepared students for democratic life.

In bald terms, the civic knowledge and capacity of American students is remarkably thin.[114] In 2010, a hefty majority (80 % and 75 %) of eighth and twelfth graders scored *below proficiency level* on the NAEP Civics exam.[115] NAEP's more recent (2014) Civics scores were deemed "flat" by most experts, although there were some positive signs within minority subgroups.[116]

Let us get specific about an important subject: the civil rights movement. Rod Paige, US Secretary of Education (2001–2005), lamented American students' lack of knowledge about the civil rights movement, its impetus, and its longstanding arguments. They know about Martin Luther King, Jr.'s famous "I Have a Dream" speech, but little else:

> In 1996, only 43 % of eighth graders gave an "appropriate" response when asked why marchers participated in Martin Luther King Jr.'s 1963 march on Washington. In 2001, only 34 % could identify that the phrase 'Jim Crow' refers to laws that 'enforced racial segregation' as opposed to laws that made liquor illegal, restricted immigration, or protected the environment.

> Then there are twelfth graders, those on the cusp of adulthood and full citizenship. In 2006, only 38 % could identify appropriately the social policy reflected by a sign declaring "COLORED ENTRANCE" above the door of a theater. In addition, only 28 % knew that the main issue in the Lincoln-Douglas debates of 1858 was whether slavery should be expanded into new US territories, and 40 % failed to identify the purpose of the punitive 'Black Codes' passed in the South during Reconstruction.[117]

Most American students know neither the basic, shameful facts about American slavery nor its enduring consequences. How can they hope to enter into contemporary debates about race and culture?

Qualitative studies also show that most students have not formed "citizen identities." For most of them, citizenship constitutes either a thin patriotism or an elaboration of good manners.[118] In the early 1990s, scholars Conover and Searing studied four very different public school communities: agricultural families in Minnesota, blue-collar workers in Philadelphia, immigrants in Texas, and suburbanites in North Carolina.[119] The researchers interviewed not only students, teachers, and principals, but also 125 additional adults from each community. They found pockets of patriotism—particularly in the immigrant group—but little evidence of coherence or depth of knowledge about what citizenship *means*. Calling their project "a sobering portrait of the 'making of Americans'," Conover and Searing summarized:

> Although most students have strong citizen identities, these identities are experienced as free-floating abstractions that are not tied to the students' understanding of what it means to be a citizen or to their behaviors. Similarly, most students have thin understandings of what it means to be a citizen, understandings dominated by a focus on rights and deficient in a sense of

obligation. For most, being a good citizen requires only that one obey the law, vote, and act patriotically. All public activity beyond this falls to the "virtuous citizen" to perform. Particularly troubling is the finding that few students have a clear sense of their "future selves" as adult citizens. Without well-defined images of who they wish to become as citizens, it will be difficult for them consciously to construct a practice of citizenship and a rich public life.[120]

Their recommendations to remedy this problem? A rigorous curriculum with academic depth and frequent classroom debate[121]—curiously, the "goods" more often associated with private schools.

In contrast to students in the public school communities above, students from private schools know more about democracy and possess more skills to participate.[122] They also volunteer at greater rates and, with one exception (discussed below), are more politically generous toward those with whom they disagree. This holds after controlling for family background.

The research to support this claim is compelling. In 2007, Patrick Wolf analyzed 21 quantitative studies on the effects of private and public schools on seven civic virtues: the four enumerated by Campbell (community service, civic skills, political knowledge, and political tolerance) plus social capital ("the extent to which a person is networked within their community"), political participation (voting, writing government representatives), and patriotism ("a visceral positive connection to one's country and respect for its national symbols and rituals").[123] Taken together, the study yielded 59 discrete findings that connected particular school types with civic outcomes and that separated school effect from family background.

The vast majority of the findings (56 out of 59) suggested a neutral-to-positive effect of non-public schools on civic outcomes. Only 3 of 59 findings were negative: "[E]vangelical Protestant schools reduce political tolerance, secular private schools decrease voluntarism, and private schooling of any sort may diminish a particularly passionate form of patriotism."[124] Among the most rigorous subset of studies, *only one of 22 findings* indicated a public school advantage: the sentiment of patriotism.[125] But patriotic attachment without commensurate knowledge of civics and history may be worrying, not comforting. Even this single positive finding is not unalloyed.

David Campbell's 2008 comparison of public and private school outcomes also concluded that private schools did a better job than public schools in nurturing his indicators of citizenship behavior: civic skills, community service, political knowledge, and political tolerance. The only negative finding was that evangelical Protestant school graduates showed slightly diminished political tolerance compared to the rest.[126] A 2011 study of graduates of American schools suggested that graduates of Catholic and Protestant schools were active participants in their communities, not separatists.[127] (The sample included too few Jewish and Muslim school graduates to be conclusive about those school sectors.)

One area needing further investigation is the variation that exists *within* each school sector. As with academic cultivation, policymakers will want to understand the differences between how a fundamentalist and a classical Christian school prepare students for democratic life, or whether independent boarding schools do a better job than day schools. The civic capacity of charters remains understudied.[128] The same is true of homeschooling. Early evidence indicates that homeschoolers, particularly non-religious ones, have low levels of social trust.[129] Does this translate directly into low levels of civic participation? Or into discriminatory voting patterns? We simply do not know enough to say.

While there are still unexplored issues within school sector research, the preponderance of data suggests that, as one political scientist wrote in 2012, "[i]t is time to move beyond the question of whether public or private schools are 'better' at civic education ... [E]mpirical evidence makes clear that private schooling is not a detriment to civic education. In many cases, private schools surpass their public counterparts." The more pertinent question, instead, is "*why* do schools differ in the civic education they offer?"[130]

THE WHY QUESTION

Why do America's private and urban charter schools frequently outpace public schools, academically and civically, with the same group of students? I think there are at least two reasons.

The first is that private and urban charter schools tend to be more academically rigorous than public schools. As Diane Ravitch describes it, a content-rich academic curriculum, "Refers ... to the systematic study of language and literature, science and mathematics, history, the arts, and foreign languages." These pursuits, she continues, "Convey important knowledge and skills, cultivate aesthetic imagination, and teach students to think critically and reflectively about the world in which they live."[131] Some of the world's highest-performing countries (including Australia, Canada, Finland, France, the Netherlands, and Singapore) require students to learn specific knowledge, year on year. Most countries allow some curricular variations. The Dutch and Austrian governments often approve equivalent, alternative curricula; France allows schools to choose the textbooks and methods by which to teach the set national curriculum; Israel lets Arab-language schools modify the curriculum in consultation with the government. In many of these countries, students also sit "exit exams" at the end of high school. These tests are comprehensive and content-specific.[132]

The tight coupling of content-rich curriculum and exit exams narrows the achievement gap. It also incentivizes students, who must take primary responsibility for their learning and results. This scenario is vastly different from the accountability structures in the United States that reward or penalize teachers maximally, but students minimally. As Martin West argued recently, "Exit exams in many European and Asian countries cover a broader swath of the curriculum, play a central role in determining students' postsecondary options, and carry significant weight in the labor market." As a consequence, "These systems provide strong incentives for student effort and valuable information to parents and other stakeholders about the relative performance of secondary schools."[133] The OECD report on excellence and equity makes the same point: teaching rigorous mathematics to *all* a country's students narrows the achievement gap between advantaged and disadvantaged.[134] The IEA's 2015 international analysis of academically resilient students, defined as "those ... who are academically successful, despite coming from the socioeconomically disadvantaged backgrounds that have typically predicted poorer educational outcomes,"[135] finds the most important driver to be, "environments of high academic achievement [that] support academic resilience among disadvantaged students."[136]

In the USA, students in Catholic and independent schools are more likely to have gone through a meaningful academic curriculum—particularly in high school. They take more advanced courses. They also attend more competitive colleges.[137] This was true when Coleman wrote, and it is true now.[138]

A common corollary of rigorous academics is what political scientists call an "open classroom," or one that welcomes frequent discussion and debate about current political issues. David Campbell examined the effect of classroom climate upon students' civic knowledge, appreciation of conflict, and likelihood of voting. He found that a classroom climate that embraced frequent and civil debate about political issues was more powerful in shaping these attributes than almost any other factor. In his words, "it is the nature of political discussion within the classroom, not simply the frequency of formal social studies instruction, which has the effect. A classroom environment which fosters a free, open, and respectful exchange of ideas is positively related to young people's level of knowledge about democratic processes."[139] A salient example is Walter Feinberg's portrait of Jewish day schools, where public deliberation becomes high art.[140] Responsibility, frequent engagement, an open classroom, reasoned debate: these are the building blocks of democratic habit.[141]

One common defense of public schools' less challenging academics is that they have to educate more students and from more diverse backgrounds. High-level coursework, in this view, is simply not possible given the exogenous factors that bear on student learning. This justification needs to be dismissed out of hand. The lower academic standards found in public schools are *not* the inevitable consequence of "mass education." It is not the case that public schools have to educate a wider range of children and therefore *need* to teach at a more basic level. On the contrary, public school leaders began to dismantle academic depth a 100 years ago, out of the intellectual conviction that the traditional curriculum was damaging to children—as Diane Ravitch's *Left Back* chronicles in great detail.[142] *Left Back* is not for the faint of heart. In its pages, Ravitch describes the deliberate dismantling of the academic curriculum in the name of social efficiency,[143] expressivism,[144] eugenics,[145] vocational preparation,[146] social activism,[147] social adjustment,[148] and most continually "child nature"—which was said to unfold so successfully, without the imposition of new knowledge, that even teaching children the "rules" of punctuation was considered suspect.[149] Ravitch summarized the trajectory she describes in her 500-page manuscript:

> The three great errors demonstrated in these pages are, first, the belief that schools should be expected to solve all of society's problems; second, the belief that only a portion of children need access to a high-quality academic education; and third, the belief that schools should emphasize students' immediate experiences and minimize (or even ignore) the transmission of knowledge.[150]

The move away from academic content may have been well intentioned, but it has been disastrous for first-generation and low-income families who, when given the opportunity, thrive in academically challenging contexts.[151] Nor is the recent move toward standards and skills sufficient; as David Steiner points out, testing for general skills places educationally disadvantaged students even further behind their better-off peers.[152]

Many Catholic, Jewish, and independent schools, on the other hand, maintain a college-preparatory curriculum that classical Protestant schools and high-performing charters emulate to good effect. A 2015 analysis of two charter networks in New York (Icahn and Success Academy) concluded that their robust intellectual curricula were a significant factor in boosting student achievement to the level of the state's independent and suburban public schools.[153] Tougher academics and higher expectations open doors for underprivileged students by expanding their background knowledge, establishing a strong academic identity, and imparting the academic skills needed in college and beyond.

When public schools embrace rigorous academics and high expectations, they also see strong results. A striking example is what happened when Chicago introduced the International Baccalaureate Diploma Program ("IB") and a pre-IB program into 13 low-performing public high schools in 1997. Long-term analysis that matched students who enrolled in the four-year program with those who did not found that the IB students were 40 % more likely to attend a four-year college and 50 % more likely to attend a selective college than their matched peers. They were also significantly more likely to persist through college.[154] Several indications may mute these results; there were no positive effects for students who left the program before completion, and the IB curriculum may have become less rigorous since the students whose results were examined. The point is that these students rose to the challenge. Given the IB's success at no additional school cost, it is tragic that so many public schools continue to under-challenge underprivileged students.

The second reason for stronger outcomes in private and charter schools: it is easier for them to construct strong school cultures in which explicit ideals permeate school life. This means something very different from a friendly school, or a high-achieving school, or a school with few discipline problems. Rather, it means a school where the moral vocabulary, rituals, discipline, academic expectations, and relationships align. Such a school can define its mission, hire faculty who concur, and attract students and parents based upon a shared vision. Of course, no school does this perfectly—and some hardly do it at all. But the entire enterprise can grow tall and deep, starting from ideals as straightforward as ensuring that all students are prepared for college and as complex as the Baltimore Catechism.

Evidence from around the world suggests that studying within "distinctive educational communities in which pupils and teachers share a common *ethos*" vastly increases the odds of acquiring academic and civic knowledge, skills, and sensibilities.[155] A review of the research on outcomes of England's schools, for instance, showed that Catholic students exhibit a keener sense of life's having meaning, higher academic achievement, and a clearer sense of belonging to a community than other students. (Interestingly, Church of England schools had no such advantages—discussed in Chap. 6.)[156] Education scholar Charles Glenn puts it this way: "Schools with a distinctive identity ... offer educational advantages deriving from their clarity of focus."[157] I want to emphasize that this asset goes above and beyond academic rigor; indeed, such schools may place intellectual formation itself within a larger moral framework that makes sense of success and failure alike.[158]

Anthony Bryk, Valerie Lee, and Peter Holland provided an in-depth description of organic community in *Catholic Schools and the Common Good* (1993). The Catholic schools they studied were organized within a "communal" framework that encompassed all areas of school life. The schools' commitment to a common, constrained, challenging academic curriculum, for instance, did not stand alone. It was, rather rooted in a Thomistic concept of a human being that sees reason as "the common inheritance of all men and women" and a vital reflection of our "being made in the image and likeness of God."[159] The community's adults shared a common responsibility to "shape adolescents' lives through personal interaction and individual example."[160] Students and faculty alike were urged toward the Christian virtues of "faith, hope, and love," which serve as "classic institutional norms, in that they motivate and inspire behavior toward a different world." They possess "the ability to bring meaning to action and thereby transcend the instrumental intent of action."[161] Bryk's team was not interested in valorizing Catholic schools per se; they were interested in discovering which factors make Catholic schools so equalizing.[162] The answer lay in the "expansive, liberating, and humanizing" beliefs about the human person that were carried throughout the community.[163]

This is profoundly not about religion or religious schools; Scott Seider found the same effects in the (non-religious) charter schools he studied in Boston. All three schools served students from low socioeconomic standing; all three produced very high student test scores; all three aimed for college matriculation; all three featured extended days, longer school years, and strict discipline.[164] But they rested on very different philosophies and produced very different cultures. Boston Prep pursued an Aristotelian approach to moral virtue; its students and faculty engaged in philosophical reflections about the good life, the nature of courage, and when one should choose compassion over justice. Roxbury Prep focused on performance virtues such as grit, resilience, and optimism. Pacific Rim grew out of Eastern thought and emphasized global character; each student learned Mandarin, and teachers rewarded "making a contribution" over "getting ahead."

These schools, wrote Seider, provided a common moral vocabulary and rationale that flowed through all of their activities: straightforward honor codes, student orientations, visits to family homes before the school year, "the back and forth conversations as an important break from the high level of structure," "social capital such as shaking hands and self-advocacy with teachers," advisory groups, the depth of ethical reflection, and the way the schools talked about community service.[165]

Some education researchers call these "effective schools." They are organized so as to create "clear school goals, rigorous academic standards, order and discipline, homework, strong leadership by the principal, teacher participation in decision-making, parental support and cooperation, and high expectations for student performance."[166]

Traditional public schools can be effective schools, but against the odds. Richard Arum has written about the legal strictures that impede student discipline.[167] Recent lawsuits describe the difficulties of faculty selection and dismissal,[168] and James Davison Hunter has analyzed the inability of public schools to articulate normative values.[169] These are discrete but related challenges to creating an effective school.

The larger problem is that bureaucracies *inevitably* create challenges of this kind, as John Chubb and Terry Moe explored in *Politics, Markets & America's Schools* (1990). The authors write from a libertarian perspective that views choice and competition as inherent goods. I have argued, against this libertarian view, that choice alone is insufficient, and that without guardrails choice can undermine excellence and equity. Nevertheless, Chubb and Moe's trenchant critique of governmental bureaucracy helps make sense of the underperformance of public schools and the difficulty of changing them.

All organizations require some administrative power to function properly, Chubb and Moe explain, but the extensive bureaucracy in the public school system is simultaneously necessary and debilitating. Why necessary? Public schools are political and therefore subject to institutional instability. "Public authority," they write, "is delegated"; it can be revoked; it is subject to change.[170] It requires compliance across a multi-layered system. Highly formalized administration exists to address the threats of non-compliance and policy change. As Chubb and Moe put it, "[e]ffective bureaucracy is commonly built around rules that specify appropriate behavior, rewards and sanctions that encourage such behavior, and monitoring to ascertain whether goals are being met, whether rules are being followed, when rewards are called for, and whether rules and incentive systems need to be adjusted."[171]

This formalization should not be interpreted as "sinister." It is, rather, the necessary outcome of the heterogeneous interests and multiple layers (federal, state, local, school, classroom) that are represented.

But the bureaucratic regime is also debilitating. Detailed procedures and verifications diminish—indeed, are designed to diminish—the role of human judgment. Bureaucracy unintentionally works *against* the creation of a coherent community. Principals cannot build their own team of teachers; teachers cannot exercise judgment in their use of time; adults "hold lower and more ambiguous expectations of their students"; instruction time gives way to the demands of compliance and reporting.[172] Principals and teachers become managers rather than leaders,[173] and a distinctive mission remains elusive.[174]

Some traditional public schools do possess the markers of effective organizations, but Chubb and Moe are pessimistic that this counts for more than an accident of geography and political quiescence.[175] They might say the same about uniform school systems that have strong academic outcomes; Japan and Korea, at the top of PISA charts, are not known for diverse or restive populations. The uniform systems in place in China's top-performing provinces are demographically diverse but may enjoy political quiescence for political reasons and, as such, do not contradict Chubb and Moe's thesis. In any case, their thesis concerns not performance but meaningful change, about which the pair is pessimistic, since (they believe) no reform, however beneficial and agreed-upon, can overwhelm the enervating aspects of a bureaucratic regime.[176] Chubb and Moe conclude that, "[even if] reformers are right about where they want to go, their institutions cannot get them there."[177] One of the major funders of education reform in the United States, the Eli and Edythe Broad Foundation, may have concluded the same thing: after decades of supporting urban education reform, the Foundation posted a list entitled, "75 Examples of how Bureaucracy Stands in the Way of America's Students and Teachers."[178]

Here, then, lies a significant and, in most contexts, insurmountable problem: Our traditional public schools act as bureaucratic agencies rather than as the organic communities that work well for so many students. Changing this fact depends not upon laws, regulations, or funding, but upon a new institutional framework, one that supports and regulates a panoply of schools. The next chapters explore the possibilities and limitations of pluralism. The bottom line of *this* chapter is that the vast majority of research, both from abroad and also from the United States, suggests that, contrary to the opinion of Horace Mann, there is *no clear advantage to a uniform system of education* in its ability to prepare students academically or civically. In fact, the advantage seems to lie elsewhere.

NOTES

1. Only white, property-owning males could be "citizens" in the early republic, and expectations about what counts as "productive adult lives" have changed substantially over time.
2. Lorraine McDonnell, "Defining Democratic Purposes," in *Rediscovering the Democratic Purposes of Education*, ed. Lorraine McDonnell, P. Michael Timpane,

and Roger Benjamin, Studies in Government and Public Policy (Lawrence, KS: University Press of Kansas, 2000), 1–14, 28.

3. Oliver Brown, Mrs. Richard Lawton, Mrs. Sadie Emmanuel, et al. v. Board of Education of Topeka, 347 United States Reports 483 (Supreme Court of the United States 1954), 493.

4. Council on Foreign Relations. Independent Task Force et al., *U. S. Education Reform and National Security* (New York, NY: Council on Foreign Relations, Independent Task Force, 2012), x.

5. Ibid., 5–6.

6. See, for instance, David Berliner, Gene V. Glass, and & Associates, *50 Myths and Lies That Threaten America's Public Schools: The Real Crisis in Education* (New York, NY: Teachers College Press, 2014), 14–15.

7. Council on Foreign Relations. Independent Task Force et al., *U. S. Education Reform and National Security*, viii–ix.

8. Charles Leslie Glenn, *The Myth of the Common School* (Amherst: University of Massachusetts Press, 1988), 9.

9. David E. Campbell, Meira Levinson, and Frederick M. Hess, *Making Civics Count: Citizenship Education for a New Generation*, 2012, 12.

10. OECD, PISA 2012 Results: What Students Know and Can Do (Volume I, Revised Edition, February 2014) (Paris: Organisation for Economic Co-operation and Development, 2014), http://www.oecd-ilibrary.org/content/book/9789264208780-en.

11. Wolfram Schulz et al., *ICCS 2009 International Report: Civic Knowledge, Attitudes, and Engagement among Lower-Secondary School Students in 38 Countries* (International Association for the Evaluation of Educational Achievement. Herengracht 487, Amsterdam, 1017 BT, The Netherlands. Tel: +31-20-625-3625; Fax: +31-20-420-7136; e-mail: department@iea.nl; Web site: http://www.iea.nl, 2010), 15.

12. http://www.oecd.org/pisa/keyfindings/pisa-2012-results.htm, downloaded June 20, 2015.

13. Schulz et al, *ICCS 2009 International Report*, 16. The United States participated in the 1999, but not in the 2008–2009, study.

14. See, for instance, Kadriye Ercikan, Wolff-Michael Roth, and Mustafa Asil, "Cautions about Inferences from International Assessments: The Case of PISA 2009," *Teachers College Record* 117, no. 010301 (January 2015): 28.

15. See, for instance, Richard Muench, "Education under the Regime of PISA & Co.: Global Standards and Local Traditions in Conflict—the Case of Germany," *Teachers College Record* 116, no. 090306 (September 2014): 16.

16. See, for instance, David Berliner, "The Many Facets of PISA," *Teachers College Record* 117, no. 010308 (January 2015): 20.

17. Editors, "Very Good on Paper," *The Economist*, December 12, 2013, http://www.economist.com/blogs/banyan/2013/12/education-vietnam.

18. See, for instance, Heinz-Dieter Meyer, "OECD's PISA: A Tale of Flaws and Hubris," *Teachers College Record*, December 19, 2013, http://www.tcrecord.org/Content.asp?ContentId=17371.

19. David H. Kamens and Connie L. McNeely, "Globalization and the Growth of International Educational Testing and National Assessment," *Comparative Education Review* 54, no. 1 (February 2010): 5–25, doi:10.1086/648471, 10.

20. Kathleen Knight Abowitz and Jason Harnish, "Contemporary Discourses of Citizenship," *Review of Educational Research* 76, no. 4 (December 1, 2006): 653–90, doi:10.2307/4124417, 656-7.
21. Ibid., 665.
22. Ibid., 666–674.
23. Peter McLaren, *Life in Schools: An Introduction to Critical Pedagogy in the Foundations of Education*, 5th ed. (Pearson, 2006), xviii, 39.
24. Abowitz and Jason Harnish, "Contemporary Discourses of Citizenship.", p. 675.
25. They do appear in some independent schools, however. See T. Alviar-Martin, "Reconciling Multiple Conceptions of Citizenship: International School Teachers' Beliefs and Practice," *Journal of Education—Boston University School of Education* 191, no. 3 (2011): 39–50.
26. Abowitz and Jason Harnish, "Contemporary Discourses of Citizenship."
27. Mark Evans, "Educating for Citizenship: What Teachers Say and What Teachers Do," *Canadian Journal of Education* 29, no. 2 (2006): 410–35, http://eric.ed.gov/?id=EJ750389, 412–13.
28. In 2009, former Supreme Court Justice Sandra Day O'Connor launched iCivics, which provided a "free, interactive, online civics curriculum": O'Connor, Sandra, "The Democratic Purpose of Education from the Founders to Horace Man to Today," in David Feith, ed. 2011. *Teaching America: The Case for Civic Education.* New York: Rowman & Littlefield. p. 10; William Galston, currently a distinguished fellow at Brookings, established the prominent CIRCLE (the Center for Information and Research upon Civic Learning and Education) http://www.civicyouth.org/about-circle/, downloaded February 27, 2015; Harvard University's Meira Levinson co-founded the Moral and Civic Education Initiative in the wake of her award-wining *No Citizen Left Behind* (2011), http://www.gse.harvard.edu/faculty/meira-levinson, downloaded February 27, 2015.
29. Sara Wallace Goodman, "Fortifying Citizenship: Policy Strategies for Civic Integration in Western Europe," *World Politics* 64, no. 4 (2012), 665, 667.
30. Ibid., pp. 659–661.
31. Geert ten Dam et al., "Measuring Young People's Citizenship Competences," *European Journal of Education* 46, no. 3 (September 1, 2011): 354–72, doi:10.1111/j.1465-3435.2011.01485.x, 354.
32. Goodman, "Fortifying Citizenship.", 660.
33. Jasmine B.-Y Sim, "Social Studies and Citizenship for Participation in Singapore: How One State Seeks to Influence Its Citizens," *Oxford Review of Education* 37, no. 6 (2011): 743–61. and Jasmine B-Y Sim and Murray Print, "Citizenship Education in Singapore: Controlling or Empowering Teacher Understanding and Practice?," *Oxford Review of Education* 35, no. 6 (2009): 705–23.
34. Schulz et al., *ICCS 2009 International Report*, 39.
35. Ibid., 44–45. The three countries that ranked citizenship as "of low priority" were New Zealand, Switzerland, and the Slovak Republic.
36. D.E Campbell, "The Civic Side of School Choice: An Empirical Analysis of Civic Education in Public and Private Schools," *Brigham Young University Law Review*, no. 2 (2008): 487–524, 489–90.
37. Schulz et al., *ICCS 2009 International Report*, 43.
38. Alan Dershowitz, "The Right to Know Your Rights: Civic Literacy, the Miranda Warnings, and Me," in *Teaching America: The Case for Civic Education*, ed. David Feith (New York: Rowman & Littlefield, 2011), 43.

39. Secretary-General of the OECD, "PISA 2012 Results in Focus: What 15-Year-Olds Know and What They Can Do" (Paris: Organisation for Economic Co-Operation and Development, 2014), http://www.oecd.org/pisa/keyfindings/pisa-2012-results-overview.pdf.

40. For example, Secretary-General of the OECD, "OECD Program for International Student Assessment 2003: Student Questionnaire" (Paris: Organisation for Economic Co-Operation and Development, 2003), http://nces.ed.gov/Surveys/PISA/pdf/quest_pisa_2003_student.pdf.

41. Eric A. Hanushek, Paul Peterson, and Ludger Woessman, "Not Just the Problems of Other People's Children: U.S. Student Performance in Global Perspective" (Boston, MA: Harvard's Program on Educational Policy and Governance, May 2014), p. 17. In the United States, only 17 % of these children are proficient—compared to a full 37 % in the Netherlands, 35 % in Germany, and 33 % in Switzerland. This means that a disadvantaged child would have *at least twice the chance* of becoming proficient if she moved to one of these nations.

42. Ibid., 19. In the United States, 26 % of such students are proficient—compared with 57 % of students in Switzerland, 52 % in Germany, 50 % in the Netherlands, 39 % in the United Kingdom, and 35 % in France.

43. Ibid., 20. In the United States, 43 % of these students are proficient—compared with 71 % in Poland, 65 % in Switzerland, and 61 % in the Netherlands and Belgium.

44. Ibid., 9–12.

45. Other social scientists use an index comprised of income, education, and occupation; ICCS measured SES by "parental occupational status, parental educational attainment, and home literacy resources." Schulz et al., *ICCS 2009 International Report*. 32.

46. OECD, *PISA 2012 Results: Excellence through Equity (Volume II)* (Paris: Organisation for Economic Co-operation and Development, 2013), http://www.oecd-ilibrary.org/content/book/9789264201132-en, 13.

47. Ibid., 37.

48. Ibid., 13.

49. Macedo, Stephen and Patrick Wolf, "Introduction: School Choice, Civic Values, and Problems of Policy Comparison," in Patrick J. Wolf and Stephen Macedo, *Educating Citizens: International Perspectives on Civic Values and School Choice* (Brookings Institution Press. 1775 Massachusetts Avenue NW, Washington, DC 20036. Tel: 202-797-6000; Fax: 202-797-6004; e-mail: webmaster@brookings.edu; Web site: http://www.brookings.edu/index/publications.htm, 2004), http://www.eric.ed.gov/ERICWebPortal/detail?accno=ED493327, p. 7.

50. Secretary-General of the OECD, "PISA 2012 Results: Excellence through Equity: Giving Every Student the Chance to Succeed, Volume II" (Paris: Organisation for Economic Co-Operation and Development, 2013), 72.

51. Ibid.

52. Ibid., 73.

53. Ibid., 36.

54. Provided the policies ensure equitable access.

55. "James Tooley: A Champion of Low-Cost Schools or a Dangerous Man?," *The Guardian*, accessed June 21, 2015, http://www.theguardian.com/education/2013/nov/12/professor-james-tooley-low-cost-schools.

56. James Tooley, "If India Can, Why Can't We?," *The New Statesman*, September 10, 2001.

57. James Tooley, *The Beautiful Tree: A Personal Journey Into How the World's Poorest People Are Educating Themselves*, 1st ed. (Cato Institute, 2009).
58. Andrews, Lewis M. "The Special Education Scare: Fact vs. Fiction," in David Salisbury and James Tooley, *What America Can Learn From School Choice In Other Countries* (Cato Institute, 2005), 71.
59. Macedo, Stephen and Patrick Wolf, "Introduction: School Choice, Civic Values, and Problems of Policy Comparison, in Wolf and Macedo, *Educating Citizens*, 4.
60. Dronkers, Jasp. Do Public and Religious Schools Really Differ? Assessing the European Evidence," in Ibid., 306–307.
61. Secretary-General of the OECD, "PISA 2012 Results: Excellence through Equity: Giving Every Student the Chance to Succeed, Volume II.", 91, 104.
62. http://www.oecdbetterlifeindex.org/topics/civic-engagement/, downloaded February 26, 2015. Of course, many factors—including whether voting is compulsory and enforced, as it is in Australia and Belgium—influence voter turn-out.
63. Schulz et al., *ICCS 2009 International Report*, 60.
64. Ibid., 61.
65. Ibid., 79. It is unfortunate that Canada, Australia, and the United States did not participate in this survey. The Netherlands, whose results would have been important, did not reach a statistically significant sample of students and thus was disqualified from the analysis.
66. Ibid., 254–55.
67. William H. Jeynes, "Religion, Intact Families, and the Achievement Gap," *Interdisciplinary Journal of Research on Religion* 3, no. 3 (2007).
68. Anthony S. Bryk, Valerie E. Lee, and Peter Blakeley Holland, *Catholic Schools and the Common Good* (Cambridge, MA: Harvard University Press, 1993), 187–193.
69. Karin Chenoweth, *It's Being Done: Academic Success in Unexpected Schools* (Cambridge, MA: Harvard Education Press, 2007).
70. James S. Coleman and Others, "Equality of Educational Opportunity," 1966, http://eric.ed.gov/?id=ED012275, 36.
71. Ibid., p. 8. Half of the first graders in these schools responded to guided questions.
72. David Steiner, "The New Common Core Assessments: How They Could Stop Patronizing Our Students," *The Huffington Post*, February 21, 2014, http://www.huffingtonpost.com/david-m-steiner/the-new-common-core-asses_b_4809973.html.
73. Coleman and Others, "Equality of Educational Opportunity.", 22, 218.
74. Ibid., 298. The home factors included the degree of urbanism, the parents' education, the structural integrity of the home, family size, items within the home as indicators of wealth, reading materials in the home as indicators of intellectual interest, and the parents' interest in the children's education and in their educational outcomes, as perceived by the child.
75. Ibid., 325.
76. James S. Coleman, Thomas Hoffer, and Sally Kilgore, *High School Achievement: Public, Catholic, and Private Schools Compared* (New York: Basic Books, 1982), 195.
77. Ibid., 48.
78. Ibid., 127.
79. Ibid., 144, 146.

80. Ibid., 144.
81. Jeynes, "Religion, Intact Families, and the Achievement Gap."
82. Bryk, Lee, and Holland, *Catholic Schools and the Common Good*, 206–209.
83. Ray Pennings, *Cardus Education Survey* (Hamilton, ON: Cardus, 2011), "Cardus Education Survey 2014: Private Schools for the Public Good," *Cardus.ca*, accessed May 29, 2015, http://www.cardus.ca/store/4291/.
84. Edmundo F. Litton et al., "The Promise of Catholic Schools for Educating the Future of Los Angeles," *Catholic Education: A Journal of Inquiry and Practice* 13, no. 3 (March 2010): 350–67, http://eric.ed.gov/?id=EJ914874.
85. Vivian S. Louie, *Keeping the Immigrant Bargain: The Costs and Rewards of Success in America* (New York: Russell Sage Foundation, 2012), 114.
86. Matthew M. Chingos et al., *The Effects of School Vouchers on College Enrollment: Experimental Evidence from New York City* (Washington, DC: Brown Center on Education Policy at Brookings, 2012).
87. This process is known as "Virtual Control Record" protocol. See p. 9 of the *Executive Summary*, Stanford University and Center for Research on Education Outcomes, *National Charter School Study 2013* (Stanford, CA: Center for Research on Education Outcomes, 2013), http://credo.stanford.edu/research-reports.html.
88. Ibid., Executive Summary, 19.
89. Ibid., Executive Summary, 17.
90. Stanford University and Center for Research on Education Outcomes, *Urban Charter School Study: Report on 41 Regions*, 2015, http://urbancharters.stanford.edu/download/Urban%20Charter%20School%20Study%20Report%20on%2041%20Regions.pdf, iv.
91. Ibid., 16.
92. Ibid., 20–21.
93. "The Economist Snapshot," accessed June 20, 2015, http://www.economist.com/node/21558265.
94. Paul Peterson, "CREDO Reveals Successful Charters' Secret Sauce," *Education Next*, Summer 2015, http://educationnext.org/credo-reveals-successful-charters-secret-sauce/.
95. Stanford University and Center for Research on Education Outcomes, *National Charter School Study 2013*, Executive Summary, 11–12.
96. Yun Xiang and Beth Tarasawa, "Propensity Score Stratification Using Multilevel Models to Examine Charter School Achievement Effects," *The Journal of School Choice: International Research and Reform* 9, no. 2 (June 2015): 179–96.
97. Andy Smarick and Kelly Robson, "Innovation in Catholic Education: New Approaches to Instruction and Governance May Revitalize the Sector," *Education Next*, March 29, 2016, http://educationnext.org/innovation-in-catholic-education-instruction-governance/.
98. Stanford University and Center for Research on Education Outcomes, *National Charter School Study 2013*, Executive Summary, 11–14.
99. Adriana Villavicencio and William Marinell, *Inside Success: Strategies of 25 Successful High Schools* (New York, NY: Research Alliance for New York City Schools, July 2014).
100. Nelson Smith, *Redefining the School District in America* (Washington, DC: Thomas B. Fordham Institute, June 2015).

101. Alan Peshkin, *God's Choice: The Total World of a Fundamentalist Christian School* (University of Chicago Press, 1988).

102. See, for instance, the curricula of two classical Christian schools (one in New York City, the other in Central Florida): http://www.genevaschool.net; http://www.genevaschool.org, downloaded June 11, 2015.

103. Walter Feinberg, *For Goodness Sake: Religious Schools and Education for Democratic Citizenry* (New York: Routledge, 2006), 21–28.

104. The Institute for Advanced Studies in Culture at the University of Virginia is currently undertaking an in-depth analysis of ten different school sectors and their outcomes. See http://www.iasc-culture.org/research_school_culture_student_formation_project.php, downloaded May 29, 2015.

105. Mai Miksic, "Is the 'Catholic School Effect' Real? New Research Challenges the Catholic Primary School Advantage," *CUNY Institute for Education Policy*, accessed June 9, 2015, http://ciep.hunter.cuny.edu/catholicschools/, downloaded June 10, 2015.

106. Todd Elder and Christopher Jepsen, "Are Catholic Primary Schools More Effective than Public Primary Schools?," *Journal of Urban Economics* 80 (March 2014): 28–38, doi:10.1016/j.jue.2013.10.001. Note that this research is also subject to challenge: http://crsi.nd.edu/evaluations/achievement-in-catholic-and-public-primary-schools-compared/, downloaded June 10, 2015.

107. Mai Miksic, "Are Montessori Pre-K Programs the Best Educational Model for Low-Income Black and Latino Children?," *CUNY Institute for Education Policy*, September 18, 2014, http://ciep.hunter.cuny.edu/are-montessori-pre-k-programs-the-best-educational-model-for-low-income-black-and-latino-children/.

108. David N. Figlio and Cassandra M. D. Hart, "Competitive Effects of Means-Tested School Vouchers," Working Paper (National Bureau of Economic Research, June 2010), http://www.nber.org/papers/w16056.

109. David Figlio, Cassandra M. D. Hart, and Molly Metzger, "Who Uses a Means-Tested Scholarship, and What Do They Choose?," *Economics of Education Review*, Special Issue in Honor of Henry M. Levin, 29, no. 2 (April 2010): 301–17, doi:10.1016/j.econedurev.2009.08.002.

110. Anders Böhlmark and Mikael Lindahl, *Independent Schools and Long-Run Educational Outcomes Evidence from Sweden's Large Scale Voucher Reform* (Munich: CESifo, 2012), 42.

111. Wolf, Patrick and Stephen Macedo, "Introduction," in Wolf and Macedo, *Educating Citizens*, 12.

112. Two researchers recently found a public school advantage (Christopher A. Lubienski and Sarah Theule Lubienski, *The Public School Advantage: Why Public Schools Outperform Private Schools* (Chicago: University of Chicago Press, 2013).), but their thesis rests upon one small sample and tests which are geared for public school consumption (David Sikkink, "The Public School Advantage: Why Public Schools Outperform Private Schools by Christopher A. Lubienski and Sarah Theule Lubienski," *Journal of School Choice* 9, no. 1 (January 2, 2015): 161–63, doi:10.1080/15582159.2014.1000784.). David Berliner's statement that there is "little evidence suggesting that private school students are better prepared academically than their public school counterparts, particularly once other factors attributed to student achievement, such as

demographics, family characteristics, and other non-school factors, are considered," does not rest upon empirical data. Berliner, Glass, and & Associates, *50 Myths and Lies That Threaten America's Public Schools: The Real Crisis in Education*, 18.

113. See this view in Stephen Prothero, *Religious Literacy: What Every American Needs to Know—And Doesn't* (New York: HarperCollins, 2007), 127; and William Damon, *Failing Liberty 101: How We Are Leaving Young Americans Unprepared for Citizenship in a Free Society* (Stanford, CA: Hoover Institution Press, 2011), 43.

114. William A Galston, "Political Knowledge, Political Engagement, and Civic Education," *Annual Review of Political Science* 4 (2001): 217–34, 222, quoting a study in Michael X Delli Carpini and Scott Keeter, *What Americans Know about Politics and Why It Matters* (New Haven: Yale University Press, 1996), 197–8.

115. Allison M. Martens and Jason Gainous, "Civic Education and Democratic Capacity: How Do Teachers Teach and What Works?," *SSQU Social Science Quarterly* 94, no. 4 (2013): 956–76, 956–7.

116. http://www.nationsreportcard.gov/hgc_2014/# downloaded May 14, 2015; "Michelle Herczog Statement on the 2014 NAEP Results," *National Council for the Social Studies*, accessed May 14, 2015, http://www.socialstudies.org/news/2015-05-04-38024. "Simpson's Paradox Hides NAEP Gains (Again)," *Education Next*, accessed May 12, 2015, http://educationnext.org/simpsons-paradox-hides-naep-gains/. http://www.wsj.com/articles/teaching-better-civics-for-better-citizens-1431471803?KEYWORDS=Sandra+Day+O%27Connor, downloaded May 14, 2015.

117. Rod Paige, "Forgetting Martin Luther King's Dream: How Politics Threatens America's Civil Rights Memory," in David Feith, *Teaching America: The Case for Civic Education* (Lanham, MD: Rowman & Littlefield, 2011), 69–70.

118. Pamela Johnston Searing and Donald Searing, "A Political Socialization Perspective," in *Rediscovering the Democratic Purposes of Education*, ed. Lorraine McDonnell (Lawrence, KS: University Press of Kansas, 2000), 91–124.

119. They defined "community" in this study as "the local communities geographically defined by a single high school district. Thus, *all* students in each community sample attended the same high school." Ibid., 120.

120. Ibid. 117.

121. Ibid. 118.

122. http://www.nationsreportcard.gov/hgc_2014/#civics/groups, downloaded May 14, 2015.

123. Patrick J. Wolf, "Civics Exam: Schools of Choice Boost Civic Values," *Education Next* 7, no. 3 (2007): 67–72, http://www.eric.ed.gov/ERICWebPortal/detail?accno=EJ767503, 67–68.

124. Ibid., 71.

125. Ibid., 68.

126. Campbell, "The Civic Side of School Choice."

127. Pennings, *Cardus Education Survey*.

128. The only major study, as I write, dates from 2004. Jack Buckley, "Do Charter Schools Promote Student Citizenship?," Occasional Paper (New York, NY: National Center for the Study of Privatization in Education, 2004). It showed

positive effects on civic skills and community service and no effects on political tolerance. It did not include a measure of political knowledge.

129. "Cardus Education Survey 2014.", p. 15; research presentation at the CUNY Institute for Education Policy round table discussion, September 10, 2014, attended by the author.

130. David Campbell, "Introduction," in *Making Civics Count: Citizenship Education for a New Generation*, ed. David Campbell, Meira Levinson, and Frederick Hess (Cambridge: Harvard University Press, 2012), 1–15, 12.

131. Diane Ravitch, *Left Back: A Century of Battles over School Reform* (Simon & Schuster, 2001), 15.

132. Ashley Berner, "School Systems and Finance," in *Balancing Freedom, Autonomy, and Accountability in Education* (Tilburg: Wolf Legal Publishers, 2012), 115–127. Of course, some such systems allow students to differentiate at age 14 or 16 between academic and vocational trainings. Thus, not everyone takes the exit exams.

133. West, Martin, "Education and Global Competitiveness," in *Rethinking Competitiveness*, ed. K. Hassett (Washington, DC: American Enterprise Institute Press, 2012), 68–94.

134. Secretary-General of the OECD, "PISA 2012 Results: Excellence through Equity: Giving Every Student the Chance to Succeed, Volume II.", 89–91.

135. "Socioeconomically Disadvantaged Students Who Are Academically Successful Examining Academic Resilience Cross-Nationally," Policy Brief (Amsterdam: International Association for the Evaluation of Educational Achievement, March 2015), 1.

136. Ibid., 9.

137. Ibid., 19–20.

138. "Cardus Education Survey 2014.", 18–19.

139. David E. Campbell, "Voice in the Classroom: How an Open Classroom Climate Fosters Political Engagement Among Adolescents," *Polit Behav Political Behavior* 30, no. 4 (2008): 437–54, 450.

140. Feinberg, *For Goodness Sake*, 21–28.

141. James Youniss, "How to Enrich Civic Education and Sustain Democracy," in *Making Civics Count: Citizenship Education for a New Generation*, ed. David Campbell, Meira Levinson, and Frederick Hess (Cambridge: Harvard University Press, 2000), 116–40, 116–118.

142. See the chronology in Chap. 2 and in Ravitch, *Left Back*. E. D. Hirsch, *The Making of Americans: Democracy and Our Schools* (New Haven: Yale University Press, 2009). E. D. Hirsch, *The Knowledge Deficit: Closing the Shocking Education Gap for American Children* (Boston: Houghton Mifflin, 2006).

143. Ravitch, *Left Back*, 64–67.

144. Ibid., 113–124.

145. Ibid., 45–47.

146. Ibid., 65–67.

147. Ibid., 203–224.

148. Ibid., 240–263.

149. Ibid., 69–74; 242–257.

150. Ibid., 465–6.

151. There are numerous examples explored in this chapter, but also see Andrea Berger et al., "Early College, Continued Success: Early College High School

Initiative Impact Study" (Washington, DC: American Institutes for Research, January 2014), v.

152. Steiner, "The New Common Core Assessments."

153. Charles Sahm, "What Explains Success at Success Academy? Charter Network Focuses on What Is Being Taught, and How," *Education Next* 15, no. 3 (Summer 2015), http://educationnext.org/what-explains-success-academy-charter-network/.

154. Vanessa Coca and Consortium on Chicago School Research, *Working to My Potential: The Postsecondary Experiences of CPS Students in the International Baccalaureate Diploma Programme*, 2012, http://bibpurl.oclc.org/web/49260   http://ccsr.uchicago.edu/sites/default/files/publications/IB%20Report1.pdf, 4.

155. Stephen Macedo and Patrick Wolf, "Introduction: School Choice, Civic Values, and Problems of Policy Comparison," in *Educating Citizens: International Perspectives on Civic Values and School Choice*, ed. Stephen Macedo and Patrick Wolf (Washington, DC: Brookings Institute, 2004), 12.

156. Elizabeth Green and Trevor Cooling, *Mapping the Field: A Review of the Current Research Evidence on the Impact of Schools with a Christian Ethos* (London: Theos, 2009). 26–30.

157. Charles Glenn, "What the United States Can Learn from Other Countries," in *What Americans Can Learn from School Choice in Other Countries*, ed. James Tooley and David Salisbury (Washington, DC: Cato Institute, 2005), 79–90, 80, 83.

158. It is a side point, but some school cultures prize spiritual or moral formation above academic rigor; their student outcomes reflect the school's purpose. See Pennings, *Cardus Education Survey*.

159. Bryk, Lee, and Holland, *Catholic Schools and the Common Good*, 144.

160. Ibid., 144.

161. Ibid., 144–145.

162. Ibid., 245.

163. Ibid., 144.

164. Scott Seider, *Character Compass: How Powerful School Culture Can Point Students Toward Success* (Harvard Education Press, 2012), 5, 13.

165. Ibid., 214–215.

166. John E. Chubb and Terry M. Moe, *Politics, Markets & America's Schools* (Washington, DC: Brookings Institution, 1990), 16.

167. Richard Arum, *Judging School Discipline: The Crisis in Moral Authority* (Cambridge, MA: Harvard University Press, 2003), 92–100. See especially his comparison of the judgments regarding expulsions in private and public schools.

168. Steven Brill, *Class Warfare: Inside the Fight to Fix America's Schools*, Reprint (Simon & Schuster, 2012). And the text of the *Vergara* judgment.

169. This is the heart of Hunter's argument in James Davison Hunter, *The Death of Character: Moral Education in an Age without Good or Evil* (New York: Basic Books, 2000). A teacher could certainly explain the wide spectrum of potential moral sources, but we know that most do not (see Chap. 2). It is furthermore unclear whether a strong school culture could be established based upon cognizance of ultimate principles, in any case. The point is to enact particular ones.

170. Chubb and Moe, *Politics, Markets & America's Schools*, 26–31.
171. Ibid., 36.
172. Ibid., 91–97.
173. Ibid., 56 and 202.
174. Ibid., 54–55.
175. Ibid., 65.
176. Chubb and Moe were pessimistic that even school-based management would mediate the negative effects of bureaucratic culture. Ibid., 200.
177. Ibid., 191.
178. "75 Examples of How Bureaucracy Stands in the Way of America's Students and Teachers," *The Eli and Edythe Broad Foundation*, August 2012, http://www.broadeducation.org/about/bureaucracy.html.

CHAPTER 6

The Limits of Educational Pluralism and How to Address Them

Educational pluralism is a necessary but insufficient component of a strong education system. It is necessary because it encourages distinctive school cultures, the *sine qua non* of strong academic and civic outcomes.[1] It is necessary because *all* schools are stronger when no one type of school dominates.[2] It is necessary because when we create openly distinctive schools, we hedge against indoctrination.[3] Finally, it is necessary because pluralism sits with our democratic ideals better than uniformity. I elaborated these points in earlier chapters.

But educational pluralism is insufficient, for at least two reasons. First, the most consistent advantages that private and charter schools have over traditional public schools—challenging academic content and strong school culture—are not guaranteed within a plural structure. Providing intellectually rigorous academic coursework rests upon the conviction that a challenging curriculum equalizes opportunity across social and racial divides[4] and forms the foundation for a shared, democratic culture.[5] Similarly, distinctive school cultures must be sustained over time, often against external and internal pressures. Instituting and maintaining robust cultures and challenging academic coursework require consistency on the part of school leaders and restraint on the part of the state, as I describe below.

Second, despite its many advantages, educational pluralism can work *against* equity, as Arizona's first tax credit program and Chile's initial voucher program seem to have done. Whether pluralism is beneficial or harmful depends upon the enabling policy framework. In this domain, there is ample research on the outcomes of policies in other countries and in the United States that might serve to guide us going forward.

What follows are two sections. The first sets out general guidelines for preserving and extending the advantages of private and charter schools, the second, a broad-brush outline of policies that advance equity for all families. State and district leaders will need to render them specific to local contexts.

© The Author(s) 2017
A.R. Berner, *Pluralism and American Public Education*,
DOI 10.1057/978-1-137-50224-7_6

STRENGTHENING AND EXPANDING THE ADVANTAGES

Part 1. Rigorous Academic Curricula

We know that a content-rich academic curriculum as Diane Ravitch defines it is vital to narrowing the achievement gap.[6] In the United States, private schools are historically more likely to offer this, and charter schools increasingly do as well.

Articulating the importance of a content-rich curriculum is more important now than ever—for all school sectors. There are indications that some of the world's high-performing nations have shifted from a traditional curriculum to a skills orientation, and from a teacher-centered to a student-focused classroom, with unfortunate results for students. Gabriel Sahlgren makes the case that this turn from intellectual content has had negative consequences for student learning in Finland.[7] In an upcoming book, E.D. Hirsch argues that a similar shift has been disastrous for student learning in France.[8] A Swedish researcher speculates that the loss of rigor and teacher-led instruction contributed to Sweden's declining PISA scores.[9] In the United States, the prestigious National Association of Independent Schools may be thinning out the traditional academic content in favor of a more nebulous "skills."[10] The general enthusiasm among educational entrepreneurs for skills and competencies is not matched with a passion for curriculum.[11]

While the evidence from here and abroad suggests that a content-rich curriculum plays a vital role in narrowing achievement gaps, this country's longstanding aversion to the traditional academic curriculum makes a federal-level curriculum difficult to contemplate; even state-level attempts have foundered. During the twentieth century, both were tried and failed—with one exception.

One notable example occurred in 1959 when a group of eminent scientists, educational psychologists, historians, and textbook authors gathered at Woods Hole, Massachusetts. As described by the group's chair, Harvard professor Jerome Bruner, the purpose was to address the poor level of scientific learning in America's schools.[12] The group's remedy: start with college content, and map mastery back through all of the grade levels. The so-called "spiral curriculum" would revisit core concepts with increasing sophistication as a child went through school.[13] The new curriculum would be intellectually demanding at every stage of a child's cognitive development and would accelerate cognitive development itself.[14]

Pulling this off would require leadership from university professors, who knew "where each subject was going" and could help textbook writers and teachers craft a systematic program.[15] It would also mean challenging the prevailing culture of American schools. As Jerome Bruner noted, "studies of American high school culture point ... to the higher value placed upon social popularity than upon academic achievement."[16] Finally, it would require significant and ongoing professional support for teachers.[17] The challenges were formidable, but generous federal funding (this was the Sputnik era) made the project viable.

The Woods Hole effort never got off the ground. Its call for sequenced, challenging science and math curricula in K-12 did not sit well with expressivist educational philosophy, already strong among educational elites and now reinforced in the broader culture. Bruner's introduction to the second edition (1977) said as much; in the cultural milieu of the 1960s, he wrote, the "school itself came to be seen as a vehicle for oppression," and "relevance became more important than training." Self-discovery, not intellectual mastery, was the name of the game.[18]

Neil Postman's 1969 bestseller, *Teaching as a Subversive Activity*, confirms Bruner's account. Postman's book targeted educational traditionalists, including Jerome Bruner whose theories Postman rejected by name.[19] Postman argued that the purpose of education was for students to make meaning out of their personal experiences. For this, they needed questions, not knowledge. Such a goal was bad news for textbooks, lesson plans, syllabi, or adult expertise; Postman wanted biology teachers to teach Spanish, German teachers math, and history teachers physics, as a way to reinforce the senselessness of received wisdom.[20] Another book that sold 200,000 copies a year throughout the 1960s and was required reading in 600 education classes across the country, A.S. Neill's *Summerhill*,[21] put forth individual self-definition as the aim of education and thoroughly rejected the academic curriculum.[22] Postman's and Neill's views were clearly not unique but, rather, resonated with and drew upon the dominant educational philosophy that was expressivist in nature. Thus, the Woods Hole attempt at coherence—at least within math and science—foundered. The Woods Hole effort assumed that the primary goal of K-12 education was to prepare students academically; the cultural majority's response, captured but not exhausted by Postman and Neill, assumed it was to empower students socially and emotionally.

Championing a sequenced curriculum has been even more fraught within the humanities. Teachers in the humanities, in contrast to those in the natural sciences, fundamentally disagree about which interpretive framework should be used to select material. In English literature, for instance, should the curriculum emphasize influential works of Western civilization, or the voices of the underprivileged? Should it address Western, Eastern, and African texts equally, or privilege the Western tradition? Should the texts be taught sequentially ("Beowulf to Sheridan") or topically ("Love and Death")? Should students read complete plays and novels, or select passages? A history curriculum can be just as contentious, as Robert Fullinwider, Lawrence Blum, and Gilbert Sewall describe in *Public Education in a Multicultural Society: Policy, Theory, Critique*. In the 1980s and early 1990s, California and New York's social studies curricula sparked public firestorms.[23] Fullinwider put it this way:

> We may all accede to the proposition that students should be presented with a realistic view of American history, but my realism may be your panegyric and another's denunciation. We may agree that curricula should be language-sensitive, but find ourselves all over the map about acceptable and unacceptable

terms and descriptions in schoolbooks and classrooms. We may all believe that students should learn that "difference does not necessarily imply inferiority," yet quarrel vigorously about the value and acceptability of particular "differences."[24]

A curriculum designed under these circumstances runs the risk of offending one or another sensitivity or becoming inclusive to the point of tedium. It also highlights, as above, that educational philosophies affect curricular choices and pedagogies. A traditionalist approach is different from a critical one.

But yet another difficulty pertains. Even if a state crafted a content-rich curriculum, preparing teachers to teach it would be another challenge altogether. Massachusetts is famous in education circles for its Herculean efforts to do both. The Massachusetts Education Reform Act of 1993 required the creation of a coherent, intellectually challenging curriculum. To this end, the State Board of Education worked with university professors to sketch out the college-ready contours of each subject, and by 1998, they had back-mapped K-12 coursework accordingly.[25] Professional development changed to reflect the new focus on subject mastery,[26] and teacher certification included new academic exams.[27] There were indeed political conflagrations in the process.[28] The reforms went through nevertheless.

Massachusetts skyrocketed to the top of the academic charts.[29] The important and sobering point is this: while other states took bits and pieces of the Massachusetts' program, no other state went to such lengths to formalize an intellectually challenging curriculum and to support teachers in delivering it. A recent report from the Center for American Progress indicated that, although instituting rigorous, content-rich curricula is cost-effective,[30] "policy decisions do not consider rigorous measures of curricula quality," and the process of selecting textbooks and instructional materials has become deeply politicized.[31]

Recent strife about the CCSS illustrates the persistent difficulty of consensus around anything, much less a curriculum. The CCSS is not a curriculum. Rather, it specifies a set of skills to be learned that, along the way, includes a few specific documents (such as the Declaration of Independence) and requires specific evidence-based skills (such as phonemic awareness).[32] The CCSS were crafted in a content-blind manner no doubt to *avoid* the political quagmires of previous debates, but they have been attacked from Left and Right regardless. Libertarians object to the "imposition" of national standards and want the whole thing scrapped. Teachers' unions resist the use of students' CCSS scores to evaluate teachers. A growing number of parents reject standardized tests.[33] Doing away with CCSS-inspired tests is unlikely; as of this writing, most states have accepted the official CCSS or an alternative version of them. There is some early evidence that CCSS have raised academic expectations and had a positive impact upon intellectual rigor.[34] My emphasis is on how politically contentious and (necessarily) intellectually limited they are.

For longstanding reasons, then, it is hard to envision a *movement* within public education or its teacher preparation programs[35] that supports a coherent academic curriculum. Reformist organizations could try, but reforming the traditional public school system from within is slow, politically fraught, and extremely expensive. It inevitably engages a clash of educational philosophies about the purpose of education itself. Most reforms, however hard-won, are reversible; witness the erosion of support for federal accountability in the post-NCLB era, and the (partial) reversion to the status quo ante in post-Bloomberg New York City.[36]

The movement for educational pluralism offers a new opportunity to emphasize content as opposed to merely skills and competencies, as part of robust public accountability and funding framework. The tax credit and voucher programs in most states already require that funded students undertake nationally- or state-normed tests each year. This could be expanded by enterprising states and districts to require the rigorous course content that some private and charter schools already use to great effect. This strategy is similar to what Finland did in the 1970s when it transposed the college preparatory curriculum to all schools and grades 1–9, or what Massachusetts did in the late 1990s when it sequenced K-12 backwards from university-level coursework.

If there were opposition to (say) a district's requiring an independent school's chronological or set-text approach, a school could opt instead for what David Steiner calls domain knowledge,[37] thus avoiding a battle over specific texts while requiring students to learn about entire periods of history and literature. Within, for example, the requirement to read and understand nineteenth century English literature, schools could select texts that reflected their *ethos*, and interpret them from within religious, gender, or economic perspectives. State or district exams on nineteenth century English literature would allow students to write on the particular texts they had analyzed and absorbed.

Along with domain knowledge and commensurate tests, a district or state could require all funded schools to make their curriculum and student outcomes public. Each school could publish its course of study including the textbooks used, the proficiency targets, and students' academic outcomes. At the same time, schools could embrace a broader understanding of "outcomes" and report upon those that fit its *ethos*. Montessori schools might want to talk about the development of democratic character, which has a very specific meaning in the Montessori culture ("valorization").[38] Evangelical Protestant schools might elevate "Christian discipleship" above all other goals, including academic achievement;[39] this, too, could be articulated in a way that mattered to parents. Schools in Northern Europe publish indicators of how their graduates fare in the workplace,[40] and some American districts would have an interest in such information, as would businesses in funding data dashboards.[41] Publishing detailed information about a school's course of study, and evidence about the outcomes of interest (not only academic but potentially social, economic, civic, and ethical/religious), would give stakeholders more information that could guide where they enrolled their children or applied for a job. Naturally, the new requirements would apply to public as well as to private and charter schools, thus giving all school sectors a chance to differentiate and to learn from one another.

While government funds would flow only to schools that ensured minimal levels of proficiency,[42] there could be some flexibility to approve alternative ways of measurement,[43] and to set proficiency goals that reflect the starting point of the students. Such flexibility within accountability is similar to what plural systems around the world, such as Alberta, the Netherlands, and France, have found effective.

Part 2. Supporting Strong School Cultures

As I argued in the previous chapter, a second factor in narrowing the achievement gap is a strong, positive school culture. Private and charter schools have an empirical advantage in this area as well. Educational pluralism cannot *ensure* distinctive school cultures; however, it merely creates the legal space for them. Distinctiveness can be eroded from the inside (by negligence) or the outside (by unreasonable policies).

A fair policy framework enables distinctive school cultures, but policy can become oppressive, too. Politicians and courts can run roughshod over beliefs that seem trivial to them but are sacred to others. A recent conflict over the school curriculum in Quebec illustrates potential risks.

Quebec is linguistically, religiously, and culturally diverse, and its school system included publicly funded Protestant, Catholic, Jewish, and non-sectarian schools in addition to the non-funded independent schools. For more than a 100 years, Quebec had allowed schools to modify the provincial curriculum in accordance with their ideals. In 2008, a new Liberal government reversed this policy and required strict adherence to an Ethics and Religious Culture (ERC) course that reflected the government's commitment to "normative pluralism." The new ERC course was intended to provide a neutral approach *about* religions and, in the process, to inculcate tolerance and respect for others.

Many religious schools objected. For many Catholic, Protestant, and Jewish schools, placing the sacred within a secular framework made no sense. In a departure for Quebec, however, the government did not allow dissenting schools to provide alternative courses that covered the same *material*.

Several lawsuits ensued, the most famous of which, *Loyola High School and John Zucchi v. Michelle Courchesne and her Ministry*, ended up at the Canadian Supreme Court.[44] In *Loyola*, the plaintiffs (a Jesuit independent school and one of its families) agreed with the ERC's aims of "'recognition of others, pursuit of the common good … and an informed understanding of religion,'" but could not accept its underlying assumption that "the secular is a space, or rather a time, in which God is not to be considered or in which belief in God somehow does not matter."[45] Thus, argued the plaintiffs, Catholic schools could not adapt ERC's ideological framework without abrogating their Catholic identity. Many Jewish schools[46] and a substantial majority (75 %) of Quebecois agreed.[47] In 2015, the Court sided with Loyola High School and ruled that Quebec had infringed the religious rights of the school.[48] Dissenting schools were freed from the obligation to teach the course material from the government's distinctive viewpoint.

But a larger point emerges here. The *Loyola* case did not occur in a vacuum but, rather, reflected longstanding debates about the hierarchy of moral claims in a plural society. On one side, the Chief Justice of the Supreme Court of Canada, Beverley McLachlin, in an essay published in 2004, argues that the claims of state law are prior to the claims of religious and civic institutions: "The law makes total claims upon the self and leaves little of human experience untouched."[49] On the other hand, an expert witness in the *Loyola* case claims that in imposing its normative pluralism upon confessional institutions, the state demands "ideological conformity."[50]

Such debates are par for the course in democratic countries. This is precisely the point: for educational pluralism to function, the government cannot impose its theory of the good, the true, and the beautiful upon schools. There must be a careful balance between civic norms and minority or countercultural beliefs.

But how countercultural is okay? It is well and good to let Montessori schools talk about "valorization," or Catholic schools to talk about servant leadership, but how should we deal with an Aryan National School? How can educational pluralism separate the wheat from the chaff?

First, educational pluralism inevitably involves funding schools that many of us would not send our own children to. Secularists feel that Catholic schools perpetuate misinformation; Evangelicals feel the same way about the public schools; Hasidic Jews do not in the main support non-theological coursework. This is not a new problem, nor is it unique to education. Taxpayers in democracies end up supporting wars, economic policies, and social programs that they do not endorse. Educationally, plural democracies crossed that bridge a long time ago.[51]

But there is a limit to what democracies should fund. How do we draw the line? Fortunately, we do not have to create the boundaries *ex nihilo*; our courts have done much of the heavy lifting already. There are broad categories that are illegal in any context. Sedition is one of them. A school could not endorse the overthrow of any branch of the US government without violating federal law.[52] Racial prejudice is likewise illegal. There is no constitutional protection for schools with racially discriminatory practices, even if the school is private. In 1973, the Supreme Court ruled that Mississippi could lend textbooks on secular subjects to religious schools, but not to those schools that discriminated on racial grounds (*Norwood v. Harrison*). In 1976, the Court ruled that private schools could not hold racially discriminatory admissions policies without violating federal law (*Runyon v. McCrary*).[53] In 1983, it upheld the Internal Revenue Service (IRS)'s revocation of the federal tax exemption from Bob Jones University, because of its policy of racial discrimination (*Bob Jones University v. United States*). Non-discriminatory practice around race has become a super-norm in American society.

Sedition and institutional racism are, from our early twenty-first century perspective, fairly easily proscribed. They do not, however, exhaust the areas of potential conflict about funded schools. What reasonable test could we apply to the others? The case against racism suggests one: whether a school policy brings psychological harm to entire categories of students.

The psychological harm threshold dates to the fight against segregation. Two New York psychologists, Mamie and Kenneth Clark, had found in multiple trials that black children chose to play with white dolls over black dolls and associated positive attributes with white dolls but not with black dolls. The Clarkses viewed this as evidence that black children had absorbed and internalized "negative self-regard" from a segregated society.

The Clarkses served as expert witnesses in the segregation cases combined by the Supreme Court in *Brown v. Board of Education* (1954). Chief Justice Earl Warren found the body of literature on internalized inferiority so compelling, that he referenced psychological harm in the unanimous decision:

> To separate them [black children] from others of similar age and qualifications solely because of their race generates a feeling of inferiority as to their status in the community that may affect their hearts and minds in a way unlikely ever to be undone. The effect of this separation on their educational opportunities was well stated by a finding in the Kansas case by a court which nevertheless felt compelled to rule against the Negro plaintiffs: Segregation of white and colored children in public schools has a detrimental effect upon the colored children. The impact is greater when it has the sanction of the law, for the policy of separating the races is usually interpreted as denoting the inferiority of the negro group. A sense of inferiority affects the motivation of a child to learn. Segregation with the sanction of law, therefore, has a tendency to [retard] the educational and mental development of negro children and to deprive them of some of the benefits they would receive in a racial[ly] integrated school system.[54]

The Court held that racial segregation was inherently damaging to black children and thus placed psychological harm at the center of race and schooling. But is psychological harm helpful on other fronts? We can test it with three culturally contested issues that play out in schools: abortion, evolution, and sexual identity.

The constitutional right to an abortion has existed since *Roe v. Wade* (1973), but Americans are still deeply divided on its merits—with younger Americans more uncomfortable than their elders.[55] The fact is that there are persistent philosophical differences about the status of a fetus: Does an unborn child possess intrinsic rights that should be protected by the state, as traditionalists believe? Or do the manifest rights of the mother trump potential rights that *might* pertain to a fetus, as progressives hold?

School cultures reflect these differences. Most religious schools teach the traditionalist view, while public and many independent schools teach the progressive view. Abortion is merely the most visible conflict about the meaning of sexuality. It is no wonder that sex education has sparked a long history of conflict and litigation in the public schools.[56]

But can one view of abortion or the other be said to cause psychological harm? Certainly, at the level of individual experience, exposure to contrary beliefs and practices can be traumatic. There is no evidence, however, that institutional support for either side of the abortion debate creates such routine psychological damage that it should be regulated by the state. An educationally plural system need not interfere with a school's chosen approach to abortion.

Evolutionary theory is another issue that sparks school controversy. Many scientists and mainline religious groups accept evolution as fact. Creationists explain human origins by starting with the book of Genesis. Creationism is thus considered a religious theory is therefore banned from public schools along with its cousin, intelligent design. But what would happen in an educationally plural system? What about government support for fundamentalist schools that taught creationism or classical schools that voted for intelligent design?

Other countries have trod this ground before. In England, funded schools are required to teach evolutionary theory in biology classes, but faith-based schools may also teach creationism in religion classes.[57] The Netherlands' approach is similarly flexible.[58] There, high school students have to take national and school-based exams. The national exam material is uniform and requires knowledge about evolution; school exams reflect the ideals of each school.[59] Thus, it is possible for creationist schools to teach *about* evolution for the national exam, but teach *against* it for the local ones.

Creationism in state-funded schools bothers some Europeans,[60] as it would many Americans. It is hard to see, however, how belief in a literal six-day creation causes inherent psychological harm. Do we know that being taught creationist views damages one's self-regard? I do not think we do. Moreover, does being taught evolutionary theory in school lead inevitably to belief that it is true? This cannot be: some 46 % of Americans are self-proclaimed creationists,[61] but most of them were educated in public schools that taught natural selection as scientific truth.

My point is not that creationism is accurate (I do not think it is), but that psychological harm is not at play. Here, the risks of allowing state-funded schools to teach a literalist creation seem *de minimis* compared to the known benefits of enabling distinctive schools to flourish. There does not seem to be the "compelling state interest" that would lead to strict court scrutiny or legal concern. Therefore, for the state to regulate private school policy in this domain would seem unreasonable. Public and charter schools, which are required to be non-religious, would continue to fall under the Supreme Court's rulings on this issue.[62]

The possibility of psychological harm looks very different when we come to sexual identity. As with abortion and human origins, Americans disagree: is sexual orientation chosen or innate? Should same-sex marriage be legal? Is gender fixed or fluid? Unlike public opinion on abortion and creationism, however, opinion on sexual orientation is shifting toward progressive consensus. In

1972, the psychiatric diagnostic manual still listed homosexuality as a mental illness.[63] Consider the difference a few decades make: in 2015, the Supreme Court made gay and lesbian marriages legal in all 50 states.[64] Health insurance covers transgender operations,[65] national organizations track laws that protect LGBT citizens,[66] and television shows and films reflect a variety of sexual orientations.[67] "Heteronormativity," a pejorative term, has entered the academic and popular lexicons.[68] These changes were unthinkable even 50 years ago.

Public and private schools are betwixt and between. One example: when a Mississippi public school denied a lesbian couple tickets to prom in 2010, the school and the resulting lawsuit made international news.[69] Similar situations have occurred across the country.[70] Most public schools now embrace non-discriminatory hiring policies and allow students to participate in LGBT activism. Many independent schools have followed suit, and the most prestigious independent school organization, the National Association of Independent Schools, requires its members to have non-discriminatory sexual orientation policies in place.[71]

Religiously conservative schools, in contrast, view homosexual behavior as morally wrong. Many of them will not hire openly gay and lesbian faculty, permit LGBT student groups on campus, or speak favorably about the gay movement in class.

How will this issue play out in tax credit and voucher programs? It is already rising to the surface. North Carolina's tax credit legislation requires participating schools to allow openly LGBT faculty and students, and at least one school pulled out of the program because it would not comply.[72] Georgia's legislation, in contrast, does *not* require non-discrimination, and progressive groups protest it for that reason.[73] This tension reaches higher education as well; the evangelical Wheaton College attracted national attention in 2011 when a chapel speaker called upon gay and lesbian Christians to remain celibate.[74] A vocal group of alumni founded an organization (OneWheaton) that supports gay and lesbian believers and campaigns for a change in the college's policy. The college holds firm to its traditional perspective. The conflict persists.[75]

The tension between conservative schools and public funding on LGBT rights will no doubt escalate. This would be unsurprising, given the cultural shifts underway. The finding of psychological harm, however, would accelerate the debate substantially. What if credible research found that heteronormative schooling damaged children who were not heterosexual, much as Mamie and Kenneth Clark found that segregated schools harmed black children? One can imagine a *Brown v. Board of Education* moment at the Supreme Court. If the Court ruled on this basis, it is hard to see how state tax credit or voucher programs could support schools that discriminated against gay and lesbian faculty or students.

How do other plural systems manage sexual orientation in their schools? Canada considers speaking against homosexuality to be a hate crime,[76] but whether this applies to K-12 education depends upon the province.[77] As of July 2015, the European Court of Human Rights had not heard a single school case on sexual orientation.[78] The English Parliament legalized same-sex marriage in 2012; schools are required to teach this fact but are not required to endorse it.[79] The Netherlands has the same laws and educational latitude.[80] Israel, on the other hand, bans discrimination against LGBT students in its funded schools as of 2014—although the degree of enforcement no doubt varies.[81] A finding that heteronormative schooling brings psychological harm to LGBT students would likely influence hiring and admissions policies across democratic nations.

A qualification is in order. Scholars have argued about the validity of the dolls test since *Brown v. Board of Education*: that Kenneth Clarks' presentation of the findings was selective and therefore "misled the courts";[82] that the dolls tests, properly administered, produced considerably more nuanced results;[83] and that the dolls test itself was culturally conditioned, its findings qualified.[84] Additionally, a core concern with psychological research that diminishes its trustworthiness, is that few projects yield the same results when replicated. In August 2015, *Science Magazine* published a paper on "a painstaking yearlong effort to reproduce 100 research projects" that had appeared in peer-reviewed journals.[85] The researchers who duplicated the psychological studies found that while reproducibility "is a defining feature of science," a majority of the replications yielded "weaker evidence." While 97 % of the original studies produced significant findings, only 36 % of the replications did so.[86]

Why bring this up? Categorical psychological harm is a promising tool for education policy and civil courts, and I support its use. However, the standard for research findings to become actionable should be exceptionally high and rest, at the least, on replication of findings across multiple labs.

There are, therefore, principles that can guide public policy so that it balances protecting distinctive schools and prohibiting psychological harm. Public policy is not the only force at play, however; individual schools have to safeguard their distinctiveness themselves. Schools that begin with a strong mission can lose their way. The responsibility to maintain a school's distinctive edge falls upon the school's management. Novel approaches to pedagogy and strategic corrections can strengthen a school, but adoption without critique can weaken it.[87] A large-scale study on faith schools in the UK (2009), for instance, indicated that Anglican schools were not particularly Anglican: very few principals could articulate what made their schools different. School leaders failed to "engage with the Christian faith as a coherent rationale for life and learning."[88]

How did this homogenization happen to the nation's largest single provider of education?[89] It could have been the tacit desire not to offend non-Anglican students.[90] It could have been a consequence of teacher preparation programs that de-emphasized philosophical differences.[91] It could have been the pursuit of other goals, such as prestige, that urged leaders to chase trends that inadvertently subverted the school mission.[92] Each of these explanations is historically plausible.

More broadly, the line between fidelity and change is a fine one. The problem comes when no one sees the line. "Mission drift" occurs when no one is paying attention. Educational pluralism cannot ensure that schools preserve their distinctiveness. It can, however, create space for them to revive or reimagine their mission—as many Church of England schools have done.[93] Maintaining a school's distinctive voice is a vital responsibility of school leaders. A fair-minded policy framework can enable but not ensure this.

Strengthening the Advantages: Conclusion

As I have argued, educational pluralism reflects democratic values better than our current system, in which the traditional neighborhood school serves as the norm against which other school models must prove their worth. We know from international and domestic research that private and charter schools, and well-designed plural systems, offer distinct advantages in terms of academic and civic outcomes. These advantages, however, are not a given; they depend upon a commitment to a strong curriculum and to the possibility of diverse school cultures. A robust policy framework would do two things: promote an intellectually demanding curriculum for all students, and enable a space in which distinctive schools can flourish. This means that the state will end up funding some beliefs and practices that differ from those of the cultural majority; any individual might find a particular school distasteful or even heinous. In this respect, educational pluralism mirrors what happens in every other domain of democratic deliberation. At the same time, the state cannot fund beliefs and practices that cause psychological harm to entire categories of students.

Advancing Equity in Plural Systems

It might seem that creating a plural system within the above constraints would sufficiently advance equal access to excellent schools. After all, private and charter schools have an empirical advantage in narrowing the achievement gap, all things being equal; why not merely open the gates via tax credits or vouchers? Studies from around the world and in the United States suggest otherwise. Not all plural mechanisms advance equity; sometimes they unintentionally reinforce socioeconomic or racial disadvantages. This betrays a key justification for public education in the first place: that it equalizes opportunities for all students. That a uniform school system has been unable to do so does not negate the importance of crafting a plural system that bends toward justice. Domestic and international research suggests ways to increase the odds that an educationally plural system helps instead of hinders equal access to opportunity. The policy framework for educational pluralism should make sure that all families have access. As American pluralism gets off the ground, it is important to acknowledge the barriers that pertain to our most disadvantaged children, and to mediate them. Research findings on the consequences of poverty upon children's life chances prove persuasive paying particular attention to these children. As Alanna Bjorklund-Young notes in her summary of recent research, the most significant academic achievement gap in America is between low-income and high-income families, which is twice that of the gap between black and white students. Children who are raised in poverty are only one-third as likely to complete high school than their peers and significantly less likely to enroll in college.[94] Adults who only attain a high school degree earn 22 % and 34 % less than those who hold Associates or Bachelor's degrees, respectively,[95] and go through life with substantially diminished non-monetary satisfaction.[96] At the same time, our current system already permits better-off families to approximate educational pluralism: they can move to more desirable public school districts or send their children to Catholic, Jewish, independent, or Montessori private schools. Giving priority to low-income families would thus begin to equalize this imbalance and place more young Americans on a positive life trajectory.

The mechanisms of educational pluralism can be tailored to do this. Arizona created the country's first individual tax credit in 1997. Two aspects of the program benefited benefited wealthier families, but not the lowest-income families: it did not include a means test as a criterion for receiving a private school scholarship, and it allowed those who gave their tax credit to the public school district to specify which school and program received support. Because the scholarships were not means-tested, middle-income families used the scholarships more frequently than did low-income families. Because the program let donors name the sponsored program, wealthy families received tax relief to support their own children's public school activities.[97]

Arizona corrected the first inequity in subsequent legislation: its two corporate tax credit programs allow scholarships only for those students who live at or below 185 % of the threshold for free or reduced lunch, who are in the foster care system, or who possess special needs. Almost all of the country's subsequent tax credit legislation has been crafted in this way, and to good effect: Florida's corporate tax credit benefited not only the lowest-income students, but also the least-able students—thus directly helping the students who used scholarships and also those who remained in public schools.[98]

The sticking point in some states seems to be that Jewish Orthodox families, whose national organizations support school choice mechanisms,[99] tend to have large families—much larger than other Jews or most Americans. Of the Jewish Orthodox who are parents, almost half (48 %) have four or more children.[100] This places a strain on the standard means test, which if in place, is usually 150 to 200 % of the qualifying income for free or reduced lunch.[101] Rather than let the means test go to the wayside, as Georgia's program does, it makes more sense to create a sliding scale of income based on the number of family members. Pennsylvania's tax credit program follows this model, thus allowing those with an absolute low income to qualify while also acknowledging that a larger family should have a higher qualifying mean.[102]

Merely requiring means tests for scholarships is not enough; other, less obvious, proxies can skew benefits toward upper-income recipients. Academic ability is one such proxy, as Chile found out when it opened the first voucher system in the world (other countries had given block grants). Chile's program

(1981) allowed schools to take students' academic record into consideration, and to interview parents, during the admission process. Both measures correlate to socioeconomic status. Therefore, Chile's system produced gains for students who were already advantaged.[103]

In 1994, Chile's government struck down all selection processes in the lower grades and parent interviews in the upper grades.[104] The country's voucher program, which now educates 39 % of Chile's students, no longer privileges the middle class—and Chile outperforms most of its neighboring countries on international exams.[105]

Sweden did things differently from the beginning. In 1992, the central government allowed municipalities to create per capita school funding to follow students to their chosen schools. Not all the municipalities did so. Still, the educational landscape has changed greatly. Before 1992, fewer than 1 % of Swedish children attended private schools; 20 years later, with per capita funding, 14 % did so nationally, with some municipalities reporting fully 45 % of students in non-public schools.[106]

Sweden's per-child funding is absolute; when students change schools, the full funding moves with them. This has not increased the cost of schooling, nor has it created uneven achievement. Rather, in cities with widespread participation, average academic achievement, attainment, and university attendance grew across the board. A 2012 study made this concrete, noting that every 10 % increase in the share of non-public students resulted in "close to a 2 percentile rank higher educational achievement at the end of compulsory school and in high school, a 2 percentage point higher probability of choosing an academic high-school track, a 2 percentage point higher probability of attending university."[107] This was *not* because independent schools produced better results. Rather, average performance and achievement grew across the system, after controlling for demographics and other reforms.[108] How did Sweden's program seem to "lift all boats," when Chile's had not? Sweden's did not allow schools to select students on the basis of ability.[109] As such, the schools resembled American charters.

There is a problem with this approach, however. Implemented in absolute terms, it would prevent schools in which high achievement is a core component of the culture, from joining the system. Exam schools, such as Stuyvesant and Hunter College High Schools in New York City, have a long history of enabling social mobility for middle- and low-income students, and some of the private schools that participate in the DC. Opportunity Scholarship program (OSP) have high academic admissions standards which scholarship applicants must meet. This is as it should be. A fully plural school system would include some of these options, as well.

SUPPORT PARENTS IN THE PROCESS

A plural educational system gives families equal access to good schools—theoretically. In practice, parents are unequally prepared to choose the right school for their children. Picture a low-income parent who, for the first time, has the option of sending her child to a school other than the assigned neighborhood public school. The choice can be overwhelming.

We know this from research on inter-district choice models. Inter-district choice programs are not equivalent to educational pluralism; these choice programs allow (or require) families to select only between district schools, not between school sectors. Nevertheless, studies of these programs offer insights into the unequal preparation that parents have to choose widely. In 2002, Charlotte-Mecklenburg Schools (CMS) in North Carolina, the country's 20th-largest school district, created an open-enrollment policy for high school. Although students could still attend their neighborhood schools if they wished, they could request up to three others. CMS launched an extensive campaign to reach parents that included kiosks in popular shopping malls, door-to-door walkathons, and brochures that described the process. In the end, 95 % of families in the district applied for alternative placement.[110] A gold standard study of the consequences showed a strong positive impact on academic attainment for low-income students.[111]

The high percentage of families in CMS who signed up for alternative placements, however, does not mean that all families felt well informed about their choices. Most research indicates that even well run public school choice programs can be confusing to families. A recent study of families in "choice-rich" districts showed that 30 % of the parents had trouble with the eligibility requirements, and 25 % with the enrollment procedures.[112] The Center on Reinventing Public Education (CPRE) studied eight such programs in Baltimore, Cleveland Denver, Detroit, Indianapolis, New Orleans, Philadelphia, and Washington, D.C., surveying a total of 4000 parents and guardians. The researchers found that "parents with less education, minority parents, and parents of special-needs children are more likely to report challenges navigating choice," and that "cities have made uneven investments" in the parental aspect of their choice programs.[113] Mere access to information was insufficient; in cities that provided extensive details about curricula, school performance, and enrollment, "parents were no more likely to report having the information they need ... than in cities with less developed information systems."[114] Not only that: even in high-choice cities, many parents were dissatisfied with the lack of *high quality* choices, adequate transportation, and access to information.[115]

Another study (2015) from CPRE examined the open enrollment policies in Denver and New Orleans. An open enrollment policy gives parents a one-stop application for district *and* charter schools, instead of having to apply to each school separately—as is the case, for instance, with charter schools in Massachusetts. Open enrollment policies that include charters are a step closer to the full-bodied pluralism I argue for in this book. Even with the expanded options (district and charter), however, researchers found that parents were not adequately informed. While the centralized enrollment process "eliminated a lot of confusion and inequities,"[116] parents "still wanted more information about school culture, the relationship between adults and students and among students, the approach teachers take in the classroom, and how their own child might react to the school's environment."[117] Denver and New Orleans, while leading the country in public school choice mechanisms, still have work to do to fully support parents and, as CPRE notes, ensuring that all schools are of high quality.[118]

The same problem applies to tax credit and voucher programs, most of which are geared for families who are experiencing choice for the first time. Patrick Wolf is the scholar of record on the OSP in Washington, DC—a voucher plan that helps a modest number of families send their children to private schools. His five-year study indicates that parents' ability to navigate the choice system "varie[d] substantially in understandable ways."[119] Wolf found, most critically, that what parents wanted for their children changed over time. Initially, they wanted a safe school that their children enjoyed. Over time, they came to want academic attainment, college preparedness, and intellectual depth. Parents, in other words, became increasingly sophisticated consumers of education "as a result of their direct experiences with parental school choice."[120] Wolf observed the lack of personal supports along the way. "Even books and guides," he wrote, are insufficient, because "40 % of most adults in D.C. are functionally illiterate. They need people."[121]

All of this reminds us that parents are unequally equipped to navigate a plural educational system. The mere presence of choice is not sufficient. Governments in Central Europe provide extensive information to parents on the academic and vocational outcomes that go with particular schools.[122] Austria created "an extensive system of educational counseling" to help families navigate their options.[123] And the developing world may be doing an even better job: the Pakistani province of Punjab, for instance, provides parent support along with vouchers, new private schools in rural districts, new measures of quality control. One of the Punjab's innovations involved giving village parents "report cards showing the test scores of their children and the average for schools nearby, both public and private." This resulted in higher test scores across the board, as parents became savvier about what to expect and even demand.[124]

It is not clear that any plural system has the magic bullet to help all parents make the most of the opportunity. We can expect, based on Wolf's research, that most parents *learn* to choose well over time, and that this learning to choose constitutes a democratic training ground.[125] The obligation remains on governments and philanthropies to provide the necessary funding and human presence to speed up this process.

MAKE SURE FUNDING FORMULAE WORK FOR EQUITY

How do we make sure that a plural system is equitably funded between wealthy and poor districts and between public and non-public students?

The first issue, of addressing the disparities between a state's wealthy and poor districts, has been a concern for decades. Unequal funding is caused by the dependence of education budgets upon local property taxes. New Hampshire and Connecticut are the most dependent upon property tax (55 % of the state's education budget) and Hawaii and Vermont least (between 0 and 1 %). In most states, between a quarter and a half of the overall education budget comes from, and stays in, local districts.[126] The problem is that this leaves poorer districts with less money to spend on their students.

State governments step into the breach to varying degrees, with Utah, New Jersey and Minnesota earning the "most progressive" and Illinois, New Hampshire and Nevada the "most regressive" ends of the spectrum, according to the Education Law Center.[127] State budgetary formulae are labyrinthine; New York State Education Department's 2008 district-level budget went on for 86 pages.[128] The federal government steps in as well, *via* Title 1 funding, a provision in the Congressional budget that supports low-income students, and *via* other federal agencies such as the Department of Agriculture, which coordinates childhood nutrition programs, and the Department of Health and Human Services, which manages HeadStart.[129]

Despite such interventions, even neighboring districts can have very different budgets. In 2014, school districts in New York's Nassau County varied in per-student expenditures from $36,426 in Long Beach City to $18,325 in Floral Park-Bellerose.[130]

State and federal additives have patently not cured such disparities, and most states have had their school funding formulae challenged in court.[131] At first, plaintiffs (usually low-income districts) attacked state distribution under the *federal* Constitution's Equal Protection Clause. The Supreme Court did not accept this reasoning and in 1973 ruled, in *San Antonio Independent School District v. Rodriguez,* that the Constitution did not guarantee a right to an education nor to "absolute equality" of educational inputs, including money.[132] The equality argument got nowhere.

Having failed under Equal Protection, litigants began to focus on *adequacy* of education and on state, not federal, constitutions.[133] An important case happened in 1989 in Kentucky, when the state's Supreme Court struck down the funding mechanism that had left poor districts with "inadequate education," in *Rose v. Council for Better Education* (1989).[134] In *Rose*, the judges ordered the legislature to fix the funding formula and to ensure specific learning goals (such as "sufficient oral and written communication skills to enable students to function in a complex and rapidly changing civilization"). In consequences, the state passed the Kentucky Education Reform Act (KERA) in 1990, which was until then the most radical systemic overhaul in the country.

Rose changed school finance litigation. As one legal scholar wrote, "For the first time, courts invalidated educational finance systems not because the expenditures were unequal (the equity theory), but because some schools lacked the money to meet minimum standards of quality (the adequacy theory)."[135] In subsequent years, 26 state cases called for changing the property tax allocations on the basis of educational adequacy, and in 21 of these cases, the state court ruled for the plaintiffs.[136]

Did Kentucky's KERA work as planned? A 2003 Mathematica study found that KERA had indeed redistributed funding equitably. By 2000, per-pupil expenditures were higher in poorer than in wealthier districts; teachers in poorer districts had higher salaries than those in wealthy districts; class sizes in poor districts had shrunk.[137] However, the same study found *no impact* upon the achievement gap between wealthy and poor students on nationally normed tests.[138] There had been a statistically significant increase in black student test scores, but this too proved complex. Because a majority of black students lived in economically stable, not depressed, districts, the funding redistribution did not affect them greatly. The researchers therefore surmised that the reform's tougher learning goals, not its improved funding standards, had caused the rise in black test scores.[139] Kentucky had not become an educational paradise; 20 years later, the learning goals remained "aspirational" rather than actual.[140]

What are we to make of this? The intent of redistributive funding is surely right, but doing so does not inevitably yield better student outcomes.[141] Equitable spending, it seems, has to keep one eye on comparative funding, the other on each budget itself. Indeed, it seems that the majority of school districts in this country—whether or not under litigated regimes—are not fiscally productive. Thus, the attempts to redistribute property taxes more fairly will not result in better student outcomes. This is a major problem which litigation thus far has not addressed.

As an example, in 2014, the Center for American Progress analyzed 7000 school districts representing 80 % of American K-12 students. After using weighted controls for low-income, special education, and English Language Learning students, and then tying expenditures to academic achievement, the research team found that "low educational productivity remains a deeply pressing problem, with billions of dollars lost in low-capacity districts."[142] What did they mean by "educational productivity?" Academic "bang per buck." In 2011, one district in New York State (Rondout Valley School District) "spent around $25,500 per student in unadjusted expenditures, which puts the district in the upper tier of the state ... but [it] gets lower achievement relative to other districts with similar demographics."[143] On a national scale, "only one in three districts that were in the top third of spending within their state (after adjusting for student populations and cost of living) were also in the top third for achievement."[144] In other words, there was no absolute correlation between the wealth of the district and its academic outcomes, nor did the states themselves investigate these connections.[145] Only Florida and Texas "regularly rated the productivity of local school dollars" through analyses of inputs and outcomes at the district level.[146]

It is therefore fruitless to campaign for more equitable funding between the districts without addressing the fiscal irresponsibility displayed by the districts. As a next step, "fair funding" between districts must take this into account.

Fair funding between public and non-public students has been no easier to achieve. Public charter schools are accused of taking money from traditional schools by progressive politicians[147] and even by Moody's, which in 2013 attributed the rise of charter schools to the fiscal instability of traditional school districts.[148] A dispute over Baltimore's charter school funding formula erupted into a lawsuit in the fall of 2015.[149] The nation's largest teachers union opposes vouchers and tax credit programs because "they divert money away from public schools to private and religious schools."[150] Diane Ravitch, who was recently named the second-most influential educational commentator on social media,[151] echoes this sentiment.[152] This sense of competition between district, charter, and private schools stands in sharp contrast to what we find in many other democratic systems and makes fair funding mechanisms difficult to consider.[153]

A way forward under an educationally plural system would at least create proxies for per capita funding and weighted formulae for high-needs students, ensure fair admissions policies, and provide in-person support for parents as they navigate the new system.

That would be the end goal. It will take time to unwind our current district infrastructure. A first step would be to allow a district's variable costs to follow students to non-public schools (in states that allow vouchers) or back into the state treasury (in states that do not). Fixed costs comprise approximately 36 % of the total and represent capital expenditures, interest, general administration, school administration, operations and maintenance, transportation, and "other" support services. The remaining 64 % is variable and includes teachers' salaries, instructional costs, nonacademic student supports, instructional staff support, materials, and food service.[154] In the long run, all costs are variable. In the short term, according to one recent study, it is possible to reallocate a significant portion of variable costs without penalizing the district's fiscal or academic health.[155]

Limits of Pluralism: Summary

We know from national and international research that educational systems that allow schools to have a distinctive ethos and also require rigorous academic curricula narrow the achievement gaps. We also know that plural systems can be as inequitable as uniform systems. The broad policy frameworks above would go a long way to ensuring excellence and equity for America's students—or at least, so it seems. But policies are designed based on our predictions of their effects. There will always be unintended consequences and unexpected variables. We do not know, for instance, what an entirely plural system would look like in Colorado or Texas, nor do we know how the effects might differ in rural Kansas and Seattle. If educational pluralism begins to take hold, our learning curve will be steep. The good news is that other democratic systems provide extensive lessons—both negative and positive—from which to draw, if we wish to heed them.

NOTES

1. James S. Coleman, Thomas Hoffer, and Sally Kilgore, *High School Achievement: Public, Catholic, and Private Schools Compared* (New York: Basic Books, 1982); Anthony S. Bryk, Valerie E. Lee, and Peter Blakeley Holland, *Catholic Schools and the Common Good* (Cambridge, MA: Harvard University Press, 1993).
2. Patrick J. Wolf and Stephen Macedo, *Educating Citizens: International Perspectives on Civic Values and School Choice* (Brookings Institution Press. 1775 Massachusetts Avenue NW, Washington, DC 20036. Tel: 202-797-6000; Fax: 202-797-6004; e-mail: webmaster@brookings.edu; Web site: http://www.brookings.edu/index/publications.htm, 2004), http://www.eric.ed.gov/ERICWebPortal/detail?accno=ED493327. *Introduction*, p. 12.
3. Elmer John Thiessen, *Teaching for Commitment: Liberal Education, Indoctrination, and Christian Nurture* (Mcgill Queens University Press, 1993). 89.
4. Diane Ravitch, *Left Back: A Century of Battles over School Reform* (Simon & Schuster, 2001), 25–29, 466.
5. Hirsch, E.D. *Why Knowledge Matters: Rescuing Our Children from Failed Educational Theories.* Cambridge, MA: Harvard Education Press, 2016.
6. See the final section of Chap. 5.
7. Gabriel Heller Sahlgren, *Real Finnish Lessons: The True Story of an Education Superpower* (London, UK: Centre for Policy Studies, 2015). 47–48; 49–62.
8. E.D. Hirsch, *The Skills Delusion: Educational Ideas and the Fate of Nations* (To be released, 2016).
9. Tino Sanandaji, "Sweden Has an Education Crisis, But It Wasn't Caused by School Choice," *National Review*, July 21, 2014, http://www.nationalreview.com/agenda/383304/sweden-has-education-crisis-it-wasnt-caused-school-choice-tino-sanandaji. This is not empirically verified.
10. Robert Witt and Jean Orvis, "A 21st Century Imperative: A Guide to Becoming a School of the Future," NAIS Commission on Accreditation (Washington, DC: National Association of Independent Schools, 2010).
11. On June 24, 2015, I attended a conference at the American Enterprise Institute on "The State of Entrepreneurship in K-12 Education." The speakers were excellent, their projects and recommendations important and strong. However, their attention to intellectually challenging content was nil; indeed, the subject never came up. http://www.aei.org/events/the-state-of-entrepreneurship-in-k-12-education/, accessed August 15, 2015. This is not a failure of entrepreneurship as much as selective attention to what closes the gap for at-risk students.
12. Jerome S. Bruner, *The Process of Education: [a Landmark in Educational Theory]* (Cambridge [u.a.]: Harvard University Press, 1978). pp. xvii–xxii; 3–14.
13. Ibid., 52.
14. Ibid., 33–39.

15. Ibid., 3, 19.
16. Ibid., 71.
17. Ibid., 89–90.
18. Ibid., x–xii.
19. Neil Postman, *Teaching As a Subversive Activity* (Random House Digital, Inc., 1969). 30, 53.
20. Ibid., 137–14.
21. Ravitch, *Left Back.*, 387.
22. Neill's other books were entitled *The Problem Child* (1927), *The Problem Parent* (1932), That *Dreadful School* (1937), *The Problem Teacher* (1939). Together, they put forth the view that adult authority was oppressive and that the ideal school allowed students to pursue their natural interests at all levels. Neill's boarding school, Summerhill, captured this educational philosophy and was detailed in the popular *Summerhill.*
23. Robert K. Fullinwider, "Multicultural Education: Concepts, Policies, and Controversies," in *Public Education in a Multicultural Society: Policy, Theory, Critique*, Cambridge Studies in Philosophy and Public Policy (Cambridge [England]; New York: Cambridge University Press, 1996), 3–22. Lawrence Blum, "Antiracist Civic Education in the California History-Social Science Framework," in *Public Education in a Multicultural Society: Policy, Theory, Critique*, Cambridge Studies in Philosophy and Public Policy (Cambridge [England]: Cambridge University Press, 1996), 23–48. Gilbert T. Sewall, "A Conflict of Visions: Multiculturalism and the Social Studies," in *Public Education in a Multicultural Society: Policy, Theory, Critique*, Cambridge Studies in Philosophy and Public Policy (Cambridge [England]: Cambridge University Press, n.d.), 49–61.
24. Fullinwider, Robert K, "Multicultural Education: Concepts, Policies, and Controversies," in *Public Education in a Multicultural Society: Policy, Theory, Critique*, 3–22, p. 12. Cambridge Studies in Philosophy and Public Policy. Cambridge [England]; New York: Cambridge University Press, 1996.
25. Anthony M. Roselli, "Chapter 2: A Close Look at Reform in One State: The Massachusetts Experiment," *Counterpoints* 283 (2005): 23–40, 33.
26. Elaine Wrisley Reed, "A New Professionalism for Massachusetts Teachers: Six Constituencies at Work," *Journal of Education* 180, no. 1 (1998): 79–88. pp. 80–82.
27. Sandra Stotsky, *An-Empty-Curriculum-The-Need-to-Reform-Teacher-Licensing-Regulations-and-Tests* (New York, NY: Rowman & Littlefield, 2015), https://rowman.com/ISBN/9781475815689/An-Empty-Curriculum-The-Need-to-Reform-Teacher-Licensing-Regulations-and-Tests.
28. Roselli, "Chapter 2." 33.
29. Paul E. Peterson et al., "Globally Challenged: Are U.S. Students Ready to Compete? The Latest on Each State's International Standing in Math and Reading. PEPG 11-03" (Program on Education Policy and Governance, Harvard University, August 2011), http://www.eric.ed.gov/ERICWebPortal/detail?accno=ED526954.
30. Grover Whitehurst, "Don't Forget Curriculum," Brown Center Letters on Education (Brookings, October 2009).
31. Ulrich Boser, Matthew Chingos, and Chelsea Straus, "The Hidden Value of Curriculum Reform" (Washington, DC: Center for American Progress, October

2015), https://cdn.americanprogress.org/wp-content/uploads/2015/10/06111518/CurriculumMatters-report.pdf. 2.

32. Common Core State Standards Initiative, "Common Core State Standards for English Language Arts & Literacy in History/Social Studies, Science and Technical Subjects" (Common Core State Standards Initiative, 2015), http://www.corestandards.org/ELA-Literacy/.

33. Elizabeth A. Harris and Ford Fessenden, "'Opt Out' Becomes Anti-Test Rallying Cry in New York State," *The New York Times*, May 20, 2015, http://www.nytimes.com/2015/05/21/nyregion/opt-out-movement-against-common-core-testing-grows-in-new-york-state.html.Valerie Strauss, "New York's Common Core Test Scores Flop yet Again—with 20 Percent of Students Opting out," *The Washington Post*, August 13, 2015, http://www.washingtonpost.com/blogs/answer-sheet/wp/2015/08/13/n-y-common-core-test-scores-flop-yet-again/.

34. Thomas Kane et al., "Teaching Higher: Educators' Perspectives on Common Core Implementation" (Cambridge, MA: Center for Education Policy Research, Harvard University, February 2016), http://cepr.harvard.edu/files/cepr/files/teaching-higher-report.pdf?m=1454988762, esp. 4–6.

35. For a survey of the general disinterest in evidence about what works in colleges of education, even in the important subject of instruction: Thomas Kane et al., "Teaching Higher: Educators' Perspectives on Common Core Implementation" (Cambridge, MA: Center for Education Policy Research, Harvard University, February 2016), http://cepr.harvard.edu/files/cepr/files/teaching-higher-report.pdf?m=1454988762.

36. There are exceptions, such as the newly created Knowledge Matters Campaign (http://knowledgematterscampaign.org), which promotes the value of specific content in the quest for educational equity.

37. David Steiner, "The New Common Core Assessments: How They Could Stop Patronizing Our Students," *The Huffington Post*, February 21, 2014, http://www.huffingtonpost.com/david-m-steiner/the-new-common-core-asses_b_4809973.html.

38. Katie Dulaney, "Institutional Commitment to Civic Education: Public Montessori Secondary Schools," *CUNY Institute for Education Policy*, May 8, 2015, http://ciep.hunter.cuny.edu/institutional-commitment-to-civic-education-public-montessori-secondary-schools/.

39. Ray Pennings, *Cardus Education Survey* (Hamilton, ON: Cardus, 2011). Especially pages 6, 11, 16–22.

40. John Bishop, "Which Secondary Education Systems Work Best? The United States or Northern Europe," *Working Papers*, January 1, 2010, http://digitalcommons.ilr.cornell.edu/workingpapers/105.

41. See, for instance, "The Central Ohio Compact: A Regional Strategy for College Completion and Career Success," Organizational (Columbus, OH: Columbus State Community College and the Educational Service Center of Central Ohio, November 2012).

42. Stephen Macedo, "In Defense of Conditional Funding of Religious Schools," *Law & Ethics of Human Rights* 1, no. 1 (2007): 382–428, doi:10.2202/1938-2545.1011. Macedo makes a strong case that conditional funding is appropriate when funding extends to non-public schools; the same reasoning applies, it seems to me, to public schools as well.

43. See the New York Performance Standards Consortium at http://performanceassessment.org, accessed August 15, 2015.
44. Douglas Farrow, "On the Ethics and Religious Culture Program, Expert Testimony, Re: Loyola High School et John Zucchi C. Michelle Courchesne, En Sa Qualite de Minister de l'Education, Du Loisir et Du Sport. Cour Superieure, District de Montreal, N. 500-17-045278-085." (D.B. Farrow, January 2010)."Loyola High School and John Zucchi, Plaintifs, v. Michelle Courchesne, in Her Capacity as Minister of Education, Recreation and Sports" (Montreal: Superior Court, Canada, Province of Quebec, District of Montreal, June 18, 2010).
45. "Loyola High School and John Zucchi, Plaintifs, v. Michelle Courchesne, in Her Capacity as Minister of Education, Recreation and Sports." 8.
46. Janice Arnold, "Frum Schools Balk at New Religious Culture Course," *Canadian Jewish News*, September 18, 2008, sec. News, http://www.cjnews.com/node/81794.
47. "Ethique et Culture Religieuse—Sondage Léger Marketing—Plus Des Trois Quarts Des Québécois Pour Le Libre Choix," News Wire (Montreal [Que.]: Coalition pour la liberté en éducation, May 26, 2009), http://archive.newswire.ca/en/story/558659/ethique-et-culture-religieuse-sondage-leger-marketing-plus-des-trois-quarts-des-quebecois-pour-le-libre-choix.
48. Megan, "Supreme Court Rules Quebec Infringed on Loyola High School's Religious Freedom," accessed October 3, 2015, http://www.cbc.ca/news/canada/montreal/supreme-court-rules-quebec-infringed-on-loyola-high-school-s-religious-freedom-1.3000724.
49. Beverley McLachlin, "Freedom of Religion and the Rule of Law: A Canadian Perspective," in *Recognizing Religion in a Secular Society: Essays in Pluralism, Religion and Public Policy* (Montreal [Que.]: McGill-Queen's University Press, 2004). 16.
50. Farrow, "On the Ethics and Religious Culture Program, Expert Testimony, Re: Loyola High School et John Zucchi C. Michelle Courchesne, En Sa Qualite de Minister de l'Education, Du Loisir et Du Sport. Cour Superieure, District de Montreal, N. 500-17-045278-085." 5.
51. Rev. Francis Close, "Cooperation with the Committee of Council on Education Vindicated and Recommended," Cheltenham College Archives (London: Hatchard & Son, 1848), in which he argued that Parliamentary funding for education was worth the likelihood of "funding error."
52. "18 U.S. Code § 2385—Advocating Overthrow of Government," n.d.
53. Runyon v. McClary, 427 United States Reports 160 (Supreme Court of the United States 1976).
54. Ibid., 494.
55. Robert D. Putnam and David E. Campbell, *American Grace: How Religion Divides and Unites Us* (Simon & Schuster, 2012). 370.
56. Eric A DeGroff, "Parental Rights and Public School Curricula: Revisiting Mozert after 20 Years," *Journal of Law & Education*. 38, no. 1 (2009): 83.
57. Jasmine Hafiz, "Creationism Banned From UK Schools," *The Huffington Post*, June 25, 2014, http://www.huffingtonpost.com/2014/06/25/creationism-banned-uk-schools_n_5529693.html.
58. Abraham C. Flipse, "The Origins of Creationism in the Netherlands: The Evolution Debate among Twentieth-Century Dutch Neo-Calvinists," *Church History* 81, no. 1 (March 2012): 104–47.

59. S. Heijnens, "Theory of Evolution in Dutch Education. History of the Theory of Evolution in Dutch Public Education, Policy, Debates and High School Examinations from 1867 until Recent." (Masters in History and Philosophy of Science, Utrecht, 2013), http://dspace.library.uu.nl/handle/1874/272751.

60. Thomas Hoffman, "Scientists Warn: Creationism Is on the Rise in Europe," *Sciencenordic*, Research & Study, February 24, 2015, http://sciencenordic.com/scientists-warn-creationism-rise-europe.; Jonny Scaramanga, "Pseudoscience I Was Taught at a British Creationist School," *The Guardian*, September 25, 2014, sec. Science, http://www.theguardian.com/science/blog/2014/sep/25/pseudoscience-creationist-schools-uk-accelerated-christian-education-ace.

61. Frank Newport, "In U.S., 46 % Hold Creationist View of Human Origins," *Gallup.com*, June 1, 2012, http://www.gallup.com/poll/155003/Hold-Creationist-View-Human-Origins.aspx.

62. Lawrence D. Weinberg, *Religious Charter Schools: Legalities and Practicalities (PB)* (Information Age Publishing, 2007). Weinberg argues that a state could construct a neutral law that enabled religious charter schools, but this has not yet been tried.

63. Ronald Bayer and Robert L. Spitzer, "Edited Correspondence on the Status of Homosexuality in DSM-III," *Journal of the History of the Behavioral Sciences* 18, no. 1 (January 1, 1982): 32–52, doi:10.1002/1520-6696(198201)18:1<32::AID-JHBS2300180105>3.0.CO;2-0.

64. Obergefell et al. v. Hodges, Director, Ohio Department of Health, Et Al., 576 United States Reports—(Supreme Court of the United States 2015).

65. "Aetna Insurance Coding," 2015, http://www.aetna.com/cpb/medical/data/600_699/0615.html.

66. "Movement Advancement Project|Our Work and Mission," accessed October 10, 2015, http://www.lgbtmap.org/our-work-and-mission.

67. "What Transgender Looks Like in Pop Culture," *US News & World Report*, accessed October 10, 2015, http://www.usnews.com/news/articles/2014/06/06/laverne-cox-and-the-state-of-trans-representation-in-pop-culture.

68. "What Is Heteronormativity?|GEA—Gender and Education Association," accessed October 10, 2015, http://www.genderandeducation.com/issues/what-is-heteronormativity/. "What Is Heteronormativity and How Is It Damaging?," *About.com News & Issues*, accessed October 10, 2015, http://civil-liberty.about.com/od/gendersexuality/g/heteronormative.htm.

69. CNN, "Mississippi School Sued for Canceling Prom over Lesbian Student," *CNN.com*, March 12, 2010, http://www.cnn.com/2010/LIVING/03/11/mississippi.prom.suit/.

70. "10 LGBT Prom Controversies from Around the US," *Ranker*, accessed October 10, 2015, http://www.ranker.com/list/10-lgbt-prom-controversies-from-around-the-us/ballerina-tatyana.

71. "National Association of Independent Schools, Principles and Best Practices," *National Association of Independent Schools*, 2015, http://www.nais.org/Articles/Pages/Principles-of-Good-Practice.aspx.

72. "Anti-Gay Policy Prompts School To Nix State Money," *The Huffington Post*, accessed October 10, 2015, http://www.huffingtonpost.com/2013/12/08/north-carolina-school-gay-policy-_n_4403722.html.

73. "Georgia's Tax Dollars Help Finance Private Schools with Severe Anti-Gay Policies, Practices, & Teachings" (Atlanta, GA: Southern Education Association, January 2013).

74. Michelle Manchir, "Wheaton College: Group Supporting LGBT Students at Wheaton College Plans Homecoming Festivities," *Tribunedigital-Chicagotribune*, September 30, 2011, http://articles.chicagotribune.com/2011-09-30/news/ct-met-wheaton-lgbt-homecoming-0930-20110930_1_wheaton-college-homecoming-kristin-winn.; "Statement on Sexual Identity—Policies|Wheaton College," June 15, 2011, http://wheatoncollege.edu/policies/sxidentity/.

75. "OneWheaton: A Community of Lesbian, Gay, Bisexual, Transgender, Queer, Questioning and Allied (LGBTQ&A) Alumni and Students of Wheaton College (Illinois)," *OneWheaton*, accessed November 7, 2015, http://www.onewheaton.com.; Herbert Pinnock, "Gay and Lesbian Graduates to Make a Statement During Wheaton College's Alumni Event? Read More at Http://www.christianpost.com/news/gay-and-Lesbian-Graduates-to-Make-a-Statement-during-Wheaton-Colleges-Alumni-Event-57635/#qYsviUoSWvYxlsOU.99," *Christian Post*, October 7, 2011, http://www.christianpost.com/news/gay-and-lesbian-graduates-to-make-a-statement-during-wheaton-colleges-alumni-event-57635/.; Julie Roys, "Wheaton College's Gay Celibate Counselor Says She Cannot Change Her Sexual Orientation," *ChristianHeadlines.com*, December 16, 2014, http://www.christianheadlines.com/news/wheaton-college-s-gay-celibate-counselor-says-she-cannot-change-her-sexual-orientation.html.; Eric Teetsel, "Wheaton College Counselor Resigns, Admits Support for Same-Sex Marriage," *Religious Write*, July 13, 2015, http://www.patheos.com/blogs/manhattanproject/2015/07/wheaton-college-counselor-resigns-admits-support-for-same-sex-marriage/.

76. Steve Weatherbe, "Canadian Parents Battle Pro-Homosexual Public Schools," *National Catholic Register*, August 12, 2011, http://www.ncregister.com/daily-news/canadian-parents-battle-pro-homosexual-public-schools/, Heather Clark, "Canadian Supreme Court Rules Biblical Speech Opposing Homosexual Behavior Is a 'Hate Crime,'" Religious publication, *Christian News Network*, (February 2013), http://christiannews.net/2013/02/28/canadian-supreme-court-rules-biblical-speech-opposing-homosexual-behavior-is-a-hate-crime/.

77. "Canada Schools Forced to Admit Gay-Straight Groups," *Christian Broadcasting Network*, June 8, 2012, http://www.cbn.com/cbnnews/world/2012/June/Canada-Schools-Forced-to-Admit-Gay-Straight-Groups/.

78. "Fact-Sheet: Sexual Orientation Issues" (European Court of Human Rights, Strasbourg, July 2015), http://www.echr.coe.int/Documents/FS_Sexual_orientation_ENG.pdf.

79. Robert Long, "Sex and Relationships Education in Schools," Briefing document (London, UK: House of Commons, July 26, 2015), 17.

80. Elsbeth Asbeek Brusse and Tanya Keenan, "'Recognize the Heterosexual' Education About Homosexuality in Dutch Secondary Schools by Elsbeth Asbeek Brusse, Tanya Keenan," *Humanity In Action*, June 27, 2008, http://www.humanityinaction.org/knowledgebase/94-recognize-the-heterosexual-education-about-homosexuality-in-dutch-secondary-schools.

81. Dan Littauer, "Israeli Parliament Bans Discrimination against LGBT Youth in Schools," *LGBTQ Nation*, March 19, 2014, http://www.lgbtqnation.com/2014/03/israeli-parliament-bans-discrimination-against-lgbt-youth-in-

schools/.; Odalis Garcia, "Israeli Parliament Bans Discrimination against LGBT Youth in Schools," Member organization, *GLAAD*, (March 21, 2014), https://www.glaad.org/blog/israeli-parliament-bans-discrimination-against-lgbt-youth-schools.

82. Ernest van den Haag, "Social Science Testimony in the Desegregation Cases—A Reply to Professor Kenneth Clark," *Villanova Law Review* 6 (1961): 69, http://heinonline.org/HOL/Page?handle=hein.journals/vllalr6&id=77&div=10&collection=journals, 77.

83. Joseph Hraba, "The Doll Technique: A Measure of Racial Ethnocentrism?," *Social Forces* 50, no. 4 (1972): 522–27, doi:10.2307/2576794.

84. Gwen Bergner, "Black Children, White Preference: Brown v. Board, the Doll Tests, and the Politics of Self-Esteem," *American Quarterly* 61, no. 2 (2009): 299–332, http://www.jstor.org/stable/27734991.

85. Benedict Carey, "Many Psychology Findings Not as Strong as Claimed, Study Says," *The New York Times*, August 27, 2015, http://www.nytimes.com/2015/08/28/science/many-social-science-findings-not-as-strong-as-claimed-study-says.html.

86. Open Science Collaboration, "Estimating the Reproducibility of Psychological Science," *Science* 349, no. 6251 (August 28, 2015): aac4716, doi:10.1126/science.aac4716, 943.

87. Eliza Shapiro, "Facing Decline, Catholic Schools Form a Charter-like Network," *Capital*, July 20, 2015, sec. Policy, http://www.capitalnewyork.com/article/city-hall/2015/07/8572070/facing-decline-catholic-schools-form-charter-network.

88. Elizabeth Green and Trevor Cooling, *Mapping the Field: A Review of the Current Research Evidence on the Impact of Schools with a Christian Ethos* (London: Theos, 2009). 33–35.

89. "Schools, Pupils and Their Characteristics: January 2015—Publications—GOV.UK," accessed August 15, 2015, https://www.gov.uk/government/statistics/schools-pupils-and-their-characteristics-january-2015.

90. Green and Cooling, *Mapping the Field*. 41–42.

91. Ashley Berner, "Metaphysics in Educational Theory: Educational Philosophy and Teacher Training in England (1839–1944)" (D.Phil., University of Oxford, 2008). 301–317.

92. Julie A Reuben, *The Making of the Modern University: Intellectual Transformation and the Marginalization of Morality* (Chicago: University of Chicago Press, 1996).

93. Julie Henry and Edward Malnick, "Church of England Schools to Be 'Rebranded,'" March 17, 2012, sec. Education, http://www.telegraph.co.uk/education/educationnews/9150817/Church-of-England-schools-to-be-rebranded.html.

94. Alanna Bjorklund-Young, "Moving to Opportunity: A Housing Experiment That Worked," *Johns Hopkins Institute for Education Policy*, January 7, 2016, http://education.jhu.edu/edpolicy/commentary/MovingtoOpportunityAHousingExperimentthatWorked.

95. "The New Forgotten Half and Research Directions to Support Them," *The William T. Grant Foundation*, January 2015, http://wtgrantfoundation.org/newforgottenhalf#_.

96. James Rosenbaum et al., "The New Forgotten Half and Research Directions to Support Them" (New York, NY: William T. Grant Foundation, January 2015), 9.

97. Glen Y. Wilson, "Effects on Funding Equity of the Arizona Tax Credit Law," *Education Policy Analysis Archives* 8, no. 0 (August 1, 2000): 38, doi:10.14507/epaa.v8n38.2000, 10; Glen Y. Wilson, "The Equity Impact of Arizona's Tax Credit Program: A Review of the First Three Years (1998–2000)," Research Report (Tempe, AZ: Arizona State University, March 2002), http://epsl.asu.edu/epru/documents/EPRU%202002-110/epru-0203-110.htm, 20. Paul Louis Melendez, "Do Education Tax Credits Improve Equity?" (Doctoral Dissertation in Educational Leadership, University of Arizona, 2009), http://arizona.openrepository.com/arizona/handle/10150/194044, 12.

98. Mai Miksic and Ashley Berner, "What Are Education Tax Credits, and Why Should We Care?," *CUNY Institute for Education Policy*, accessed June 17, 2015, http://ciep.hunter.cuny.edu/education-tax-credits-care/.; David Figlio, Cassandra M. D. Hart, and Molly Metzger, "Who Uses a Means-Tested Scholarship, and What Do They Choose?," *Economics of Education Review*, Special Issue in Honor of Henry M. Levin, 29, no. 2 (April 2010): 301–17, doi:10.1016/j.econedurev.2009.08.002.; David N. Figlio and Cassandra M. D. Hart, "Competitive Effects of Means-Tested School Vouchers," Working Paper (National Bureau of Economic Research, June 2010), http://www.nber.org/papers/w16056.; David Figlio and Cassandra Hart, "Competitive Effects of Means-Tested Vouchers," *American Economic Journal: Applied Economics* 6, no. 1 (January 2014): 133–56, doi:10.1257/app.6.1.133.

99. "Tuition Affordability," *OU Advocacy Center*, current, http://advocacy.ou.org/issues/tuition-crisis/.; Josh Nathan-Kazis, "How Orthodox Agudah and Wal-Mart Money United To Back School Vouchers—News," *The Forward*, July 22, 2014, http://forward.com/news/202290/how-orthodox-agudah-and-wal-mart-money-united-to-b/.; Josh Nathan-Kazis, "Did Jewish Groups Push Too Hard on N.Y. Education Tax Credit?—News," *The Forward*, July 3, 2015, http://forward.com/news/311348/pushin-too-hard/.

100. Pew Research Center, "A Portrait of American Orthodox Jews," *Pew Research Center's Religion & Public Life Project*, August 26, 2015, http://www.pewforum.org/2015/08/26/a-portrait-of-american-orthodox-jews/.; Asher Elbein, "Grappling With the Rising Cost of Being an Orthodox Jew," *Tablet Magazine*, July 11, 2014, http://www.tabletmag.com/jewish-life-and-religion/177127/rising-cost-of-being-orthodox.

101. "Scholarship Tax Credits," *National Conference of State Legislatures*, April 2014, http://www.ncsl.org/research/education/school-choice-scholarship-tax-credits.aspx.

102. "Overview of the Opportunity Education Tax Credit Program," *Pennsylvania Department of Education*, April 2015, http://www.education.pa.gov/Documents/K-12/Opportunity%20Scholarship%20Tax%20Credit%20Program/OSTCP%20Overview.pdf.

103. G. Elacqua, D. Contreras, and F. Salazar, "Scaling Up in Chile: Networks of Schools Facilitate Higher Student Achievement," *Education Next* 8, no. 3 (2008): 62–68, 64.

104. Ibid., 65.

105. Ibid., 62.

106. Anders Böhlmark and Mikael Lindahl, *Independent Schools and Long-Run Educational Outcomes Evidence from Sweden's Large Scale Voucher Reform* (Munich: CESifo, 2012), 6, 10.
107. Ibid., 31.
108. Ibid., 3.
109. Ibid., 9.
110. David S. Deming et al., "School Choice, School Quality and Post-Secondary Attainment" (National Bureau of Economic Research, 2011), 6.
111. Ibid., 5, 21.
112. Ashley Jochim, "Lessons from the Trenches on Making School Choice Work," *The Brookings Institution*, August 12, 2015, http://www.brookings.edu/blogs/brown-center-chalkboard/posts/2015/08/12-school-choice-lessons-jochim.
113. Ashley Jochim et al., "How Parents Experience Public School Choice," Making School Choice Work Series (University of Washington Bothell: Center on Reinventing Public Education, December 2014), 1.
114. Ibid., 2.
115. Ibid., 3.
116. Betheny Gross, Michael DeArmond, and Patrick Denice, "Common Enrollment, Parents, and School Choice: Early Evidence from Denver and New Orleans," Making School Choice Work Series (University of Washington Bothell: Center on Reinventing Public Education, May 2015), 1.
117. Ibid., 2.
118. Ibid., 2.
119. Patrick J. Wolf and Thomas Stewart, "The Evolution of Parental School Choice," in *Customized Schooling: Beyond Whole-School Reform*, ed. Frederick Hess and Bruno V. Manno (Cambridge, MA: Harvard Education Press, 2011), 91–105, 92.
120. Ibid., 103–104.
121. Ibid., 105.
122. Bishop, "Which Secondary Education Systems Work Best?"
123. Berner, "School Systems and Finance."
124. Editors, "Learning Unleashed," *Economist*, August 1, 2015, http://www.economist.com/news/briefing/21660063-where-governments-are-failing-provide-youngsters-decent-education-private-sector.
125. See, for instance, Patrick J. Wolf and Brian Kisida, "School Governance and Information: Does Choice Lead to Better-Informed Parents?," *American Politics Research* 38, no. 5 (September 2010): 783–805.
126. "Public School Revenue Sources," *Institute of Education Sciences: National Center for Education Statistics*, May 2015, http://nces.ed.gov/programs/coe/indicator_cma.asp, Figure 3.
127. Bruce D. Baker, David G. Sciarra, and Danielle Farrie, "Is School Funding Fair? A National Report Card" (Newark, NJ: Education Law Center, September 2010), http://www.schoolfundingfairness.org/National_Report_Card.pdf, Figure 2.
128. "2008–09 Executive Budget Proposal: Preliminary Estimate of 2007–08 and 2008–09 State Aids Payable under Sectionn 3609 plus Other Aids," State Government Proposal (Albany, NY: New York State Education Department, 2008), https://www.budget.ny.gov/pubs/archive/fy0809archive/eBudget0809/fy0809localities/schoolaid/schoolruns.pdf.

129. "Atlas New America," Foundation, *New America*, (June 29, 2015), http://atlas. newamerica.org/school-finance.
130. Steve Billmyer, "NY State School Budgets 2014–15: Look Up, Compare Any District in the State," *Syracuse.com*, May 19, 2014, http://www.syracuse.com/ news/index.ssf/2014/05/nys_school_budgets_2014-15_look_up_compare_ any_district.html.
131. Rob Reich, "Equality, Adequacy, and K-12 Education," in *Education, Justice, and Democracy*, ed. Rob Reich and Danielle Allen (Chicago: University of Chicago Press, 2013), 43–62, 45.
132. San Antonio Independent School District v. Rodriguez, 411 US 1 (1973) (Supreme Court of the United States 1973).
133. Benjamin Michael Superfine, *Equality in Education Law and Policy, 1954–2010* (New York: Cambridge University Press, 2013), 100–101.
134. Rose v. Council for Better Education, Inc., 790 Kentucky Court of Justice 186 (Supreme Court of Kentucky 1989).
135. William Thro, "Judicial Humility: The Enduring Legacy of Rose v. Council for Better Education" (Prepared for "Rose at 20: The Past and Future of School Finance Litigation," Louisville, KY, October 21, 2009), http://law-apache.uky. edu/wordpress/wp-content/uploads/2012/06/Thro-II.pdf, 764.
136. Superfine, *Equality in Education Law and Policy, 1954–2010*, 125.
137. Melissa A. Clark, "Education Reform, Redistribution, and Student Achievement: Evidence From the Kentucky Education Reform Act" (Princeton, NJ: Mathematica Policy Research, October 2003), 2; 16–23.
138. Ibid., 23–34.
139. Ibid., 33–34.
140. Thro, "Judicial Humility: The Enduring Legacy of Rose v. Council for Better Education.", 766.
141. Superfine, *Equality in Education Law and Policy, 1954–2010*, 79, 92.
142. Ulrich Boser and Center for American Progress, "Return on Educational Investment: A District-by-District Evaluation of U.S. Educational Productivity" (Washington, DC: Center for American Progress. 1333 H Street NW 10th Floor, Washington, DC 20005. Tel: 202-682-1611; Web site: http://www.american-progress.org, 2011), 2.
143. Ibid., 26.
144. Halley Potter, "Pathways to Smarter, Fairer Funding: Three Reports in Review," *Journal of School Choice Journal of School Choice* 9, no. 2 (2015): 310–14, 311.
145. Boser and Center for American Progress, "Return on Educational Investment.", 2.
146. Ibid., 14–15.
147. Karen Matthews, "Charter Schools Worry About De Blasio's Plans," News, *The Huffington Post*, (December 26, 2013), http://www.huffingtonpost. com/2013/12/26/bill-de-blasio-charter-schools_n_4503518.html.Andrew J. Rotherham and Richard Whitmire, "De Blasio vs. Everyone Else," *Slate*, March 12, 2014, http://www.slate.com/articles/news_and_politics/educa-tion/2014/03/bill_de_blasio_vs_charter_schools_a_feud_in_new_york_city_ has_broad_national.html.
148. Michael D'Arcy and Naomi Richman, "Moody's: Charter Schools Pose Greatest Credit Challenge to School Districts in Economically Weak Urban Areas," Investor Service, *Moodys.com*, (October 15, 2013), https://www.moodys.com/

research/Moodys-Charter-schools-pose-greatest-credit-challenge-to-school-districts—PR_284505.

149. Erica Green, "City Charter Schools File Lawsuit against School System over Funding," *Baltimoresun.com*, September 10, 2015, http://www.baltimoresun.com/news/maryland/education/blog/bs-md-ci-charter-funding-lawsuit-20150910-story.html.

150. "The Case Against Vouchers," Membership Organization, *The National Education Association*, (2015), http://www.nea.org/home/16378.htm.

151. Mike Petrilli, "Top K-12 Education Policy People on Social Media 2015," Journal, *Education Next*, (August 26, 2015), http://educationnext.org/top-k-12-education-policy-people-on-social-media-2015/.

152. Diane Ravitch, "Bernie and Hillary on Charters," opinion, *Diane Ravitch's Blog*, (October 1, 2015), http://dianeravitch.net/2015/10/01/bernie-and-hillary-on-charters/.

153. Berner, "School Systems and Finance."

154. Benjamin Scafidi, "The Fiscal Effects of School Choice Programs on Public School Districts. National Research" (Friedman Foundation for Educational Choice. Available from: Foundation for Educational Choice. One American Square Suite 2420, Indianapolis, IN 46282. Tel: 317-681-0745; Fax: 317-681-0945; e-mail: info@edchoice.org; Web site: http://www.edchoice.org, March 2012), http://www.eric.ed.gov/ERICWebPortal/detail?accno=ED529881, 2.

155. Ibid., 1.

CHAPTER 7

Changing the Frame

No One Way to School calls for a change in the American framework for public education such that pluralism becomes the cultural norm. This would involve utterly new reference points, such that when Americans heard the words "public education," they would picture not the neighborhood school but rather a dynamic array of schools that answered to the common good and fulfilled the civic and academic demands we have always assigned them.

Change at the level of culture is different in kind than change at the level of politics or the law. A law may reflect or challenge the dominant cultural framework, but it is not the thing itself. The federal No Child Left Behind law and its accompanying regulations on teacher and school accountability did not change the dominant cultural framework of American education. They represented one view of schooling that has not yet won the day.

Cultural change is the process by which novelty moves from the foreground, where it is noticed and contested, into the background—where it is not.[1] It is thus deeper not only than the law but also than acknowledged belief: it is tacit, not explicit. The uniform school system at first appeared to contradict American values, but over time, it became the norm, the ideal against which innovation justifies itself. We *notice* culture only by comparison with other contexts or when we come to dispute its imperatives.[2]

For example, notice *how* Americans disagree about abortion: the "rights of the mother" versus the "rights of the fetus." These two sides sound diametrically opposed, but they actually share a philosophical commitment to individualism and autonomy. Mary Ann Glendon elaborates on this point in *Abortion and Divorce in Western Law* (1987), contrasting debates on abortion in the United States with those that occur in other countries and that rest upon entirely different premises.[3] I noticed the culture-bounded-ness of America's rhetoric on abortion only after reading Glendon's book. I noticed the culture-bounded-ness of our school system only after studying those in other countries.

Or take the rising up of the LGBTQIA community and the legitimization of marriage equality in the Supreme Court's *Obergefell v. Hodges* (2015).

© The Author(s) 2017
A.R. Berner, *Pluralism and American Public Education,*
DOI 10.1057/978-1-137-50224-7_7

Obergefell would not have happened, had it not been for decades of concerted protest against the criminalization of homosexuality and the social *mores* that rendered it shameful. This protest wound its way through religious and medical institutions, the arts, entertainment and media outlets, and law, calling upon the deep tenets of American democracy to upend the status quo. Future generations may not remember the battle, but they will experience sexual orientation and marriage on very different terms. We are speaking not at the level of the law but of the imagination.

Changing the underlying cultural expectations is therefore complicated. It requires, minimally: overlapping networks of individuals with high financial, political, intellectual, and social capital; who articulate a common goal over a long period of time; and create new institutions that embody those ideals; which must be plausible and morally compelling to the audiences they seek to persuade. We have seen that the tacit norms about the structures of education in the United States and the Netherlands changed over time (see Chap. 3). Recent history offers other examples.

For instance, Finland. In 1950, most Finns left school after sixth grade, and less than one-third of Finnish students attended the selective grammar schools that served as gateways to higher education.[4] Elementary school teachers trained in small seminaries instead of universities. No one would have considered Finland an exemplary education nation.

Between 1950 and 1970, however, the structure and content of the school system were transformed to spectacular effect. By 1970, *all* schools, not merely the elite grammars, delivered a rigorous academic curriculum to all students, who could then choose academic or vocational paths at age 16 instead of 12. The teaching profession began to model medicine in its selectivity and *ethos*.[5] Today, Finland's students score near the top of international exams,[6] and immigrant children score 50 % higher on the PISA test in Finland than they do elsewhere.[7]

How did the Finns change their school system so drastically in such a short period of time? The Finns' experience was not "tinkering towards utopia;"[8] radical innovations were put in place rapidly.[9] As one observer put it,

> Most governments enact education reforms through new programs—smaller class sizes, more ambitious external assessments, increased professional development. Reforms like these take the basic features of the system as given. The Finnish reforms, by contrast, especially the creation of the comprehensive school, created a sector that functioned in a radically different way.[10]

Even in this small country, the barriers to change had been formidable: grammar schools had remained small and selective for more than a century, and some educators feared that no one would benefit by an expanded system.[11] Two factors, however, made a unified and academically rigorous school system plausible: the Finnish war effort against the Soviets, and a pilot scholarship program that gave low-income students access to grammar schools.

In the winter of 1939, Finland had to marshal its *"suomalainen sisu,"* or "Finnish fighting spirit," to fend off the invading Soviet army. Against overwhelming odds, the Finns proved successful.[12] Their collective national effort, in which farmers and railway workers fought alongside of patricians, set the stage for a more equitable school system. When Finland passed the Basic School Act expanding the system in 1968, many members of Parliament had participated in the war, personally or through collective memory.[13]

Second, the government had begun to give scholarships for low-income students to attend grammar schools. The results were good, and the program grew. By 1960, with this support, fully 270,000 pupils were attending grammar school—up from 34,000 in 1950.[14] A college-preparatory curriculum began to seem appropriate for all, instead of only some, of Finland's children.

During this time, the government tasked prominent political and educational leaders with examining the structure and content of schooling.[15] One such committee met 200 times between 1956 and 1959. Its recommendation, that Finland create a nine-year school system with a rigorous curriculum for all children, became law. Teacher preparation moved from local seminaries to universities,[16] and master's degrees became required for all teachers.[17] Throughout these structural and curricular changes, the Finnish system remained pluralistic, with most private schools still funded equally with state schools.[18]

The reforms have become a part of society's fabric. Providing high-quality intellectual content to all students is not in dispute; teacher preparation is still demanding; pluralism is in place.[19]

Cultural change can happen within a subsector, such as teacher preparation. Between 1880s and 1930s, the dominant educational philosophy in England's teacher preparation programs changed from an intellectual and theological orientation to a psychological one.[20] Many factors contributed, including the development of education psychology as a distinctive field; a network of well-placed individuals who championed the methods of the laboratory; new institutions that embodied these ideals; and changes within the administrative structures governing teacher preparation. The movement's cornerstone was the University of London's Institute of Education that, founded in 1903, certified a quarter of England's teachers by World War II.[21] Its leaders carried educational psychology into journals, scholars, membership organizations, and Parliamentary committees.[22] By the 1930s, England's teacher preparation programs emphasized psychological development far more than academic content or spiritual formation.[23] In the United States, Teachers College/Columbia played a similar role, urging teacher preparation away from a focus on academic content and toward developmental psychology and vocational skills.[24] In both cases, innovation became default.

The dominant culture within a subsector can be an important factor in the success or failure of larger education reforms. The "Reading Wars" of the early 2000s can be explained in part by a clash of cultural norms: one side, traditionalist and phonics based, the other, constructivist and theoretically reliant upon whole language. The differences between these two were not so much between conflicting pedagogical strategies as between contrasting beliefs about the purpose of education and the process by which children learn.[25]

It is more difficult to assess whether novelty has become stable when reforms are more recent. Alberta provides an example of a transformation in the 1980s and 1990s whose future remains uncertain, but Alberta stands out even in a high-performing country[26] for its strong curriculum and high PISA scores,[27] expansive educational pluralism,[28] and equitable school funding.

None of these features could have been anticipated—not by a long stretch. On curriculum: Alberta's educational establishment began to jettison intellectual content in the early twentieth century.[29] By the 1950s, high schools only required two subjects for graduation (social studies and English),[30] and by the 1970s, the activities of the classroom focused largely on students' self-actualization and on psychological history ("Why did Hitler behave as he did?").[31] On pluralism: education was plural, but limited, with the government funding only Catholic and Protestant in addition to public schools. On school funding: local property taxes made up roughly 30 % of each district's funding, resulting in inequitable spending across the province.

However, within a brief time frame, leaders in Alberta changed the content, structures, and funding of education. All three developments were tied to the neoconservative movement that came to power in the 1980s. Widespread dissatisfaction with government delivery had led to the creation of free enterprise-oriented think tanks and organizations,[32] which held round tables and consultations that convened business owners, parents, and policymakers.[33] This work reflected general disillusionment with government delivery and propelled the Conservative Progressive Party into office.[34] The Conservative Progressives used their mandate to change public education, often against the objections of the teachers unions and the district leadership.[35]

By 2000, education in Alberta looked quite different than it had in 1980. The government had put a strong academic curriculum in place.[36] School funding had expanded to include conservative Protestant, Jewish, Islamic, Sikh, and Inuit schools;[37] even homeschoolers received a stipend.[38] Property taxes had become centrally controlled.[39]

The resulting system is both common (in terms of curriculum) and plural (in terms of school types). For instance, all schools follow the same civics curriculum[40] but discuss its content within a vocabulary and understanding that fits their distinctive communities.[41] Proficiency in civics is above 80 % across all school types.[42] The funding structure, meanwhile, ensures that geographically or economically disadvantaged districts receive support commensurate to their needs.[43]

The structures and content changed, but have cultural expectations? Are a strong curriculum, pluralism, and equalized funding now to be assumed, after two decades? There seems to be lingering mistrust between the government and educators, to be sure.[44] But educational pluralism enjoys widespread support across the province, and school funding remains central instead of local. My guess is that the high expectations, expanded pluralism, and redistributive funding, would be difficult to roll back—especially given Alberta's educational success. However, it is too soon to deem these changes part of the taken-for-granted backdrop of Alberta's educational culture.[45]

In these various cases, we can point to networks of high-capital leaders who rejected the dominant narrative about education, articulated a counter-narrative, and formed prestigious institutions that embodied and promoted their ideals. There is more: the new narratives made sense in contemporary terms.[46] Horace Mann's vision for common schooling was anathema to New England's leaders in the 1840s, but it became plausible once Catholic immigrants overwhelmed the Eastern seaboard. Finland's decision to give all students access to a prep school curriculum happened after the national effort to repel the Soviets, not before.

Finally, the innovative ideals proved morally compelling to those outside the activist circles. A movement may possess all other criteria for success, but founder here.

England's Moral Instruction League (1897–1917) falls in this latter category. The League aimed to change the ethical program in schools from religious to secular.[47] Its membership read like a *Who's Who* of political, academic, financial, and (progressive) religious elites.[48] The members produced a detailed curriculum,[49] lobbied in Parliament,[50] and conferred regularly with education leaders across the country.[51] Despite its *cachet*, however, the League failed to change the atmosphere of schools. Why? Its own extensive, international survey of educators tells us why: teachers did not believe that secular ethics *worked in a school context*.[52] The League's message was not morally compelling to the professional actors who would have enforced it, and all the political and social influence in England could not make it so.

This calls to mind the federal, bi-partisan accountability movement that took hold in the 1990s and 2000s, represented so well in the Obama Administration's Race to the Top Initiative. It may not hold, and for similar reasons. Despite the confluence of support from Left and Right, government and philanthropy, and federal and state leadership, the accountability movement's momentum seems to have foundered in key states and, with the December 2015 passage of the Every Student Succeeds Act, at the federal level.[53] The law, of itself, cannot drive change into the fabric of culture.

Is it possible to intentionally "create the conditions" under which educational pluralism (or any novel institution) could become the norm? Yes and no. Even a radically mechanistic account of the world (which the theory above is not) cannot possibly predict all factors and their interactions.[54] We do not have to look far for examples. Hurricane Katrina's (2005) devastation of New Orleans gave unprecedented space for leaders to rewrite the school system; the Internet and its delivery systems make innovations that upend traditional classrooms, such as the Khan Academy,[55] possible. Neither could have been predicted. And even successful movements will have unforeseen, even adverse consequences—as Chile found in the first iteration of its voucher program (see p. 128)

AMERICA AND EDUCATIONAL PLURALISM

This book argues that our country took a wrong turn when we forced educational uniformity upon our diverse democracy, and that we should self-correct by implementing a well-designed plural system instead. Where are we on the path toward a full-scale pluralistic system?

Some districts and states have been moving toward pluralism for some time. The introduction of vouchers in 1990, charter schools in 1992, tax credits in 1997, and ESAs in 2011 has changed many students' experience with public education, in many parts of the country.

But cultural expectations die hard. Struggles no doubt lie ahead, even in educationally plural cities. In Washington, DC, for instance, the charter sector is alive and well but the tiny, and successful, Opportunity Scholarship Fund must fight repeatedly for its survival.[56] Denver is held up as a model of collaboration between traditional and charter schools, but this "détente" was hard won and does not yet extend to non-public schools.[57] In vast tracts of the country, such debates have not even started. Indeed, one is hard pressed to think of a district outside of New Orleans, and a state outside of Vermont, in which pluralism is not still required to defend and justify itself against the common school norm.[58]

Changing the frame requires a clear vision and a logical goal. There need not be a single message on behalf of pluralism: a set of compelling narratives will strengthen the process of change. For some constituencies, educational pluralism is a social justice issue; others support pluralism because it seems to boost student scores; communitarians find the emphasis on strengthening civil society important; still others find the language of "choice" compelling.

There are some narratives that risk being counter-productive. Although it resonates, the language of the market, used by some who support this direction in policy, comes with liabilities. John Chubb and Terry Moe, whose work on bureaucracies is favorably cited in Chap. 5, also produced such passages as these: "Public authority must be put to use in creating a system that is almost entirely beyond the reach of public authority."[59] Their recommendation was to devolve decision-making authority to "schools, parents, and students," with only minimal guidance (such as on safety) left to state actors.[60]

Or Andrew Coulson, whose *Market Education* (1999) held that America's education system had stalled in large part because, "Competition ha[d] been stifled by the 90 per cent share of the education market held by 'free' government schools."[61] He recommended five innovations that would enable America's schools to improve: "Choice and financial responsibility for parents, and freedom, competition, and profit for schools—in essence, a free market in education."[62]

This approach, while potentially beneficial to some school children, inadvertently minimizes the public aspects of education and risks alienating left-of-center pluralists. In fact, the progressive argument for pluralism is longstanding; it began in 1970s Berkeley and continues through the leadership of Martin Luther King, III. In 2015, the education reform organization ReDefined hosted a series on progressive support for pluralism,[63] which Ron Matus summarized in April 2016.[64] Finally, "choice" is used to describe inner-district choice, that is, choice between public schools, which is necessary but insufficient within pluralism. The language of choice is powerfully woven into the discourse of reform and clearly speaks to some advocates, but it should be used with care.

The specific language of competition bears particular risk. In a uniform system such as ours, departures from the norm have to justify public support by invoking their students' superior test scores or college completion rates. Countries with plural systems do not tend to pit one school sector against another by, for example, comparing student outcomes in Jewish, Catholic, Montessori, and state schools to assess the merits of each type. Charles Glenn has made this point repeatedly in his analyses of international systems.[65] Jonathan Sharples, Senior Researcher at the UK's Education Endowment Foundation, echoed this view recently.[66] I asked whether his research institution had studied "school sector effects," and he replied that no one had ever posed that question before.[67] In an educationally plural system, all schools should be excellent—but no one sector is deemed inherently so. Even where we find (as in Sweden and Florida)[68] that a plural system benefited all sectors, it is unclear whether the mechanism at work was competition *per se*.[69] Thus, an argument that rests on the value of competition may unintentionally subvert the good that lies on the other side of debate.

No One Way to School attempts to draw a more inclusive argument that rests upon the foundational goals of the common school, while affirming that they are better met by plural education, than by uniformity. Excellence, equity, opportunity, and citizenship resonate across America's educational history. An argument framed in these terms challenges both the philosophical thinness of the libertarian approach to education reform and also the state orientation of the status quo.

Sometimes the message of change requires a prequel. Americans worry that pluralism is unconstitutional or that it would divide an already-divided population. Clearing the underbrush means explaining the conditions under which pluralism is constitutional, academically beneficial, and civically responsible. Once the permissibility and desirability of pluralism are established, it becomes possible to talk about next steps.

One next step might be to carry the message of pluralism into films, television shows, and articles in the popular press. Most Americans are surprised to learn that pluralism is the norm in other liberal democracies. Contrasting the educational options available to families in (say) Canada or Sweden with the zoned common school in America, could prove morally compelling. Films such as *Waiting for Superman* and *Won't Back Down*, whatever their weaknesses, provide vivid depictions of the desperation in inner city schools and of the courage it takes to change the structures. We need more such films and more local coverage of the possibilities educational pluralism offers.

What about the networks that matter so much in cultural change? A broad tent for pluralism would invite new coalitions that aimed to challenge the structures of the common school. Something similar happened with the accountability movement that propelled Arne Duncan into leadership at the US Education Department and that enabled the Race to the Top campaign.[70] Commissioners of education, prominent academics, business leaders, philanthropists, worked to align expectations, standards, and accountability structures. These groups defied political patterns.

When we turn to the case for educational pluralism, non-partisanship has already been necessary for state legislatures to pass education tax credits, vouchers, and education savings accounts.[71] In 2016, the General Assembly in Maryland voted for a $5 million scholarship fund for low-income students to attend private schools. The bill was backed by members from both parties and supported by a cross-section of the state's racial, religious, and economic interests.[72] The coalition behind New York's Opportunity Tax Credit includes the Association of Historic Black Independent Schools, the Sergeants Benevolent Association, the Buffalo Boys and Girls Club, the Brooklyn Chamber of Commerce, and the New York Hispanic Clergy Organization.[73] Educational pluralists can continue to create opportunities for collaboration. Another area ripe for expansion is educational research. Dozens of research–practice partnerships provide analytic support for school districts,[74] and major conferences showcase innovative studies in education.[75] It is rare to find research in such circles that includes non-public school students or that compares teacher expectations for students in different school sectors. Coalition building could mean simply funding more inclusive research.

Making educational pluralism the norm as opposed to the exception, however, requires something more: creating authoritative institutions that have moral ballast. In this case, the new institution is not a new charter network or a political organization but rather a school district or state that functions like its counterparts in the Netherlands or Alberta. This new institution would be a fully functioning, pluralistic community of schools that are open to all students, not merely to those with special needs or those stuck in failing schools.

Such a change would be remarkable. In his book on restructuring the urban school district, Andy Smarick sets out "a system of schools" and the chancellorship model that would organize them.[76] Smarick's first premise is that school districts were designed to "operate a large, stable set of similar schools each of which is tied to a discrete geographic area." They were not, in contrast, designed to create innovative schools, close failing schools, replicate strong schools, or oversee non-public schools—whether Catholic, charter, or otherwise.[77]

The solution: dissolve the district as such and institute a new structure in its place. At the helm would be the Chancellor of City Schools, whose chief responsibility would be ensuring high quality across the system and a diversity of school offerings commensurate with the needs of parents and students. The chancellor's office would superintend authorizers for each sector (charter, public, Catholic, and otherwise), which in turn certified operators, such as the Diocese, charter management organizations, and the former district—reconstituted.[78] The goal would be a mosaic of high-performing schools that are available to all children without reference to their parents' income. Although the model was designed for urban centers, there is no reason why it could not be constituted in rural settings by combining several districts, or by bringing rural districts into suburban or urban systems.

There are other important factors in effecting cultural change, such as plausibility and moral urgency. The plausibility is not immediately obvious, but it lies in the broader American experience with pluralism. The government is not the only entity to dispense social welfare; hospitals, churches, synagogues, mosques, and the plethora of non-profit organizations do so as well, sometimes serving even as deliverers of government aid. Even in daily life, we make decisions to mail a package from the US Post Office, Federal Express (FedEx), or United Parcel Service (UPS). The American experience assigns a high value (some would say, too high a value) upon human judgment. The oddity is that in the field of education, this judgment does not pertain—unless we happen to have the money to select our children's schools. At the same time, we have accepted the need for public accountability with respect to safety standards, child labor, crime, and finance, and the availability of new medications. Thus, in terms of plausibility, the case for educational pluralism *fits* with American culture; we have only to draw those connections explicitly. Marry this with the growing number of Americans who are, often for the first time, *experiencing* educational pluralism, and we have a coalescing movement on our hands.

When it comes to moral urgency, the question is not whether but how much. Does educational pluralism possess sufficient moral urgency to persuade key actors such as teachers and parents? Some legislators, parents, and leaders are convinced; others are not. Tim Scott, the African-American Republican Senator from South Carolina, argued for Title I funding to become portable, so that it could follow low-income children to non-public schools. In his speech, he urged his fellow Senators to enlarge their conception of "public education," concluding with the words:

> All of our kids—yes, all of our kids—have amazing potential. I believe there are good people on the other side of this argument. I know the other side believes school choice, as I am describing it, is wrong. I believe they have good intentions. This Senator is speaking from personal experience. This Senator is speaking from the statistical realities that we see across this country. This Senator is speaking on behalf of those kids who have been trapped too long, locked out too often, and said no to too many times. It is up to us as policymakers to create an environment where we unlock their potential. I hope we will continue to have a robust debate, leaving politics behind and figuring out how to improve educational opportunities for all of our children.[79]

Sen. Scott is convinced. So were the 15,000 charter school parents who marched in Albany in March 2015, wearing t-shirts with the words, "Don't Steal Possible," and asking the legislature to raise the charter school cap.[80] So is Martin Luther King, III, defending Florida's tax credit program *and* the public schools, claiming that, "The freedom to choose for your family is ... about justice. About righteousness."[81] Will this level of moral urgency eventually drive change so substantial that the cultural landscape transforms? None of us could know the answer yet.

So where are we? Many of the necessary preludes to cultural change seem in place. When we contemplate the growth of charters, vouchers, tax credits, and education savings accounts; the spectrum of support from diverse organizations; and the increase in litigation that pushes against the common school structures: it seems that momentum is on pluralism's side. I am not sanguine about the outcomes, however. At least two factors work against the movement's eventual success, although there are certainly more.

There is the teacher unions' opposition to changing the model. The (Democrat-led) Maryland General Assembly passed a modest scholarship bill in March 2016, but the State Education Association, the Association of Boards of Education, and the State Superintendents' Union, opposed it. This is typical. One of the more interesting developments has occurred in New York State, where the education tax credit bill has won support from all of the state's major public sector unions *except* the teachers.[82] This is rare.

The teacher unions' efforts to maintain the status quo are not unopposed.[83] High-profile lawsuits, designed to diminish the unions' economic and political power, are at play.[84] Unions have their defenders, though,[85] and their resistance to structural change gives no sign of abating.[86]

Would anything alter the unions' stance on pluralism? Unions are designed to protect what exists. Ideally, public school teachers themselves would find pluralism professionally attractive. Pluralism has the potential to generate innovative working environments and strong school cultures that could match each teacher's individual commitments and pedagogical style. By its very nature, a civil society model for education removes many layers of compliance and restores the dignity of teachers' judgment and leadership. It is hard for me to believe that, given the choice between, a nimble Montessori school and a large, district-run operation, some teachers would not choose the former. Others who chose the latter could do so, since an educationally plural system would continue to provide state-run schools as well.

Even under these optimal conditions, the thorny, fiscal question would remain: how should districts navigate existing teacher contracts under the new structure? District chancellors might have to maintain benefit packages for the first generation of teachers who moved to non-public schools. These teachers, however, might have to accept shorter-term contracts in line with non-public schools' cultures, as has been true in most charter school programs. All developments would doubtless entail a series of bargains between non-public schools and the chancellorship, and between the chancellorship and the former district structure. Ideally, freeing up resources from the old district structure would enable per capita funding for kids that, if managed well, could be channeled into higher salaries for teachers. One can realistically hope that the teacher unions will come to support pluralism because it is beneficial for teachers and their students. In the meantime, the competitive animus is likely to continue.

The second factor that could scupper meaningful pluralism comes from the opposite pole: the libertarian resistance to government, period. Libertarian organizations have been tireless supporters of school choice. At the same time, this support often comes with wariness about state power:

> To realize the positive effects of a competitive education market, school choice programs must ensure autonomy and independence for private schools and flexibility for public schools. Therefore, states should not impose regulations on existing private schools or create regulatory barriers that prevent new private school operators from entering the market. Only in this way will school choice produce the better education American children deserve.[87]

Educational pluralism requires meaningful governmental regulation of non-public schools. As I argued in Chap. 6, this regulation should be loose instead of tight, focused on academic standards and performance rather than on school culture. But some will chafe even at this. A Texas policy institute reports positively that tax credit and voucher programs would not result in additional regulations of private schools.[88] Jay Greene, Distinguished Professor and Head of the Department of Education Reform at the University of Arkansas, writes often about the negative consequences of state accountability measures on tax credits and vouchers.[89] Similar anti-state sentiments emerged in the characterization of the Common Core State Standards as federal overreach.[90] Mike Petrilli, Director of the Thomas B. Fordham Institute, calls individuals in this camp "choice purists" who "reject results-based accountability because it conflicts with the will of parents and the right of schools to serve their customers as they think best."[91]

What might soften the anti-government stance? Perhaps encountering a plural system in which accountability worked for the benefit of children, ensuring high-quality academic standards on the one hand and distinctive missions on the other. Such an encounter could come through visiting strong plural systems that manage mission and regulation well and in hearing first-generation parents describe their own learning curve in choosing schools and the protective role that the state's quality control played. Stewart and Wolf's *The School Choice Journey*, for instance, illustrates the importance of external structures for families navigating educational opportunity for the first time.[92] By their own admission, parents new to the non-public school world learned to evaluate school quality only with experience and help, not right out of the starting gate.

The convictions of both sides are based in experience. Teacher unions doubt that plural systems would provide security for their members, and with good reason: private and charter schools do not, as a rule, offer tenure. Libertarians doubt that government oversight could be positive, and with good reason: bureaucratic formalism can indeed stifle freedom. In the best of circumstances, such convictions might serve as policy guardrails in a pluralizing system, monitoring excess on either side and holding school systems to high standards of accountability and liberty alike. More likely, at least in the short term, the commitments of teacher unions and libertarians are incommensurate with pluralism and may generate resistance to the pluralizing process.[93]

What commends a plural structure in such cases is the opportunity it gives to disagree in concrete ways. If teacher unions remain set against pluralism, they need not participate; chancellors could fund state schools that operate under collective bargaining agreements and also enter fiscal and accountability partnerships with parents and with non-public schools. If libertarians find government regulations onerous, their children and schools need not join state tax credit or voucher programs.

Educational pluralism allows, even anticipates, the reality of deep disagreement. The freedom to differ, as the Supreme Court's decision in *West Virginia v. Barnette* (1943) set out, is "not limited to things that do not matter. That would be a mere shadow of freedom. The test of its substance is the right to differ as to things that touch the heart of the existing order."[94]

Which, after all, is what democratic life is all about.

NOTES

1. James Davison Hunter, *To Change the World: The Irony, Tragedy, and Possibility of Christianity in the Late Modern World* (New York: Oxford University Press, 2010). 32, 33.
2. See Christian Smith, *The Secular Revolution: Power, Interests, and Conflict in the Secularization of American Public Life* (Berkeley: University of California Press, 2003), for an excellent account of struggle, e.g., "The historical secularization of the institutions of American public life was not a natural, inevitable, and abstract by-product of modernization; rather, it was the outcome of a struggle between contending groups within conflicting interests seeking to control social knowledge and institutions." vii.
3. Mary Ann Glendon, *Abortion and Divorce in Western Law* (Cambridge, Mass.: Harvard University Press, 1987). See, for instance, 18–22 for her discussion of abortion laws in France, Germany, and Switzerland. Of course, much has changed in America and in those countries since 1987.
4. Pasi Sahlberg, *Finnish Lessons: What Can the World Learn from Educational Change in Finland?*, Unabridged (Blackstone Audio, Inc., 2012), 15, 16, 71; Robert B. Schwartz and Jal D. Mehta, "Finland: Superb Teachers—How to Get Them, How to Keep Them.," in *Surpassing Shanghai: An Agenda for American Education Built on the World's Leading Systems*, ed. Marc Tucker (Cambridge, MA: Harvard Education Press, 2011), 51–78, 52.

5. Sahlberg, *Finnish Lessons*.81, 73; Schwartz and Mehta, "Finland: Superb Teachers—How to Get Them, How to Keep Them." 67.

6. Sahlberg, *Finnish Lessons*. 54; Schwartz and Mehta, "Finland: Superb Teachers—How to Get Them, How to Keep Them." 10.

7. Sahlberg, *Finnish Lessons*. 68–69. While Finland's overall percentage of first- and second-generation immigrants is much lower than in the United States and Canada (2.8–19.4 % and 24.4 %, respectively), its policy is to hold the percentage of immigrant children per classroom below 20 %, the ratio which seems to advance language learners while not impairing native speakers.

8. A reference to David B Tyack and Larry Cuban, *Tinkering toward Utopia: A Century of Public School Reform* (Cambridge, MA: Harvard University Press, 1995).

9. Jarkko Hautamäki, *Pisa06 Finland: Analyses, Reflections and Explanations* ([Helsinki]: Ministry of Education, 2008), 197.

10. Schwartz and Mehta, "Finland: Superb Teachers—How to Get Them, How to Keep Them." 73.

11. Private correspondence with Risto Ikonen, Senior Lecturer, University of Eastern Finland, June 28, 2013.

12. The eastern, industrialized region of Finland became de facto Soviet territory.

13. Private correspondence with Risto Ikonen, Senior Lecturer, University of Eastern Finland, June 28, 2013. Personal note: I spent the summer of 1983 in Finland and noted, even then, the frequency with which the war was referenced.

14. Schwartz and Mehta, "Finland: Superb Teachers—How to Get Them, How to Keep Them." 52.

15. One new institution, the Primary School Committee (est. 1945), systematically deepened the national curriculum and developed far-reaching educational objectives. Its 1952 "internationally comparable" curriculum "paved the way to educational success some half a century later." A second, the Education System Committee (est. 1946), was comprised of representatives from all major political parties. It recommended creating a comprehensive school in which children would spend eight years, after which they would diverge into academic and vocational tracks. The plan was not implemented immediately but proved nonetheless useful in stimulating further debate about equal educational opportunities. Two decades later, its recommendations were realized. Sahlberg, *Finnish Lessons.*, 17, 18, 20.

16. Initially, the faculty remained the same; they simply changed affiliations and in some cases continued to use the same lectures and textbooks as before. Private correspondence with Risto Ikonen, Senior Lecturer, University of Eastern Finland, June 28, 2013.

17. Sahlberg, *Finnish Lessons*. 78.

18. Religion is also part of the national curriculum for all schools. Center on International Education Benchmarking, http://www.ncee.org/programs-affiliates/center-on-international-education-benchmarking/top-performing-countries/finland-overview/finland-system-and-school-organization/ Additionally, the government sets a minimum amount of time that schools must spend on religious education; most recently that minimum was 5 % of instructional hours, down from 11 % in the early twentieth century. Saine, http://www.ortoweb.fi/religedsaine.htm. Education.stateuniversity.com/pages/469/Finland-

Educational-System-Overview.htm. Religious curricula must be approved by the State. Harri Saine, "Religious Teaching in Finland," accessed June 1, 2013, www.ortoweb.fi/religedsaine.htm.

19. At least one analysis claims, plausibly, that Finnish pedagogy is moving away from the teacher-led to the child-led classroom, and that this will have adverse effects upon learning. Nevertheless, on neither side of the pedagogical debate do we find a voice arguing for a less rigorous education. Gabriel Heller Sahlgren, *Real Finnish Lessons: The True Story of an Education Superpower* (London, UK: Centre for Policy Studies, 2015).

20. This simplifies the chronology; there were intermediate stages. See Ashley Berner, "Metaphysics in Educational Theory: Educational Philosophy and Teacher Training in England (1839–1944)" (D.Phil., University of Oxford, 2008).

21. "Report of Inspectors of Research, Training and Equipment," January 26, 1925, IE.TPN.1.1. (1925–1928), The Percy Nunn Papers, University of London.

22. Adrian Wooldridge, *Measuring the Mind: Education and Psychology in England, C. 1860–C. 1990* (Cambridge [England]; New York: Cambridge University Press, 1994), 1.: James Sully (1843–1923), Francis Warner (1847–1926), John Adams (1857–1934), W.H. Winch (1864–1955), P.B. Ballard (1865–1950), Charles Spearman (1863–1945), Thomas Percy Nunn (1870–1944), C.W. Valentine (1879–1964), Godfrey Thomson (1881–1955), Susan Isaacs (1885–1948), and Cyril Burt (1883–1971).

23. In 1932, the Training College Association, the member organization to which all training colleges belonged, reported that: "A new orientation has occurred because of the advancing knowledge of psychology ... these psychological principles apply in the teaching of all subjects to the children. The academic subjects and the crafts take their rightful place as a means of helping children towards a full realization of themselves and also as a means of enriching the students' own personalities." "The Training of Teachers: Memorandum Drawn up by the Joint Standing Committee of the Training College Association and Council of Principals, Confidential to Members of the TCA and Council of Principals," 1938, Pri/1/3/18, "Principal"s Correspondence', (1938), St Mary's Training College Archives, St Mary's, Twickenham.

24. Diane Ravitch's description of the progressive movement's ascendancy in teacher preparation programs is similar. See her description of the network: 99–102, in Diane Ravitch, *Left Back: A Century of Battles over School Reform* (Simon & Schuster, 2001).

25. See especially ED Hirsch, *The Knowledge Deficit: Closing the Shocking Education Gap for American Children* (Boston: Houghton Mifflin, 2006).

26. Canada's provinces shifted from progressive to academic curricula in the 1980s. There is now no gap between native-born and immigrant students' test scores. Only one American state (Massachusetts) is on par with Canada in international math scores, and only two (Massachusetts and Vermont) in reading. This holds even when considering students from college-educated families. Jal D. Mehta and Robert Schwartz, "Canada: Looks a Lot like Us but Gets Much Better Results," in *Surpassing Shanghai: An Agenda for American Education Built on the World's Leading Systems*, ed. Marc Tucker (Cambridge, MA: Harvard Education Press, 2011), 141–71, 145 and 150; Paul E. Peterson et al., "Globally

Challenged: Are U.S. Students Ready to Compete? The Latest on Each State's International Standing in Math and Reading. PEPG 11-03" (Program on Education Policy and Governance, Harvard University, August 2011), http://www.eric.ed.gov/ERICWebPortal/detail?accno=ED526954, 8, 18, 20, 26.

27. Peterson et al., "Globally Challenged: Are U.S. Students Ready to Compete? The Latest on Each State's International Standing in Math and Reading. PEPG 11-03." Note that Albertans attribute this success to their particularly rigorous curriculum matched with assessments.

28. Mark Milke, "School Choice in Canada: Lessons for America" (Washington, DC: The Heritage Foundation, November 8, 2010). 3.

29. Amy Jeanette Von Heyking, *Creating Citizens: History And Identity in Alberta's Schools, 1905–1980* (University of Calgary Press, 2006). 9, 65.

30. Ibid. 95.

31. Ibid. 125, 140.

32. Foremost were the Fraser Institute, Canada West, the Conference Board of Canada, and Albertans for Quality Education.

33. Opponents held that teachers and unions were not invited to the table. Trevor Harrison, *Contested Classrooms Education, Globalization, and Democracy in Alberta* (Edmonton [Alta.]: University of Alberta Press: Parkland Institute, 1999), http://site.ebrary.com/id/10203260.

34. Nelly McEwen, "Educational Accountability in Alberta," *Canadian Journal of Education / Revue Canadienne de L'éducation* 20, no. 1 (1995): 27–44. 27; Linda Matsumoto, "A Brief History—The Education Reform Movement in Alberta," *Alberta Teachers' Association Magazine* 83 (March 2002), http://www.teachers.ab.ca/Publications/ATA%20Magazine/Volume%2083/Number%201/Articles/Pages/A%20Brief%20History%20The%20Education%20Reform%20Movement%20in%20Alberta.aspx.

35. The teachers union was not opposed to equalized funding, per se, but rather to the accompanying demise of the district system—seen as rigid and bureaucratic by reformers but familiar and necessary to many teachers and their union.

36. These included the Achievement Testing Program for grades 3, 6, and 9 (1982); a reinstated Diploma Examination Program as a requirement for high school graduation (1984); and five different evaluation protocols for students, teachers, programs, schools, and systems (1984). McEwen, "Educational Accountability in Alberta." 27, 28. By "curriculum" was meant "broad learning, sequenced into grades, that students are expected to achieve ... includ[ing] specific statements of knowledge, skills, and attitudes against which student achievement is to be judged"; "assessment" were "scores to be achieved by a student on a specific test"; and "achievement" was defined as "official expectations for students, schools, and jurisdictions." Ibid., 32, 39.

37. Allison, Derek J., and Deani A. Neven Van Pelt. "Canada," in *Balancing Freedom, Autonomy and Accountability in Education*, ed. Charles L. Glenn and Jan deGroof, Vol. 3. Tilburg: Wolf Legal Publishers, 2012. Such schools become eligible for up to 70% of per-pupil funding if compliant with standards and assessments.

38. Private correspondence with Amy Van Heyking, June 2013. If parents wish to homeschool, they register their child with an associated school board (whether public or private), and the province disburses the official per-pupil amount to

the board, which in turn gives 50 % of it to the homeschooling parent for educational expenses.

39. Alison Taylor, *The Politics of Educational Reform in Alberta* (Toronto, Ont.: University of Toronto Press, 2001), http://site.ebrary.com/id/10218999. 75–77.

40. David E. Campbell, "The Civic Implications of Canada's Education System," in *Educating Citizens:*, ed. Patrick Wolf et al. (Washington, DC: Brookings Institute, 2004), 186–220, 205

41. "'Social studies encompasses a view of the person and society as perceived through the eyes of Christ and His Church … It is recognized that with the gift of free will, individual and communal choices are made. In many instances our choices help build a better world, but in many other circumstances they lead to a breakdown in relationships, sometimes on a catastrophic scale.'" Ibid., 204–05.

42. Ibid., 207.

43. http://www.education.alberta.ca/admin/funding/booklet.aspx, downloaded 11/28/2013.

44. Burger, J. AitkenA., Brandon, J., Klinck, P., McKinnon, G., Mutch, S. The Next Generation of Basic Education Accountability in Alberta, Canada: A Policy Dialogue, 5(19). IEJLL: International Electronic Journal for Leadership in Learning, North America, 5, Jan. 2001. Available at: <http://iejll.synergiesprairies.ca/iejll/index.php/ijll/article/view/511>. Date accessed: May 10, 2013. This report represents an official conversation between government ministries and school superintendents. Its aim was a better balance between accountability and collaboration. While the report noted widespread acceptance of "accountability and quality," it also mentioned superintendents' and teachers' "powerful feelings of distrust, powerlessness, and fear of misplaced or unjustified negative judgment." The language was at times quite strong: "Alberta Learning has tried to implement policy without adequately attending to the emotions experienced at all levels of the Department and the field."

45. In May 2015, a left-of-center government came into power. There is no indication that the new leadership will roll back any of the reforms. "Alberta Votes 2015," *CBC News*, May 7, 2015, http://live.cbc.ca/Event/Alberta_Votes_2015.

46. See Peter L. Berger, *The Heretical Imperative: Contemporary Possibilities of Religious Affirmation* (Garden City, NY: Anchor Press, 1979). Esp. 16, for his account of military cultures and moving apart from them.

47. G. Spiller, *The Ethical Movement in Great Britain: A Documentary History* (London: The Fairleigh Press, 1934), esp. 111. The League later modified its aim, stating that secular moral instruction should supplement, not replace, religious ethics.

48. Michael Sadler, *Moral Instruction and Training in Schools: Report of an International Inquiry*, vol. I, 2 vols. (London: Longmans, Green & Co., 1908), xi.

49. F. J. Gould, *Moral Instruction: Its Aim and Practice* (London: Longmans, Green & Co., 1913), esp. 145–160.

50. Spiller, *The Ethical Movement in Great Britain: A Documentary History.*, 139.

51. Ibid., 126, 128; R. Berard, "Frederick James Gould and the Transformation of Moral Education," *British Journal of Educational Studies* 35, no. 3 (1987): 233–47, 236.

52. Sadler, *Moral Instruction and Training in Schools: Report of an International Inquiry.*, 259, 257, 303, 356.

53. Arguably, the Every Student Succeeds Act (ESSA) maintains the accountability movement's focus on standards and evidence. ESSA certainly provides seven funding streams through which states and districts may receive federal dollars. However, ESSA also returns the formation and the management of these standards to the states.

54. Structuralists (such as Charles Beard or Shulamith Firestone) would disagree. I am persuaded with Christian Smith, that however constrained, human agency and innovations matter. As Anthony Giddens put it, "Social systems have no needs, and to suppose that they do is to apply an illegitimate teleology to them." Tom Loveless, "Common Core's Major Political Challenges for the Remainder of 2016," *The Brookings Institution*, March 30, 2016, http://www.brookings.edu/blogs/brown-center-chalkboard/posts/2016/03/30-common-core-political-challenges-loveless., 10.

55. Website: https://www.khanacademy.org.

56. See two opposing views about this: Editors, "A School Voucher Surrender," *Wall Street Journal*, December 17, 2015, http://www.wsj.com/articles/a-school-voucher-surrender-1450397585, and Valerie Strauss, "The Weird Obsession in Congress with D.C. School Vouchers," *Washington Post*, October 15, 2015, https://www.washingtonpost.com/news/answer-sheet/wp/2015/10/15/the-weird-obsession-in-congress-with-d-c-school-vouchers/. Patrick Wolf reports on the parents' defense for the program in Thomas Stewart and Patrick J. Wolf, *The School Choice Journey: School Vouchers and the Empowerment of Urban Families* (New York, NY: Palgrave Macmillan, 2014).

57. "Denver Expands Choice and Charters: Elected School Board Employs Portfolio Strategy to Lift Achievement," *Education Next* 16, no. 3 (Summer 2016), http://educationnext.org/denver-expands-choice-and-charters/. See also Daniela Doyle, Christen Holly, and Bryan C Hassel, "Is Detente Possible?: District-Charter School Relations in Four Cities" (Washington, DC: Thomas B. Fordham Institute and Public Impact, November 2015), http://edex.s3-us-west-2.amazonaws.com/publication/pdfs/Is_Détente_Possible_Report_Final.pdf.

58. Vermont has a longstanding history of using government funds for non-public schools under particular circumstances. This, too, is contested at the time of writing, under a district consolidation plan. Josh O'Gorman, "Lawmakers Talk School Choice and District Mergers," *Vermont Press Bureau*, April 7, 2016.

59. John E. Chubb and Terry M. Moe, *Politics, Markets & America's Schools* (Washington, DC: Brookings Institution, 1990), 218.

60. Ibid., 219.

61. Andrew J. Coulson, *Market Education: The Unknown History* (New Brunswick, NJ: Transaction Publishers, 1999), 283.

62. Ibid., 289–90.

63. For example, Matus, Ron. "From Sit-Ins to School Choice." *redefinED*, September 15, 2015. https://www.redefinedonline.org/2015/09/from-sit-ins-to-school-choice/.

64. Ron Matus, "Opinion: The Progressive Split Over Education, as Democrats Go Back to the Future Over School Choice," *The74*, April 19, 2016, https://www.the74million.org/article/opinion-the-progressive-split-over-education-as-democrats-go-back-to-the-future-over-school-choice.

65. Private conversations with the author over several years.

66. https://educationendowmentfoundation.org.uk/about/.

67. In conversation with the author at the Palomar Hotel in Washington, DC, on April 21, 2016.

68. Anders Böhlmark and Mikael Lindahl, *Independent Schools and Long-Run Educational Outcomes Evidence from Sweden's Large Scale Voucher Reform* (Munich: CESifo, 2012), David N. Figlio and Cassandra M. D. Hart, "Competitive Effects of Means-Tested School Vouchers," Working Paper (National Bureau of Economic Research, June 2010), http://www.nber.org/papers/w16056, David Figlio and Cassandra Hart, "Competitive Effects of Means-Tested Vouchers," *American Economic Journal: Applied Economics* 6, no. 1 (January 2014): 133–56, doi:10.1257/app.6.1.133.

69. See Andy Smarick's analysis of the lack of statistical evidence to support the claim that vouchers and charters spurred public schools to higher performance. Andy Smarick, *The Urban School System of the Future: Applying the Principles and Lessons of Chartering* (R&L Education, 2012), 20–23.

70. Sarah Reckhow, *Follow the Money: How Foundation Dollars Change Public School Politics* (New York: Oxford University Press, 2013). Her analysis of networks of elected officials, activists, and philanthropists in New York City is striking.

71. The 2016 Maryland General Assembly voted for a $5 million scholarship program for low-income students to attend private schools.

72. Liz Bowie, "Maryland to Help Pay Private School Tuition," *The Baltimore Sun*, April 19, 2016, http://www.baltimoresun.com/news/maryland/education/blog/bs-md-voucher-20160415-story.html., Ovetta Wiggins, "After 10-Year Fight, Maryland Lawmakers Vote to Fund Private-School Scholarships," *The Washington Post*, March 29, 2016.

73. http://www.investined.org/coalition-supporters/.

74. The partnerships have recently formed a network at Rice University: the National Network of Education Research Practice Partnerships. https://kinder.rice.edu/NERPP/.

75. Prominent among them are the Society for Research on Educational Effectiveness (SREE) and the American Educational Research Association.

76. Smarick, *The Urban School System of the Future*. 2012, esp. 42, 119. See also his article on Washington, DC school reform: Andy Smarick, "Laying the Foundations for the Next Decade of DC School Reform," *Flypaper at the THomas B. Fordham Institute*, March 10, 2016, http://edexcellence.net/articles/laying-the-foundation-for-the-next-decade-of-dc-reform?utm_source=Fordham+Updates&utm_campaign=7d91f9bda3-20150313_LateLateBell3_11_2016&utm_medium=email&utm_term=0_d9e8246adf-7d91f9bda3-71557525&mc_cid=7d91f9bda3&mc_eid=cb4d7b26b3.

77. Smarick, *The Urban School System of the Future*., 148.

78. Ibid., 149–162.

79. Sen. Timothy Scott, "Senator Tim Scott's Impassioned Speech on Behalf of School Choice" (United States Senate, Washington, DC, July 18, 2015), http://edexcellence.net/articles/senator-tim-scott's-impassioned-speech-on-school-choice.

80. Aaron Short, Matthew Abrahams, and Laura Italiano, "Charter School Parents, Teachers, Students Rally in Albany," *New York Post*, March 4, 2015, http://nypost.com/2015/03/04/charter-school-parents-teachers-students-rally-in-albany/.

81. B. K. Marcus, "Martin Luther King III on Freedom, Justice, and School Choice|B.K. Marcus," January 25, 2016, https://fee.org/articles/martin-luther-king-iii-on-educational-freedom/.

82. See the list of supporters: http://www.investined.org/coalition-supporters/. As of writing, the bill has passed the Senate but continues to languish in the Assembly.

83. Steven Brill, *Class Warfare: Inside the Fight to Fix America's Schools*, Reprint (Simon & Schuster, 2012).; Terry M. Moe, *Special Interest: Teachers Unions and America's Public Schools*, Reprint (Brookings Institution Press, 2011).; Daniel DiSalvo, *Government against Itself: Public Union Power and Its Consequences* (Oxford; New York: Oxford University Press, 2015). To name but a few.

84. As of writing, the *Vergara* case (Beatriz Vergara v. State of California (Superior Court of the State of California 2014), has been overturned by the California Appeals Court (Jennifer Medina and Motoko Rich, "California Appeals Court Reverses Decision to Overturn Teacher Tenure Rules," *The New York Times*, April 14, 2016, http://www.nytimes.com/2016/04/15/us/californiaappealscourt-reverses-decision-to-overturn-teacher-tenure-rules.html.). Similar litigation is under way in New York (Davids v. New York Education Quality (Staten Island Supreme Court, New York 2014), and in Forslund et. al., v. State of Minnesota (n.d.). and Motoko Rich, "Teacher Tenure Is Challenged Again in a Minnesota Lawsuit," *The New York Times*, April 13, 2016, http://www.nytimes.com/2016/04/14/us/teacher-tenure-is-challenged-again-in-a-minnesota-lawsuit.html.) See also the turmoil around *Friedrichs (Friedrichs v. California Teachers Association, United States Reports (Supreme Court of the United States 2016)*, Dmitri Mehlhorn, "Mehlhorn: How the Unions Lost Three Swing Votes and Pushed the Supreme Court Towards Historic Friedrichs Ruling," *The74*, January 12, 2016, https://www.the74million.org/article/mehlhorn-how-the-unions-lost-three-swing-votes-and-pushed-the-supreme-court-towards-historic-friedrichs-ruling.)

85. See, for instance, Henry Smith, "Review of Government Against Itself: Union Power and Its Consequences by Daniel DiSalvo," *The Journal of School Choice: International Research and Reform* 10, no. 1 (2016): 132–33, and Ben Spielberg, "Friedrichs v. California Teachers Association: A Deceptive Attack on Organized Labor," *The Huffington Post*, January 4, 2016, http://www.huffingtonpost.com/ben-spielberg/friedrichs-v-california-t_b_8910396.html.

86. Some models of change, such as the receivership in Lawrence, MA, are careful to protect the terms of collective bargaining within certain conditions (The Editorial Board, "Massachusetts Takes On a Failing School District," *The New York Times*, June 17, 2015, http://www.nytimes.com/2015/06/17/opinion/massachusetts-takes-on-a-failing-school-district.html.).

87. "School Choice," *Cato Institute*, accessed April 23, 2016, http://www.cato.org/research/school-choice.

88. "TPPF Releases 'Avoiding Government Regulation: Why Parental School Choice Is Possible Without Destructive Control of Private Schools,'" accessed April 24, 2016, http://www.texaspolicy.com/press_release/detail/tppf-releases-avoiding-government-regulation-why-parental-school-choice-is-possible-without-destructive-control-of-private-schools.

89. See, for instance, the series of posts on regulation: Jay Greene, "The High-Regulation Approach to School Choice," *Jay P. Greene's Blog*, October 1, 2015, https://jaypgreene.com/2015/10/01/the-high-regulation-approach-to-school-choice/.

90. Jim Stergios, "Testimony to the Texas Select Committee on State Sovereignty," *The Pioneer Institute*, April 14, 2011, http://pioneerinstitute.org/wp-content/uploads/dlm_uploads/TX_Stergios.pdf, Peter Wood, "The Core Between the States," *The Chronicle of Higher Education*, May 23, 2011.

91. Michael J. Petrilli, "The School Choice Moveement's Schisms, Explained," *The Flypaper*, January 27, 2016, http://edexcellence.net/articles/the-school-choice-movements-schisms-explained.

92. Stewart and Wolf, *The School Choice Journey*.

93. These categories are not meant to be absolute. Teacher unions are not all of a piece, and neither are libertarians.

94. West Virginia State Board of Education v. Barnette, 319 United States Reports 624 (Supreme Court of the United States 1943).

BIBLIOGRAPHY

10 LGBT Prom Controversies from Around the US. *Ranker*. http://www.ranker. com/list/10-lgbt-prom-controversies-from-around-the-us/ballerina-tatyana. Accessed 10 Oct 2015.

18 U.S. Code § 2385—Advocating Overthrow of Government. n.d.

75 Examples of How Bureaucracy Stands in the Way of America's Students and Teachers. *The Eli and Edythe Broad Foundation*, August 2012. http://www. broadeducation.org/about/bureaucracy.html

2008–09 Executive Budget Proposal: Preliminary Estimate of 2007–08 and 2008–09 State Aids Payable under Section 3609 plus Other Aids. 2008. State Government Proposal. Albany, NY: New York State Education Department. https://www. budget.ny.gov/pubs/archive/fy0809archive/eBudget0809/fy0809localities/ schoolaid/schoolruns.pdf

Abowitz, Kathleen Knight, and Jason Harnish. 2006. Contemporary Discourses of Citizenship. *Review of Educational Research* 76(4): 653–690. doi:10.2307/4124417.

Abo-Zena, Mona M., and Ben Mardell. 2014. When the Children Asked to Study God, What Did the Parents Say: Building Family Engagement Around Sensitive Topics. *Religion & Education Religion & Education* 42(3): 289–307.

Aetna Insurance Coding. 2015. http://www.aetna.com/cpb/medical/data/600_699 /0615.html

A Growing Movement: America's Largest Charter School Communities. Washington, DC: National Alliance for Public Charter Schools, December 2013.

Alberta Votes. 2015. *CBC News*, May 7. http://live.cbc.ca/Event/Alberta_ Votes_2015

Allison, Derek J., and Deani A. Neven Van Pelt. "Canada." In *Balancing Freedom, Autonomy and Accountability in Education*, edited by Charles L. Glenn and Jan deGroof, Vol. 3. Tilburg: Wolf Legal Publishers, 2012.

Alviar-Martin, T. 2011. Reconciling Multiple Conceptions of Citizenship: International School Teachers' Beliefs and Practice. *Journal of Education—Boston University School of Education* 191(3): 39–50.

Anti-Gay Policy Prompts School to Nix State Money. *The Huffington Post*. http:// www.huffingtonpost.com/2013/12/08/north-carolina-school-gay- policy-_n_4403722.html. Accessed 10 Oct 2015.

© The Author(s) 2017
A.R. Berner, *Pluralism and American Public Education*,
DOI 10.1057/978-1-137-50224-7

Arch R. Everson v. Board of Education of the Township of Ewing, 330 United States Reports 1 (Supreme Court of the United States 1947).

Arizona Christian School Tuition Organization v. Winn et al., 563 United States Reports 125 (Supreme Court of the United States 2011).

Arnold, Janice. 2008. Frum Schools Balk at New Religious Culture Course. *Canadian Jewish News*, September 18, sec. News. http://www.cjnews.com/node/81794

Arum, Richard. 2003. *Judging School Discipline: The Crisis in Moral Authority*. Cambridge, MA: Harvard University Press.

Atlas New America. 2015. Foundation. *New America*, June 29. http://atlas.newamerica.org/school-finance

Baker, Bruce D., David G. Sciarra, and Danielle Farrie. 2010. *Is School Funding Fair? A National Report Card*. Newark, NJ: Education Law Center. http://www.schoolfundingfairness.org/National_Report_Card.pdf

Bayer, Ronald, and Robert L. Spitzer. 1982. Edited Correspondence on the Status of Homosexuality in DSM-III. *Journal of the History of the Behavioral Sciences* 18(1): 32–52. doi:10.1002/1520-6696(198201)18:1<32::AID-JHBS2300180105>3.0.CO;2-0.

Beatriz Vergara v. State of California, (Superior Court of the State of California 2014).

Berard, R. 1987. Frederick James Gould and the Transformation of Moral Education. *British Journal of Educational Studies* 35(3): 233–247.

Berger, Peter L. 1979. *The Heretical Imperative: Contemporary Possibilities of Religious Affirmation*. Garden City, NY: Anchor Press.

Berger, Andrea, Lori Turk-Bicakci, Michael Garet, Joel Knudson, and Gur Hoshen. 2014, January. *Early College, Continued Success: Early College High School Initiative Impact Study*. Washington, DC: American Institutes for Research.

Bergner, Gwen. 2009. Black Children, White Preference: Brown v. Board, the Doll Tests, and the Politics of Self-Esteem. *American Quarterly* 61(2): 299–332. http://www.jstor.org/stable/27734991

Berliner, David. 2015. The Many Facets of PISA. *Teachers College Record* 117(010308): 20.

Berliner, David, and Gene V. Glass. 2014. *and Associates. 50 Myths and Lies That Threaten America's Public Schools: The Real Crisis in Education*. New York: Teachers College Press.

Bermann, George A. 1994. Taking Subsidiarity Seriously: Federalism in the European Community and the United States. *Columbia Law Review* 94(2): 331–456. doi:10.2307/1123200.

Berner, Ashley. 2008. Metaphysics in Educational Theory: Educational Philosophy and Teacher Training in England (1839–1944). D.Phil. Oxford: University of Oxford.

Berner, Ashley. "Funding Schools." In *Balancing Freedom, Autonomy, and Accountability in Education*, edited by Charles Glenn and Jan De Groof, 1:115–29. Tilburg: Wolf Legal Publishers, 2012.

———. 2013. Persuasion in Education. *Comment*, Spring, 28–33. https://www.cardus.ca/comment/article/4609/persuasion-in-education/

Bernhard, Michael. 1993. Civil Society and Democratic Transition in East Central Europe. *Political Science Quarterly* 108(2): 307–326.

Billmyer, Steve. 2014. NY State School Budgets 2014–15: Look Up, Compare Any District in the State. *Syracuse.com*, May 19. http://www.syracuse.com/news/index.ssf/2014/05/nys_school_budgets_2014-15_look_up_compare_any_district.html

Bishop, John. 2010. *Which Secondary Education Systems Work Best? The United States or Northern Europe.* Working Papers, January 1. http://digitalcommons.ilr.cornell. edu/workingpapers/105

Bjorklund-Young, Alanna. 2016. Moving to Opportunity: A Housing Experiment That Worked. *Johns Hopkins Institute for Education Policy,* January 7. http://education. jhu.edu/edpolicy/commentary/MovingtoOpportunityAHousing ExperimentthatWorked

Blum, Lawrence. 1996. Antiracist Civic Education in the California History-Social Science Framework. In *Public Education in a Multicultural Society: Policy, Theory, Critique,* Cambridge Studies in Philosophy and Public Policy, 23–48. Cambridge, UK: Cambridge University Press.

Board of Education of Kiryas Joel Village School District v. Grumet, 512 United States Reports 687 (United States Supreme Court 1994).

Böhlmark, Anders, and Mikael Lindahl. 2012. *Independent Schools and Long-Run Educational Outcomes Evidence from Sweden's Large Scale Voucher Reform.* Munich: CESifo.

Boser, Ulrich, and Center for American Progress. 2011. Return on Educational Investment: A District-by-District Evaluation of U.S. Educational Productivity. Washington, DC: Center for American Progress. 1333 H Street NW 10th Floor, Washington, DC 20005. Tel: 202-682-1611; Web site: http://www. americanprogress.org

Boser, Ulrich, Matthew Chingos, and Chelsea Straus. 2015. *The Hidden Value of Curriculum Reform.* Washington, DC: Center for American Progress. https://cdn. americanprogress.org/wp-content/uploads/2015/10/06111518/Curri culumMatters-report.pdf

Bowie, Liz. 2016. Maryland to Help Pay Private School Tuition. *The Baltimore Sun.* April 19. http://www.baltimoresun.com/news/maryland/education/blog/ bs-md-voucher-20160415-story.html

Bowman, Karl Desportes, James Davison Hunter, Jeffrey S. Dill, and Megan Juelfs-Swanson. 2012. *Culture of American Families Executive Report.* Charlottesville, VA: Institute for Advanced Studies in Culture.

Brill, Steven. 2012. *Class Warfare: Inside the Fight to Fix America's Schools.* Reprint. Simon & Schuster.

Brooks, David. 2012. Flood the Zone. *The New York Times.* February 6. http://www. nytimes.com/2012/02/07/opinion/brooks-flood-the-zone.html

Bruner, Jerome S. 1978. *The Process of Education: [A Landmark in Educational Theory].* Cambridge [u.a.]: Harvard University Press.

Brusse, Elsbeth Asbeek, and Tanya Keenan. 2008. 'Recognize the Heterosexual' Education About Homosexuality in Dutch Secondary Schools by Elsbeth Asbeek Brusse, Tanya Keenan. *Humanity In Action,* June 27. http://www.humanityinaction. org/knowledgebase/94-recognize-the-heterosexual-education-about-homosexuality-in-dutch-secondary-schools

Bryk, Anthony S., Valerie E. Lee, and Peter Blakeley Holland. 1993. *Catholic Schools and the Common Good.* Cambridge, MA: Harvard University Press.

Buckley, Jack. 2004. *Do Charter Schools Promote Student Citizenship?* Occasional Paper. New York: National Center for the Study of Privatization in Education.

Button, Mark. 2005. Arendt, Rawls, and Public Reason. *Social Theory and Practice* 31 (2): 257–280. http://www.jstor.org/stable/23558465

Cahn, Steven M. 1997. *Classic and Contemporary Readings in the Philosophy of Education.* New York: McGraw-Hill.

Campbell, David E. 2004. The Civic Implications of Canada's Education System. In *Educating Citizens*, ed. Patrick Wolf, Stephen Macedo, David J. Ferrero, and Charles Venegone, 186–220. Washington, DC: Brookings Institute.

———. 2008. The Civic Side of School Choice: An Empirical Analysis of Civic Education in Public and Private Schools. *Brigham Young University Law Review* 2008(2): 487–524.

———. 2008. Voice in the Classroom: How an Open Classroom Climate Fosters Political Engagement Among Adolescents. *Political Behavior* 30(4): 437–454.

———. 2012. Introduction. In *Making Civics Count: Citizenship Education for a New Generation*, ed. David Campbell, Meira Levinson, and Frederick Hess, 1–15. Cambridge: Harvard University Press.

Campbell, David E., Meira Levinson, and Frederick M. Hess. 2012. *Making Civics Count: Citizenship Education for a New Generation.*

Canada Schools Forced to Admit Gay-Straight Groups. 2012. *Christian Broadcasting Network.* June 8. http://www.cbn.com/cbnnews/world/2012/June/Canada-Schools-Forced-to-Admit-Gay-Straight-Groups/

Cardus Education Survey 2014: Private Schools for the Public Good. *Cardus.ca*, 2014. http://www.cardus.ca/store/4291/

Carey, Benedict. 2015. Many Psychology Findings Not as Strong as Claimed, Study Says. *The New York Times*, August 27. http://www.nytimes.com/2015/08/28/science/many-social-science-findings-not-as-strong-as-claimed-study-says.html

Chenoweth, Karin. 2007. *It's Being Done: Academic Success in Unexpected Schools.* Cambridge, MA: Harvard Education Press.

Chingos, Matthew M., Paul E. Peterson, Brookings Institution, Brown Center on Education Policy, John F. Kennedy School of Government, and Program on Education Policy and Governance. 2012. *The Effects of School Vouchers on College Enrollment: Experimental Evidence from New York City.* Washington, DC: Brown Center on Education Policy at Brookings.

Chubb, John E., and Terry M. Moe. 1990. *Politics, Markets & America's Schools.* Washington, DC: Brookings Institution.

Clark, Melissa A. 2003. *Education Reform, Redistribution, and Student Achievement: Evidence from the Kentucky Education Reform Act.* Princeton, NJ: Mathematica Policy Research.

Clark, Heather. 2013. Canadian Supreme Court Rules Biblical Speech Opposing Homosexual Behavior Is a 'Hate Crime.' Religious publication. *Christian News Network.* http://christiannews.net/2013/02/28/canadian-supreme-court-rules-biblical-speech-opposing-homosexual-behavior-is-a-hate-crime/

Close, Rev Francis. 1848. *Cooperation with the Committee of Council on Education Vindicated and Recommended.* Cheltenham College Archives. London: Hatchard & Son.

CNN. 2010. Mississippi School Sued for Canceling Prom over Lesbian Student. *CNN.com*, March 12. http://www.cnn.com/2010/LIVING/03/11/mississippi.prom.suit/

Coca, Vanessa, and Consortium on Chicago School Research. 2012. *Working to My Potential: The Postsecondary Experiences of CPS Students in the International Baccalaureate Diploma Programme.* http://bibpurl.oclc.org/web/49260, http://ccsr.uchicago.edu/sites/default/files/publications/IB%20Report1.pdf

Coleman, James S. 1966. Equality of Educational Opportunity. Washington, DC: Department of Health, Education, and Welfare. http://eric.ed.gov/?id=ED012275

Coleman, James S., Thomas Hoffer, and Sally Kilgore. 1982. *High School Achievement: Public, Catholic, and Private Schools Compared.* New York: Basic Books.

Collaboration, Open Science. 2015. Estimating the Reproducibility of Psychological Science. *Science* 349(6251): aac4716. doi:10.1126/science.aac4716.

Common Core State Standards Initiative. 2015. Common Core State Standards for English Language Arts & Literacy in History/Social Studies, Science and Technical Subjects. Common Core State Standards Initiative. http://www.corestandards.org/ELA-Literacy/

Copley, Terence. 2005. *Indoctrination, Education and God: The Struggle for the Mind.* London: Society for Promoting Christian Knowledge.

Coulson, Andrew J. 1999. *Market Education: The Unknown History.* New Brunswick, NJ: Transaction Publishers.

Council on Civil Society. 1998. *A Call to Civil Society: Why Democracy Needs Moral Truths.* New York: Institute for American Values and the University of Chicago School of Divinity.

Council on Foreign Relations, Independent Task Force, Joel I. Klein, Condoleezza Rice, and Julia Levy. 2012. *U. S. Education Reform and National Security.* New York: Council on Foreign Relations, Independent Task Force.

CREDO. 2013. *National Charter School Study 2013.* Stanford, CA: Center for Research on Education Outcomes.

Curren, Randall R. 2003. *A Companion to the Philosophy of Education.* Malden, MA: Blackwell http://public.eblib.com/choice/publicfullrecord.aspx?p=214150.

D'Arcy, Michael, and Naomi Richman. 2013. Moody's: Charter Schools Pose Greatest Credit Challenge to School Districts in Economically Weak Urban Areas. Investor Service. *Moodys.com,* October 15. https://www.moodys.com/research/Moodys-Charter-schools-pose-greatest-credit-challenge-to-school-districts-PR_284505

Damon, William. 2011. *Failing Liberty 101: How We Are Leaving Young Americans Unprepared for Citizenship in a Free Society.* Stanford, CA: Hoover Institution Press.

Davids v. New York Education Quality, (Staten Island Supreme Court, New York 2014).

Davis, Joseph P. 2009, Spring. Pathologies of the Achieving Self. *The Hedgehog Review* 9(2): 37–49.

Decker, Janet, and Kari A. Carr. n.d. Church-State Entanglement at Religiously Affiliated Charter Schools. *Brigham Young University Education and Law Journal* 2015(1): 77–107.

DeGirolami, Marc. 2013. Testimony Before the United States Commission on Civil Rights. March 1. https://centerforlawandreligion.files.wordpress.com/2013/03/us-commission-on-civil-rights-testimony-degirolami-1.pdf

DeGroff, Eric A. 2009. Parental Rights and Public School Curricula: Revisiting Mozert After 20 Years. *Journal of Law & Education* 38(1): 83.

Delli Carpini, Michael X., and Scott Keeter. 1996. *What Americans Know About Politics and Why It Matters.* New Haven: Yale University Press.

Deming, David S., Justine S. Hastings, Thomas J. Kane, and Douglas O. Staiger. 2011. *School Choice, School Quality and Post-Secondary Attainment.* Cambridge, MA, National Bureau of Economic Research.

Dent, H.C. 1977. *The Training of Teachers in England and Wales, 1800–1975*. London: Hodder and Stoughton.

Dershowitz, Alan. 2011. The Right to Know Your Rights: Civic Literacy, the Miranda Warnings, and Me. In *Teaching America: The Case for Civic Education*, ed. David Feith. New York: Rowman & Littlefield.

de Tocqueville, Alexis. 1988. *Democracy in America*. Ed. J.P. Mayer and Trans. George Lawrence. New York: HarperCollins.

deWiel, Boris. 1997. A Conceptual History of Civil Society: From Greek Beginnings to the End of Marx. *Past Imperfect* 6: 3–42.

DiSalvo, Daniel. 2015. *Government Against Itself: Public Union Power and Its Consequences*. Oxford and New York: Oxford University Press.

Douglas County School District v. Larue. *Becket Fund*, October 28, 2015. http://www.becketfund.org/douglas-county-school-district-v-larue-2011-present/

Doyle, Daniela, Christen Holly, and Bryan C Hassel. 2015. *Is Detente Possible?: District-Charter School Relations in Four Cities*. Washington, DC: Thomas B. Fordham Institute and Public Impact. http://edex.s3-us-west-2.amazonaws.com/publication/pdfs/Is_Détente_Possible_Report_Final.pdf

Dulaney, Katie. 2015. Institutional Commitment to Civic Education: Public Montessori Secondary Schools. *CUNY Institute for Education Policy*, May 8, 2015. http://ciep.hunter.cuny.edu/institutional-commitment-to-civic-education-public-montessori-secondary-schools/

Editors. 2015. A School Voucher Surrender. *Wall Street Journal*. http://www.wsj.com/articles/a-school-voucher-surrender-1450397585

———. 2015. Learning Unleashed. *Economist*, August 1. http://www.economist.com/news/briefing/21660063-where-governments-are-failing-provide-youngsters-decent-education-private-sector

Elacqua, G, D. Contreras, and F. Salazar. 2008. Scaling Up in Chile: Networks of Schools Facilitate Higher Student Achievement. *Education Next* 8(3): 62–68.

Elbein, Asher. 2014. Grappling With the Rising Cost of Being an Orthodox Jew. *Tablet Magazine*, July 11. http://www.tabletmag.com/jewish-life-and-religion/177127/rising-cost-of-being-orthodox

Elder, Todd, and Christopher Jepsen. 2014. Are Catholic Primary Schools More Effective than Public Primary Schools? *Journal of Urban Economics* 80: 28–38. doi:10.1016/j.jue.2013.10.001.

Ercikan, Kadriye, Wolff-Michael Roth, and Mustafa Asil. 2015. Cautions About Inferences from International Assessments: The Case of PISA 2009. *Teachers College Record* 117(010301): 28.

E, R (on the application of) v Governing Body of JFS & Anor [2009] UKSC 15, (UKSC (2009)).

Ethique et Culture Religieuse—Sondage Léger Marketing—Plus Des Trois Quarts Des Québécois Pour Le Libre Choix. News Wire. Montreal [Que.]: Coalition pour la liberté en éducation, May 26, 2009. http://archive.newswire.ca/en/story/558659/ethique-et-culture-religieuse-sondage-leger-marketing-plus-des-trois-quarts-des-quebecois-pour-le-libre-choix

Evans, Mark. 2006. Educating for Citizenship: What Teachers Say and What Teachers Do. *Canadian Journal of Education* 29(2): 410–435. http://eric.ed.gov/?id=EJ750389

Fact-Sheet: Sexual Orientation Issues. 2015. European Court of Human Rights, Strasbourg. http://www.echr.coe.int/Documents/FS_Sexual_orientation_ENG.pdf

Farrow, Douglas. 2010. On the Ethics and Religious Culture Program, Expert Testimony, Re: Loyola High School et John Zucchi C. Michelle Courchesne, En Sa Qualite de Minister de l'Education, Du Loisir et Du Sport. Cour Superieure, District de Montreal, N. 500-17-045278-085. D.B. Farrow.

Feinberg, Walter. 2006. *For Goodness Sake: Religious Schools and Education for Democratic Citizenry.* New York: Routledge.

Feith, David. 2011. *Teaching America: The Case for Civic Education.* Lanham, MD: Rowman & Littlefield.

Figlio, David N., and Cassandra M.D. Hart. 2010. *Competitive Effects of Means-Tested School Vouchers.* Working Paper. National Bureau of Economic Research. http://www.nber.org/papers/w16056

Figlio, David, and Cassandra M.D. Hart. 2014, January. Competitive Effects of Means-Tested Vouchers. *American Economic Journal: Applied Economics* 6(1): 133–156. doi:10.1257/app.6.1.133.

Figlio, David, Cassandra M.D. Hart, and Molly Metzger. 2010. Who Uses a Means-Tested Scholarship, and What Do They Choose? *Economics of Education Review*, Special Issue in Honor of Henry M. Levin, 29(2): 301–317. doi:10.1016/j.econedurev.2009.08.002.

Fiscal Year 2015 Budget: Summary and Background Information. United States Department of Education, March 4, 2014. http://www2.ed.gov/about/overview/budget/budget15/summary/15summary.pdf

Fleming, James E., and Linda C. McClain. 2000. Foreword: Legal and Constitutional Implications of the Calls to Revive Civil Society. *Chicago-Kent Law Review* 75(2). http://scholarship.kentlaw.iit.edu/cgi/viewcontent.cgi?article=3193&context=cklawreview

Flipse, Abraham C. 2012. The Origins of Creationism in the Netherlands: The Evolution Debate among Twentieth-Century Dutch Neo-Calvinists. *Church History* 81(1): 104–147.

Florida School Choice. *Institute for Justice.* https://ij.org/case/florida-school-choice/. Accessed 6 Dec 2015.

Forslund et. al., v. State of Minnesota, (n.d.).

Friedman, Milton. 1955. The Role of Government in Education. In *Economics and the Public Interest*, ed. Robert A. Solo, 123–144. New Brunswick, NJ: Rutgers University Press.

Friedrichs v. California Teachers Association, United States Reports, (Supreme Court of the United States 2016).

Fullinwider, Robert K. 1996. Multicultural Education: Concepts, Policies, and Controversies. In *Public Education in a Multicultural Society: Policy, Theory, Critique*, Cambridge Studies in Philosophy and Public Policy, 3–22. Cambridge, UK: Cambridge University Press.

———. 1996. *Public Education in a Multicultural Society: Policy, Theory, Critique.* Cambridge, UK: Cambridge University Press.

Gadamer, Hans-Georg. 1998. *Truth and Method.* New York: Continuum. http://site.ebrary.com/id/10727513

Galston, William A. 2001. Political Knowledge, Political Engagement, and Civic Education. *Annual Review of Political Science* 4: 217–234.

———. 2002. *Liberal Pluralism: The Implications of Value Pluralism for Political Theory and Practice.* Cambridge, UK: Cambridge University Press. doi:10.1017/CBO9780511613579.

Garcia, Odalis. 2014. Israeli Parliament Bans Discrimination against LGBT Youth in Schools. Member organization. *GLAAD*, March 21. https://www.glaad.org/blog/israeli-parliament-bans-discrimination-against-lgbt-youth-schools

Gaudiani, Claire. 2003. *The Greater Good: How Philanthropy Drives the American Economy and Can Save Capitalism*. New York: Times Books/Henry Holt.

Gedicks, Frederick. 2012. *Incorporation of the Establishment Clause Against the States: A Logical, Textual, and Historical Account*. SSRN Scholarly Paper. Rochester, NY: Social Science Research Network, February 5. http://papers.ssrn.com/abstract=1997807

Georgia's Tax Dollars Help Finance Private Schools with Severe Anti-Gay Policies, Practices, & Teachings. Atlanta, GA: Southern Education Association, January 2013.

Gibson, James L. 2001. Social Networks, Civil Society, and the Prospects for Consolidating Russia's Democratic Transition. *American Journal of Political Science* 45(1): 51–68. doi:10.2307/2669359.

Giddens, Anthony, and Fred R. Dallmayr. 1982. *Profiles and Critiques in Social Theory*. London: Macmillan.

Glendon, Mary Ann. 1987. *Abortion and Divorce in Western Law*. Cambridge, MA: Harvard University Press.

Glenn, Charles L. 1988. *The Myth of the Common School*. Amherst, MA: University of Massachusetts Press.

———. 2005. What the United States Can Learn from Other Countries. In *What Americans Can Learn from School Choice in Other Countries*, ed. James Tooley, and David Salisbury, 79–90. Washington, DC: Cato Institute.

———. 2011. *Contrasting Models of State and School: A Comparative Historical Study of Parental Choice and State Control*, 1st edn. New York: Continuum.

———. 2012, December. *Religious Freedom in Education?*

———. 2013, April. The Discriminatory Origins of New Hampshire's 'Blaine' Amendment, Unpublished Testimony.

Goodman, Sara Wallace. 2012. Fortifying Citizenship: Policy Strategies for Civic Integration in Western Europe. *World Politics* 64(4): 659–698.

Good News Club v. Milford Central School, 533 United States Reports 98. Accessed October 12, 2016.

Gould, F.J. 1913. *Moral Instruction: Its Aim and Practice*. London: Longmans, Green & Co.

Goyette, Kimberly A., and Annette Lareau. 2014. *Choosing Homes, Choosing Schools*. New York: Russell Sage Foundation.

Greene, Jay. 2015. The High-Regulation Approach to School Choice. *Jay P. Greene's Blog*, October 1. https://jaypgreene.com/2015/10/01/the-high-regulation-approach-to-school-choice/

Green, Elizabeth, and Trevor Cooling. 2009. *Mapping the Field: A Review of the Current Research Evidence on the Impact of Schools with a Christian Ethos*. London: Theos.

Green, Erica. 2015. City Charter Schools File Lawsuit against School System over Funding. *Baltimoresun.com*. September 10. http://www.baltimoresun.com/news/maryland/education/blog/bs-md-ci-charter-funding-lawsuit-20150910-story.html

Gross, Betheny, Michael DeArmond, and Patrick Denice. 2015. *Common Enrollment, Parents, and School Choice: Early Evidence from Denver and New Orleans. Making*

School Choice Work Series. University of Washington Bothell: Center on Reinventing Public Education.

Gutmann, Amy. 1987. *Democratic Education.* Princeton, NJ: Princeton University Press.

Habermas, Jurgen. 1995. Reconciliation Through the Public Use of Reason: Remarks on John Rawls's Political Liberalism. *The Journal of Philosophy* 92(3): 109–131. doi:10.2307/2940842.

Hafiz, Jasmine. 2014. Creationism Banned from UK Schools. *The Huffington Post,* June 25. http://www.huffingtonpost.com/2014/06/25/creationism-banned-uk-schools_n_5529693.html

Hamburger, Philip. 2002. *Separation of Church and State.* Cambridge, MA: Harvard University Press.

———. 2011. Privileges or Immunities. *Northwestern University Law Review* 105(1): 61–147.

Hansen, David T. 1992. The Emergence of a Shared Morality in a Classroom. *Curriculum Inquiry* 22(4): 345–361.

———. 1993. From Role to Person: The Moral Layeredness of Classroom Teaching. *American Educational Research Journal* 30(4): 651–674.

Hanushek, Eric A., Paul Peterson, and Ludger Woessman. 2014. *Not Just the Problems of Other People's Children: U.S. Student Performance in Global Perspective.* Boston, MA: Harvard's Program on Educational Policy and Governance.

Harris, Elizabeth A., and Ford Fessenden. 2015. 'Opt Out' Becomes Anti-Test Rallying Cry in New York State. *The New York Times,* May 20. http://www.nytimes.com/2015/05/21/nyregion/opt-out-movement-against-common-core-testing-grows-in-new-york-state.html

Harrison, Trevor. 1999. *Contested Classrooms Education, Globalization, and Democracy in Alberta.* Edmonton, AB: University of Alberta Press, Parkland Institute. http://site.ebrary.com/id/10203260

Hautamäki, Jarkko. 2008. *Pisa06 Finland: Analyses, Reflections and Explanations.* Helsinki: Ministry of Education.

Heijnens, S. 2013. Theory of Evolution in Dutch Education. History of the Theory of Evolution in Dutch Public Education, Policy, Debates and High School Examinations from 1867 until Recent. Masters in History and Philosophy of Science, Utrecht. http://dspace.library.uu.nl/handle/1874/272751

Heller Sahlgren, Gabriel. 2015. *Real Finnish Lessons: The True Story of an Education Superpower.* London, UK: Centre for Policy Studies.

Heyking, Amy Jeanette Von. 2006. *Creating Citizens: History and Identity in Alberta's Schools, 1905–1980.* Calgary, AB: University of Calgary Press.

Hillman, Benjamin Siracusa. 2008. Is There a Place for Religious Charter Schools? *Yale Law School Review* 118(554): 814–848. http://www.yalelawjournal.org/note/is-there-a-place-for-religious-charter-schools

Hirsch, E.D. 2006. *The Knowledge Deficit: Closing the Shocking Education Gap for American Children.* Boston, MA: Houghton Mifflin.

———. 2009. *The Making of Americans: Democracy and Our Schools.* New Haven, CT: Yale University Press.

Hirsch, E.D. *Why Knowledge Matters: Rescuing Our Children from Failed Educational Theories.* Cambridge, MA: Harvard Education Press, 2016.

Hoffman, Thomas. 2015. Scientists Warn: Creationism is on the Rise in Europe. Why Knowledge Matters: Rescuing Our Children from Failed Educational Theories,

Research & Study, February 24. http://sciencenordic.com/scientists-warn-creationism-rise-europe

Hraba, Joseph. 1972. The Doll Technique: A Measure of Racial Ethnocentrism? *Social Forces* 50(4): 522–527. doi:10.2307/2576794.

Hunter, James Davison. 2000. *The Death of Character: Moral Education in an Age Without Good or Evil*. New York: Basic Books.

———. 2010. *To Change the World: The Irony, Tragedy, and Possibility of Christianity in the Late Modern World*. New York: Oxford University Press.

Editors. Very Good on Paper. *The Economist*, December 12, 2013. http://www.economist.com/blogs/banyan/2013/12/education-vietnam

Illinois ex rel. Vashti McCollum v. Board of Ed. of School Dist. No. 71, Champaign County, Illinois, 333 United States Reports 203 (Supreme Court of the United States 1948).

Inazu, John D. 2012. *The Four Freedoms and the Future of Religious Liberty*. SSRN Scholarly Paper. Rochester, NY: Social Science Research Network, October 8. http://papers.ssrn.com/abstract=2158861

James B. Stockdale. 1995. Master of My Fate: A Stoic Philosopher in a Hanoi Prison. Essay. Center for the Study of Professional Military Ethics. http://www.usna.edu/Ethics/_files/documents/Stoicism2.pdf

James Tooley. 2015. A Champion of Low-Cost Schools or a Dangerous Man? *The Guardian*. http://www.theguardian.com/education/2013/nov/12/professor-james-tooley-low-cost-schools. Accessed 21 Jun 2015.

Jeynes, William H. 2007. Religion, Intact Families, and the Achievement Gap. *Interdisciplinary Journal of Research on Religion* 3(3).

Jochim, Ashley. 2015. Lessons from the Trenches on Making School Choice Work. *The Brookings Institution*, August 12. http://www.brookings.edu/blogs/brown-center-chalkboard/posts/2015/08/12-school-choice-lessons-jochim

Jochim, Ashley, Michael DeArmond, Betheny Gross, and Robin Lake. 2014. *How Parents Experience Public School Choice, Making School Choice Work Series*. Bothell, WA: University of Washington Bothell, Center on Reinventing Public Education.

John Ellis "Jeb" Bush, etc., et al., v. Ruth D. Holmes, et al.; Charles J. Crist, Jr., etc., v. Ruth D. Holmes, et al.; Brenda McShane, etc., et al., v. Ruth D. Holmes, et al., (Supreme Court of Florida 2006).

Kamens, David H., and Connie L. McNeely. 2010. Globalization and the Growth of International Educational Testing and National Assessment. *Comparative Education Review* 54(1): 5–25. doi:10.1086/648471.

Kane, Thomas, Antoniya Owens, William Marinell, Daniel Thal, and Douglas Staiger. 2016. *Teaching Higher: Educators' Perspectives on Common Core Implementation*. Cambridge, MA: Center for Education Policy Research, Harvard University. http://cepr.harvard.edu/files/cepr/files/teaching-higher-report.pdf?m=1454988762

Lamb's Chapel v. Ctr. Moriches Union Free School District, 508 United States Reports 384 (Supreme Court of the United States 1993).

Legislature of Kansas. 1879. *An Act to Incorporate Cities of the First Class*. 5242.

Lemon v. Kurtzman, 403 United States Reports 602 (Supreme Court of the United States 1971).

Levin, Betsy. 1976. Between Scylla and Charybdis: Title I's 'Comparable Services' Requirement and State and Federal Establishment Clauses. *Duke Law Journal* 1976(39): 39–67.

Levitt v. Committee for Public Education, 413 United States Reports 472 (Supreme Court of the United States 1973).

Littauer, Dan. 2014. Israeli Parliament Bans Discrimination Against LGBT Youth in Schools. *LGBTQ Nation*, March 19. http://www.lgbtqnation.com/2014/03/israeli-parliament-bans-discrimination-against-lgbt-youth-in-schools/

Litton, Edmundo F., Shane P. Martin, Ignacio Higareda, and Julie A. Mendoza. 2010. The Promise of Catholic Schools for Educating the Future of Los Angeles. *Catholic Education: A Journal of Inquiry and Practice* 13(3): 350–367. http://eric.ed.gov/?id=EJ914874

Ljubownikow, Sergej, Jo Crotty, and Peter W. Rodgers. 2013. The State and Civil Society in Post-Soviet Russia: The Development of a Russian-Style Civil Society. *Progress in Development Studies* 13(2): 153–166. doi:10.1177/1464993412466507.

Long, Robert. 2015, July 26. Sex and Relationships Education in Schools. Briefing Document. London, UK: House of Commons.

Louie, Vivian S. 2012. *Keeping the Immigrant Bargain: The Costs and Rewards of Success in America*. New York: Russell Sage Foundation.

Loyola High School and John Zucchi, Plaintifs, v. Michelle Courchesne, in Her Capacity as Minister of Education, Recreation and Sports. Montreal: Superior Court, Canada, Province of Quebec, District of Montreal, June 18, 2010.

Lubienski, Christopher A., and Sarah Theule Lubienski. 2013. *The Public School Advantage: Why Public Schools Outperform Private Schools*. Chicago: University of Chicago Press.

Macedo, Stephen. 2007. In Defense of Conditional Funding of Religious Schools. *Law & Ethics of Human Rights* 1(1): 382–428. doi:10.2202/1938-2545.1011.

Macedo, Stephen, and Patrick Wolf. 2004. Introduction: School Choice, Civic Values, and Problems of Policy Comparison. In *Educating Citizens: International Perspectives on Civic Values and School Choice*, ed. Stephen Macedo, and Patrick Wolf. Washington, DC: Brookings Institute.

MacIntyre, Alasdair C. 1990. *Three Rival Versions of Moral Inquiry: Encyclopaedia, Genealogy and Tradition : Being Gifford Lectures Delivered in the University of Edinburgh in 1988*. London: Duckworth.

Maclure, Jocelyn, and Charles Taylor. 2011. *Secularism and Freedom of Conscience*. Trans. Jane Marie Todd. Cambridge, MA: Harvard University Press.

Malnick, Edward, and Julie Henry. 2012. Church of England Schools to Be 'Rebranded,' March 17, sec. Education. http://www.telegraph.co.uk/education/educationnews/9150817/Church-of-England-schools-to-be-rebranded.html

Manchir, Michelle. 2011. Wheaton College: Group Supporting LGBT Students at Wheaton College Plans Homecoming Festivities. *Tribunedigital-Chicagotribune*, September 30. http://articles.chicagotribune.com/2011-09-30/news/ct-met-wheaton-lgbt-homecoming-0930-20110930_1_wheaton-college-homecoming-kristin-winn

Marcus, B. K. 2016. Martin Luther King III on Freedom, Justice, and School Choice|B.K. Marcus, January 25. https://fee.org/articles/martin-luther-king-iii-on-educational-freedom/

Mardell, Ben, and Mona M. Abo-Zena. 2010. 'The Fun Thing about Studying Different Beliefs Is That ... They Are Different': Kindergartners Explore Spirituality. *Young Children* 65(4): 12–17.

Martens, Allison M., and Jason Gainous. 2013. Civic Education and Democratic Capacity: How Do Teachers Teach and What Works? *SSQU Social Science Quarterly* 94(4): 956–976.

Matsumoto, Linda. 2002. A Brief History—The Education Reform Movement in Alberta. *Alberta Teachers' Association Magazine*, 83. http://www.teachers.ab.ca/Publications/ATA%20Magazine/Volume%2083/Number%201/Articles/Pages/A%20Brief%20History%20The%20Education%20Reform%20Movement%20in%20Alberta.aspx

Matthews, Karen. 2013. Charter Schools Worry About De Blasio's Plans. News. *The Huffington Post*, December 26. http://www.huffingtonpost.com/2013/12/26/bill-de-blasio-charter-schools_n_4503518.html

Matus, Ron. "From Sit-Ins to School Choice." *redefinED*, September 15, 2015. https://www.redefinedonline.org/2015/09/from-sit-ins-to-school-choice/.

Matus, Ron. 2016. Opinion: The Progressive Split Over Education, as Democrats Go Back to the Future Over School Choice. *The 74*, April 19. https://www.the74million.org/article/opinion-the-progressive-split-over-education-as-democrats-go-back-to-the-future-over-school-choice

McCann, Phillip. 1977. *Popular Education and Socialization in the Nineteenth Century*. London: Methuen.

McCrudden, Christopher. 2011. Religion and Education in Northern Ireland: Voluntary Segregation Reflecting Historical Divisions. In *Law, Religious Freedoms and Education in Europe*, ed. Myriam Hunter-Hénin. Burlington, VT: Ashgate Publishing.

McDonnell, Lorraine. 2000. Defining Democratic Purposes. In *Rediscovering the Democratic Purposes of Education*, Studies in Government and Public Policy, ed. McDonnell Lorraine, P. Michael Timpane, and Roger Benjamin, 1–14. Lawrence, KS: University Press of Kansas.

McEwen, Nelly. 1995. Educational Accountability in Alberta. *Canadian Journal of Education/Revue Canadienne de L'éducation* 20(1): 27–44.

McLachlin, Beverley. 2004. Freedom of Religion and the Rule of Law: A Canadian Perspective. In *Recognizing Religion in a Secular Society: Essays in Pluralism, Religion and Public Policy*. Montreal, QC: McGill-Queen's University Press.

McLaren, Peter. 2006. *Life in Schools: An Introduction to Critical Pedagogy in the Foundations of Education*. 5th edn. Washington, DC: Postman, New York.

McShane, Michael, and Brittany Wagner. 2016, January 20. *Course Access for Missouri Students*. St. Louis, MO: Show-Me Institute. http://showmeinstitute.org/blog/school-choice/course-access-missouri-students

Medina, Jennifer, and Motoko Rich. 2016. California Appeals Court Reverses Decision to Overturn Teacher Tenure Rules. *The New York Times*, April 14. http://www.nytimes.com/2016/04/15/us/californiaappealscourt-reverses-decision-to-overturn-teacher-tenure-rules.html

Megan. 2015. Supreme Court Rules Quebec Infringed on Loyola High School's Religious Freedom. http://www.cbc.ca/news/canada/montreal/supreme-court-rules-quebec-infringed-on-loyola-high-school-s-religious-freedom-1.3000724. Accessed 3 Oct 2015.

Mehlhorn, Dmitri. 2016. Mehlhorn: How the Unions Lost Three Swing Votes and Pushed the Supreme Court Towards Historic Friedrichs Ruling. *The 74*, January 12. https://www.the74million.org/article/mehlhorn-how-the-unions-lost-three-swing-votes-and-pushed-the-supreme-court-towards-historic-friedrichs-ruling

Mehta, Jal D., and Robert Schwartz. 2011. Canada: Looks a Lot Like Us But Gets Much Better Results. In *Surpassing Shanghai: An Agenda for American Education Built on the World's Leading Systems*, ed. Marc Tucker, 141–171. Cambridge, MA: Harvard Education Press.

Melé, Domènec. 2005. Exploring the Principle of Subsidiarity in Organisational Forms. *Journal of Business Ethics* 60(3): 293–305. http://www.jstor.org/stable/25123581

Melendez, Paul Louis. 2009. Do Education Tax Credits Improve Equity? Doctoral Dissertation in Educational Leadership, University of Arizona. http://arizona.openrepository.com/arizona/handle/10150/194044

Meyer, Heinz-Dieter. 2013. OECD's Pisa: A Tale of Flaws and Hubris. *Teachers College Record*, December 19. http://www.tcrecord.org/Content.asp?ContentId=17371

Michelle Herczog Statement on the 2014 NAEP Results. *National Council for the Social Studies*. http://www.socialstudies.org/news/2015-05-04-38024. Accessed 14 May 2015.

Miksic, Mai. 2014. Are Montessori Pre-K Programs the Best Educational Model for Low-Income Black and Latino Children? *CUNY Institute for Education Policy*, September18.http://ciep.hunter.cuny.edu/are-montessori-pre-k-programs-the-best-educational-model-for-low-income-black-and-latino-children/

———. 2014. Is the 'Catholic School Effect' Real? New Research Challenges the Catholic Primary School Advantage. *CUNY Institute for Education Policy*. http://ciep.hunter.cuny.edu/catholicschools/. Accessed 9 Jun 2015.

Miksic, Mai, and Ashley Berner. 2014. What Are Education Tax Credits, and Why Should We Care? *CUNY Institute for Education Policy*, February 21. http://ciep.hunter.cuny.edu/education-tax-credits-care/

Milke, Mark. 2010. *School Choice in Canada: Lessons for America*. Washington, DC: The Heritage Foundation.

Miller, Lisa. 2000. Religiosity and Substance Use and Abuse Among Adolescents in the National Comorbidity Survey. *Journal of the American Academy of Child & Adolescent Psychiatry* 39(9): 1190–1197.

Miller, Helena. 2001. Meeting the Challenge: The Jewish Schooling Phenomenon in the UK. *Oxford Review of Education* 27(4): 501–513. doi:http://www.tandfonline.com/doi/abs/10.1080/03054980120086202.

Miller, Lisa. 2015. *The Spiritual Child: The New Science on Parenting for Health and Lifelong Thriving.*

Minogue, Kenneth R. 1985. *Alien Powers: The Pure Theory of Ideology*. New York: St. Martin's Press.

Moe, Terry M. 2011. *Special Interest: Teachers Unions and America's Public Schools*. Reprint. Washington, DC: Brookings Institution Press.

Movement Advancement Project | Our Work and Mission. http://www.lgbtmap.org/our-work-and-mission. Accessed 10 Oct 2015.

Mueller v. Allen, 463 United States Reports 388 (Supreme Court of the United States 1983).

Muench, Richard. 2014. Education under the Regime of PISA & Co.: Global Standards and Local Traditions in Conflict – The Case of Germany. *Teachers College Record* 116(090306): 16.

Müller, Detlef K., Fritz K. Ringer, and Brian Simon. 1987. *The Rise of the Modern Educational System: Structural Change and Social Reproduction*. Cambridge/Paris: Cambridge University Press/Editions de la maison des sciences de l'homme.

Murphy, James. 1971. *Church, State and Schools in Britain, 1800–1970*. London: Routledge & K. Paul.

Murray, Charles A. 2012. *Coming Apart: The State of White America, 1960–2010*. New York: Crown Forum.

Nathan-Kazis, Josh. 2014. How Orthodox Agudah and Wal-Mart Money United To Back School Vouchers—News. *The Forward*, July 22. http://forward.com/news/202290/how-orthodox-agudah-and-wal-mart-money-united-to-b/

———. 2015. Did Jewish Groups Push Too Hard on N.Y. Education Tax Credit?—News. *The Forward*, July 3. http://forward.com/news/311348/pushin-too-hard/

National Association of Independent Schools, Principles and Best Practices. *National Association of Independent Schools*, 2015. http://www.nais.org/Articles/Pages/Principles-of-Good-Practice.aspx

National Commission on Civic Renewal. 1997. *A Nation of Spectators: How Civic Disengagement Weakens America and What We Can Do about It*. Final Report of the National Commission on Civic Renewal. College Park, MD: National Commission on Civic Renewal. http://eric.ed.gov/?id=ED424174

Newport, Frank. 2012. In U.S., 46% Hold Creationist View of Human Origins. *Gallup.com*, June 1. http://www.gallup.com/poll/155003/Hold-Creationist-View-Human-Origins.aspx

Nunn, T. Percy. 1920. *Education: Its Data and First Principles*. London: Edward Arnold.

Obergefell et al. v. Hodges, Director, Ohio Department of Health, Et Al., 576 United States Reports—(Supreme Court of the United States 2015).

OECD. 2013. *PISA 2012 Results: Excellence Through Equity (Volume II)*. Paris: Organisation for Economic Co-operation and Development. http://www.oecd-ilibrary.org/content/book/9789264201132-en

———. 2014, February. *PISA 2012 Results: What Students Know and Can Do* (vol. I, Revised edn.). Paris: Organisation for Economic Co-operation and Development. http://www.oecd-ilibrary.org/content/book/9789264208780-en

O'Gorman, Josh. 2016. Lawmakers Talk School Choice and District Mergers. *Vermont Press Bureau*, April 7.

Oliver Brown, Mrs. Richard Lawton, Mrs. Sadie Emmanuel, et al. v. Board of Education of Topeka, 347 United States Reports 483 (Supreme Court of the United States 1954).

OneWheaton: A Community of Lesbian, Gay, Bisexual, Transgender, Queer, Questioning and Allied (LGBTQ&A) Alumni and Students of Wheaton College (Illinois). *OneWheaton*. http://www.onewheaton.com. Accessed 7 Nov 2015.

Overview of the Opportunity Education Tax Credit Program. *Pennsylvania Department of Education*, April 2015. http://www.education.pa.gov/Documents/K-12/Opportunity%20Scholarship%20Tax%20Credit%20Program/OSTCP%20Overview.pdf

Osborne, David. 2016, Summer. Denver Expands Choice and Charters: Elected School Board Employs Portfolio Strategy to Lift Achievement. *Education Next* 16(3). http://educationnext.org/denver-expands-choice-and-charters/

Owen, David. 1964. *English Philanthropy, 1660–1960*. Cambridge: Belknap Press.

Pangle, Thomas L. 1988. *The Spirit of Modern Republicanism: The Moral Vision of the American Founders and the Philosophy of Locke*. Chicago, IL: University of Chicago Press. https://catalyst.library.jhu.edu/catalog/bib_1092578

Pennings, Ray. 2011. *Cardus Education Survey*. Hamilton, ON: Cardus.

Peshkin, Alan. 1988. *God's Choice: The Total World of a Fundamentalist Christian School*. Chicago, IL: University of Chicago Press.

Peterson, Paul. 2015, Summer. CREDO Reveals Successful Charters' Secret Sauce. *Education Next*. http://educationnext.org/credo-reveals-successful-charters-secret-sauce/

Peterson, Paul E., Ludger Woessmann, Eric A. Hanushek, and Carlos X. Lastra-Anadon. 2011. Globally Challenged: Are U.S. Students Ready to Compete? The Latest on Each State's International Standing in Math and Reading. PEPG 11-03. Program on Education Policy and Governance, Harvard University, August 2011. http://www.eric.ed.gov/ERICWebPortal/detail?accno=ED526954

Petition: Douglas County School District, et al., v. Taxpayers for Public Education, et al., (Supreme Court of the United States 2015).

Petrilli, Mike. 2015. Top K-12 Education Policy People on Social Media 2015. Journal. *Education Next*, August 26. http://educationnext.org/top-k-12-education-policy-people-on-social-media-2015/

Petrilli, Michael J. 2016. The School Choice Moveement's Schisms, Explained. *The Flypaper*, January 27. http://edexcellence.net/articles/the-school-choice-movements-schisms-explained

Pew Research Center. 2015. A Portrait of American Orthodox Jews. *Pew Research Center's Religion & Public Life Project*, August 26. http://www.pewforum.org/2015/08/26/a-portrait-of-american-orthodox-jews/

Pierce v. Society of the Sisters of the Holy Names of Jesus and Mary, 268 United States Reports 510 (Supreme Court of the United States 1925).

Pinnock, Herbert. 2011. Gay and Lesbian Graduates to Make a Statement During Wheaton College's Alumni Event? *Christian Post*, October 7. http://www.christianpost.com/news/gay-and-lesbian-graduates-to-make-a-statement-during-wheaton-colleges-alumni-event-57635/

Pocock, J.G.A. (John Greville Agard). 1924–1989. *Politics, Language, and Time: Essays on Political Thought and History*. Chicago, IL: University of Chicago Press. https://catalyst.library.jhu.edu/catalog/bib_1205109

Polanyi, Michael. 1958. *Personal Knowledge; Towards a Post-Critical Philosophy*. Chicago, IL: University of Chicago Press.

Pope Leo XIII. 1981. Rerum Novarum: On Capital and Labor. Papal Encyclical. Vatican City, Italy, May 15. http://www.papalencyclicals.net/Leo13/l13rerum.htm

Postman, Neil. 1969. *Teaching as a Subversive Activity*. New York: Random House Digital, Inc.

Potter, Halley. 2015. Pathways to Smarter, Fairer Funding: Three Reports in Review. *Journal of School Choice* 9(2): 310–314.

Prothero, Stephen. 2007. *Religious Literacy: What Every American Needs to Know— And Doesn't*. New York: HarperCollins.

Prothero, Arianna. 2015. School Vouchers for All? Nevada Law Breaks New Ground. *Education Week—Charters & Choice*, June 4. http://blogs.edweek.org/edweek/charterschoice/2015/06/school_vouchers_nevada_law_breaks_new_ground.html?cmp=SOC-SHR-FB

Public School Revenue Sources. 2015. *Institute of Education Sciences: National Center for Education Statistics*, May 2015. http://nces.ed.gov/programs/coe/indicator_cma.asp

Putnam, Robert D., and David E. Campbell. 2012. *American Grace: How Religion Divides and Unites Us*. New York: Simon & Schuster.

Ravitch, Diane. 2001. *Left Back: A Century of Battles Over School Reform*. New York: Simon & Schuster.

———. 2015. Bernie and Hillary on Charters. Opinion. *Diane Ravitch's Blog*, October 1. http://dianeravitch.net/2015/10/01/bernie-and-hillary-on-charters/

Rawls, John. 1987. The Idea of an Overlapping Consensus. *Oxford Journal of Legal Studies* 7(1): 1–25. http://www.jstor.org/stable/764257

———. 1997. The Idea of Public Reason. In *Deliberative Democracy: Essays on Reason and Politics*, ed. James Bohman, and William Rehg, 93–145. Cambridge, MA: MIT Press.

Reckhow, Sarah. 2013. *Follow the Money: How Foundation Dollars Change Public School Politics*. New York: Oxford University Press.

Reed, Elaine Wrisley. 1998. A New Professionalism for Massachusetts Teachers: Six Constituencies at Work. *Journal of Education* 180(1): 79–88.

Reich, Rob. 2013. Equality, Adequacy, and K-12 Education. In *Education, Justice, and Democracy*, ed. Rob Reich, and Danielle Allen, 43–62. Chicago, IL: University of Chicago Press.

———. 2013. Not Very Giving. *The New York Times*, September 4, sec. Opinion. http://www.nytimes.com/2013/09/05/opinion/not-very-giving.html

Report of Inspectors of Research, Training and Equipment, January 26, 1925. IE. TPN.1.1. (1925–1928). The Percy Nunn Papers, University of London.

Reuben, Julie A. 1996. *The Making of the Modern University: Intellectual Transformation and the Marginalization of Morality*. Chicago, IL: University of Chicago Press.

Rich, Motoko. 2016. Teacher Tenure Is Challenged Again in a Minnesota Lawsuit. *The New York Times*, April 13. http://www.nytimes.com/2016/04/14/us/teacher-tenure-is-challenged-again-in-a-minnesota-lawsuit.html

Rose, Nikolas. 2003. Neurochemical Selves. *Society* 41(1): 46–59.

Rose v. Council for Better Education, Inc., 790 Kentucky Court of Justice 186 (Supreme Court of Kentucky 1989).

Roselli, Anthony M. 2005. Chapter 2: A Close Look at Reform in One State: The Massachusetts Experiment. *Counterpoints* 283: 23–40.

Rosenbaum, James, Caitlin Ahearn, Kelly Becker, and Janet Rosenbaum. 2015. *The New Forgotten Half and Research Directions to Support Them*. New York: William T. Grant Foundation.

Rosenberger v. Rector and Visitors of the University of Virginia, 515 United States Report 819 (Supreme Court of the United States 1995).

Rosin, Hanna. "Did Christianity Cause the Crash?" *The Atlantic*, December 2009. http://www.theatlantic.com/magazine/archive/2009/12/did-christianity-cause-the-crash/307764/.

Rotherham, Andrew J., and Richard Whitmire. 2014. De Blasio vs. Everyone Else. *Slate*, March 12. http://www.slate.com/articles/news_and_politics/education/2014/03/bill_de_blasio_vs_charter_schools_a_feud_in_new_york_city_has_broad_national.html

Roys, Julie. 2014. Wheaton College's Gay Celibate Counselor Says She Cannot Change Her Sexual Orientation. *ChristianHeadlines.com*, December 16. http://www.christianheadlines.com/news/wheaton-college-s-gay-celibate-counselor-says-she-cannot-change-her-sexual-orientation.html

Runyon v. McClary, 427 United States Reports 160 (Supreme Court of the United States 1976).

Sadler, Michael. 1908. *Moral Instruction and Training in Schools: Report of an International Inquiry.* London: Longmans, Green & Co.

Sahlberg, Pasi. 2012. *Finnish Lessons: What Can the World Learn from Educational Change in Finland? Unabridged.* Ashland, OR: Blackstone Audio Inc.

Sahm, Charles. 2015, Summer. What Explains Success at Success Academy? Charter Network Focuses on What Is Being Taught, and How. *Education Next* 15(3). http://educationnext.org/what-explains-success-academy-charter-network/

Saine, Harri. Religious Teaching in Finland. www.ortoweb.fi/religedsaine.htm. Accessed 1 Jun 2013.

Salisbury, David, and James Tooley. 2005. *What America Can Learn from School Choice in Other Countries.* Washington, DC: Cato Institute.

Sanandaji, Tino. 2014. Sweden Has an Education Crisis, But It Wasn't Caused by School Choice. *National Review*, July 21. http://www.nationalreview.com/agenda/383304/sweden-has-education-crisis-it-wasnt-caused-school-choice-tino-sanandaji

San Antonio Independent School District v. Rodriguez, 411 US 1 (1973) (Supreme Court of the United States 1973).

Sandel, Michael J. 1982. *Liberalism and the Limits of Justice.* Cambridge: Cambridge University Press.

Scafidi, Benjamin. 2012. The Fiscal Effects of School Choice Programs on Public School Districts. National Research. Friedman Foundation for Educational Choice. Available from: Foundation for Educational Choice. One American Square Suite 2420, Indianapolis, IN 46282. Tel: 317-681-0745; Fax: 317-681-0945; e-mail: info@edchoice.org; Web site: http://www.edchoice.org, March 2012. http://www.eric.ed.gov/ERICWebPortal/detail?accno=ED529881

Scaramanga, Jonny. 2014. Pseudoscience I Was Taught at a British Creationist School. *The Guardian*, September 25, sec. Science. http://www.theguardian.com/science/blog/2014/sep/25/pseudoscience-creationist-schools-uk-accelerated-christian-education-ace

Scholarship Tax Credits. 2014, April. National Conference of State Legislatures. http://www.ncsl.org/research/education/school-choice-scholarship-tax-credits.aspx

School Choice. Cato Institute. http://www.cato.org/research/school-choice. Accessed 23 Apr 2016.

School Choice Now: The Power of Educational Choice. *School Choice Yearbook.* Washington, DC: Alliance for School Choice, 2013. http://s3.amazonaws.com/assets.allianceforschoolchoice.com/admin_assets/uploads/167/School%20Choice%20Yearbook%202012-13.pdf

Schools, Pupils and Their Characteristics: January 2015—Publications—GOV.UK. https://www.gov.uk/government/statistics/schools-pupils-and-their-characteristics-january-2015. Accessed 15 Aug 2015.

Schulz, Wolfram, John Ainley, Julian Fraillon, David Kerr, Bruno Losito, and International Association for the Evaluation of Educational Achievement. 2010. *ICCS 2009 International Report: Civic Knowledge, Attitudes, and Engagement among Lower-Secondary School Students in 38 Countries.* International Association for the Evaluation of Educational Achievement. Herengracht 487, Amsterdam, 1017 BT, The Netherlands. Tel: +31-20-625-3625; Fax: +31-20-420-7136; e-mail: department@iea.nl; Web site: http://www.iea.nl

Schwartz, Robert B., and Jal D. Mehta. 2011. Finland: Superb Teachers—How to Get Them, How to Keep Them. In *Surpassing Shanghai: An Agenda for American Education Built on the World's Leading Systems*, ed. Marc Tucker, 51–78. Cambridge, MA: Harvard Education Press.

Searing, Pamela Johnston, and Donald Searing. 2000. A Political Socialization Perspective. In *Rediscovering the Democratic Purposes of Education*, ed. Lorraine McDonnell, 91–124. Lawrence, KS: University Press of Kansas.

Secretary-General of the OECD. 2003. *OECD Program for International Student Assessment 2003: Student Questionnaire*. Paris: Organisation for Economic Co-Operation and Development. http://nces.ed.gov/Surveys/PISA/pdf/quest_pisa_2003_student.pdf

———. 2013. *PISA 2012 Results: Excellence Through Equity: Giving Every Student the Chance to Succeed, Volume II*. Paris: Organisation for Economic Co-Operation and Development.

———. 2014. *PISA 2012 Results in Focus: What 15-Year-Olds Know and What They Can Do*. Paris: Organisation for Economic Co-Operation and Development. http://www.oecd.org/pisa/keyfindings/pisa-2012-results-overview.pdf

Seider, Scott. 2012. *Character Compass: How Powerful School Culture Can Point Students Toward Success*. Harvard Education Press.

Sen. Timothy Scott. 2015. Senator Tim Scott's Impassioned Speech on Behalf of School Choice. United States Senate, Washington, DC, July 18. http://edexcellence.net/articles/senator-tim-scott's-impassioned-speech-on-school-choice

Sewall, Gilbert T.A. n.d. Conflict of Visions: Multiculturalism and the Social Studies. In *Public Education in a Multicultural Society: Policy, Theory, Critique*, Cambridge Studies in Philosophy and Public Policy, 49–61. Cambridge, UK: Cambridge University Press.

Shapiro, Eliza. 2015. Facing Decline, Catholic Schools Form a Charter-like Network. *Capital*, July 20, sec. Policy. http://www.capitalnewyork.com/article/city-hall/2015/07/8572070/facing-decline-catholic-schools-form-charter-network

Short, Aaron, Matthew Abrahams, and Laura Italiano. 2015. Charter School Parents, Teachers, Students Rally in Albany. *New York Post*, March 4. http://nypost.com/2015/03/04/charter-school-parents-teachers-students-rally-in-albany/

Sikkink, David. 2015. The Public School Advantage: Why Public Schools Outperform Private Schools by Christopher A. Lubienski and Sarah Theule Lubienski. *Journal of School Choice* 9(1): 161–163. doi:10.1080/15582159.2014.1000784.

Sim, Jasmine B.-Y. 2011. Social Studies and Citizenship for Participation in Singapore: How One State Seeks to Influence Its Citizens. *Oxford Review of Education* 37(6): 743–761.

Sim, Jasmine B.-Y., and Murray Print. 2009. Citizenship Education in Singapore: Controlling or Empowering Teacher Understanding and Practice? *Oxford Review of Education* 35(6): 705–723.

Simon, Katherine G. 2001. *Moral Questions in the Classroom: How to Get Kids to Think Deeply about Real Life and Their Schoolwork*. New Haven: Yale University Press.

Simpson's Paradox Hides NAEP Gains (Again). *Education Next*. http://education-next.org/simpsons-paradox-hides-naep-gains/. Accessed 12 May 2015.

Skillen, James W. 2004. *In Pursuit of Justice: Christian-Democratic Explorations.* Lanham, MD: Rowman & Littlefield Publishers.

Sloan v. Lemon, 413 United States Reports 825 (Supreme Court of the United States 1973).

Smarick, Andy. 2012. *The Urban School System of the Future: Applying the Principles and Lessons of Chartering.* Lanham, MD: Rowman & Littlefield Publishers.

———. 2016. Laying the Foundations for the Next Decade of DC School Reform. *Flypaper at the Thomas B. Fordham Institute*, March 10. http://edexcellence.net/ articles/laying-the-foundation-for-the-next-decade-of-dc-reform?utm_ source=Fordham+Updates&utm_campaign=7d91f9bda3-20150313_ LateLateBell3_11_2016&utm_medium=email&utm_term=0_d9e8246adf- 7d91f9bda3-71557525&mc_cid=7d91f9bda3&mc_eid=cb4d7b26b3

Smarick, Andy, and Kelly Robson. 2016. Innovation in Catholic Education: New Approaches to Instruction and Governance May Revitalize the Sector. *Education Next*, March 29. http://educationnext.org/innovation-in-catholic-education- instruction-governance/

Smith, Christian. 2003. *The Secular Revolution: Power, Interests, and Conflict in the Secularization of American Public Life.* Berkeley: University of California Press.

Smith, Nelson. 2015. *Redefining the School District in America.* Washington, DC: Thomas B. Fordham Institute.

Smith, Henry. 2016. Review of Government Against Itself: Union Power and Its Consequences by Daniel DiSalvo. *The Journal of School Choice: International Research and Reform* 10(1): 132–133.

Socioeconomically Disadvantaged Students Who Are Academically Successful Examining Academic Resilience Cross-Nationally. Policy Brief. Amsterdam: International Association for the Evaluation of Educational Achievement, March 2015.

Spielberg, Ben. 2016. Friedrichs v. California Teachers Association: A Deceptive Attack on Organized Labor. *The Huffington Post*, January 4. http://www.huffingtonpost. com/ben-spielberg/friedrichs-v-california-t_b_8910396.html

Spiller, G. 1934. *The Ethical Movement in Great Britain: A Documentary History.* London: The Fairleigh Press.

Stanford University, and Center for Research on Education Outcomes. 2015. *Urban Charter School Study: Report on 41 Regions.* http://urbancharters.stanford.edu/ download/Urban%20Charter%20School%20Study%20Report%20on%2041%20 Regions.pdf

Statement on Sexual Identity—Policies|Wheaton College, June 15, 2011. http:// wheatoncollege.edu/policies/sxidentity/

Statistics About Non-Public Education in the United States. Information Analyses. Washington, DC: United States Department of Education, June 9, 2015. http:// www2.ed.gov/about/offices/list/oii/nonpublic/statistics.html

Stears, Marc, and Mathew Humphrey. 2012. Public Reason and Political Action: Justifying Citizen Behavior in Actually Existing Democracies. *The Review of Politics* 74(2): 285–306. http://www.jstor.org/stable/23263303

Steiner, David M. 2002. Review of Review of Moral and Political Education, Making Good Citizens: Education and Civil Society, by Stephen Macedo, Yael Tamir, Diane Ravitch, and Joseph P. Viteritti. *The Journal of Education* 183(1): 101–106. http:// www.jstor.org/stable/42742464

———. 2014. The New Common Core Assessments: How They Could Stop Patronizing Our Students. *The Huffington Post*, February 21. http://www.huffingtonpost.com/david-m-steiner/the-new-common-core-asses_b_4809973.html

Stergios, Jim. 2011. Testimony to the Texas Select Committee on State Sovereignty. *The Pioneer Institute*, April 14. http://pioneerinstitute.org/wp-content/uploads/dlm_uploads/TX_Stergios.pdf

Stewart, Thomas, and Patrick J. Wolf. 2014. *The School Choice Journey: School Vouchers and the Empowerment of Urban Families*. New York: Palgrave Macmillan.

Stotsky, Sandra. 2015. An-Empty-Curriculum-the-Need-to-Reform-Teacher-Licensing-Regulations-and-Tests. New York: Rowman & Littlefield. https://rowman.com/ISBN/9781475815689/

Strauss, Valerie. 2015. New York's Common Core Test Scores Flop Yet Again—with 20 Percent of Students Opting out. *The Washington Post*, August 13. http://www.washingtonpost.com/blogs/answer-sheet/wp/2015/08/13/n-y-common-core-test-scores-flop-yet-again/

———. 2015. The Weird Obsession in Congress with D.C. School Vouchers. *Washington Post*, October 15. https://www.washingtonpost.com/news/answer-sheet/wp/2015/10/15/the-weird-obsession-in-congress-with-d-c-school-vouchers/

Superfine, Benjamin Michael. 2013. *Equality in Education Law and Policy, 1954–2010*. New York: Cambridge University Press.

Taylor, Alison. 2001. *The Politics of Educational Reform in Alberta*. Toronto, ON: University of Toronto Press. http://site.ebrary.com/id/10218999

Teetsel, Eric. 2015. Wheaton College Counselor Resigns, Admits Support for Same-Sex Marriage. *Religious Write*, July 13. http://www.patheos.com/blogs/manhattanproject/2015/07/wheaton-college-counselor-resigns-admits-support-for-same-sex-marriage/

ten Dam, Geert, Femke Geijsel, Rene Reumerman, and Guuske Ledoux. 2011. Measuring Young People's Citizenship Competences. *European Journal of Education* 46(3): 354–372. doi:10.1111/j.1465-3435.2011.01485.x.

The Case Against Vouchers. 2015. Membership Organization. *The National Education Association*. http://www.nea.org/home/16378.htm

The Central Ohio Compact: A Regional Strategy for College Completion and Career Success. Organizational. Columbus, OH: Columbus State Community College and the Educational Service Center of Central Ohio, November 2012.

The Economist Snapshot. http://www.economist.com/node/21558265. Accessed 20 Jun 2015.

The Editorial Board. 2015. Massachusetts Takes on a Failing School District. *The New York Times*, June 17. http://www.nytimes.com/2015/06/17/opinion/massachusetts-takes-on-a-failing-school-district.html

The New Forgotten Half and Research Directions to Support Them. *The William T. Grant Foundation*, January 2015. http://wtgrantfoundation.org/newforgottenhalf#_

The People Fight Back. 1948. Citizens Committee on Civil Rights. http://www.kansasmemory.org/item/213389/page/1

The Training of Teachers: Memorandum Drawn up by the Joint Standing Committee of the Training College Association and Council of Principals, Confidential to Members of the TCA and Council of Principals, 1938. Pri/1/3/18, "Principal"s

Correspondence', (1938), St Mary's Training College Archives, St Mary's, Twickenham.

Thiessen, Elmer John. 1993. *Teaching for Commitment: Liberal Education, Indoctrination, and Christian Nurture.* Montreal, QC: McGill-Queen's University Press.

Thro, William. 2009. Judicial Humility: The Enduring Legacy of Rose v. Council for Better Education. Presented at the Prepared for "Rose at 20: The Past and Future of School Finance Litigation," Louisville, KY, October 21. http://law-apache.uky.edu/wordpress/wp-content/uploads/2012/06/Thro-II.pdf

Tooley, James. 2001. If India Can, Why Can't We? *The New Statesman*, September 10.

———. 2009. *The Beautiful Tree: A Personal Journey into How the World's Poorest People Are Educating Themselves.* 1st edn. Washington, DC: Cato Institute.

TPPF Releases 'Avoiding Government Regulation: Why Parental School Choice Is Possible Without Destructive Control of Private Schools.' http://www.texaspolicy.com/press_release/detail/tppf-releases-avoiding-government-regulation-why-parental-school-choice-is-possible-without-destructive-control-of-private-schools. Accessed 24 Apr 2016.

Tuition Affordability. OU Advocacy Center, Current. http://advocacy.ou.org/issues/tuition-crisis/

Tyack, David B., and Larry Cuban. 1995. *Tinkering Toward Utopia: A Century of Public School Reform.* Cambridge, MA: Harvard University Press.

United Nations. 1966. International Covenant on Economic, Social and Cultural Rights. Human Rights Office of the High Commissioner, December 16. http://www.ohchr.org/EN/ProfessionalInterest/Pages/CESCR.aspx

United States Department of Education. 2009. The NCES Fast Facts Tool Provides Quick Answers to Many Education Questions (National Center for Education Statistics). *National Center for Education Statistics.* https://nces.ed.gov/fastfacts/display.asp?id=6

———. 2015. The Condition of Education at a Glance. *National Center for Education Statistics.* https://nces.ed.gov/programs/coe/ataglance.asp

van den Haag, Ernest. 1961. Social Science Testimony in the Desegregation Cases—A Reply to Professor Kenneth Clark. *Villanova Law Review* 6: 69. http://heinonline.org/HOL/Page?handle=hein.journals/vllalr6&id=77&div=10&collection=journals

Vickers, Lucy. 2011. Religious Discrimination and Schools: The Employment of Teachers and the Public Sector Duty. In *Law, Religious Freedoms and Education in Europe*, ed. Myriam Hunter-Hénin. Burlington, VT: Ashgate Publication.

Villavicencio, Adriana, and William Marinell. 2014, July. *Inside Success: Strategies of 25 Successful High Schools.* New York: Research Alliance for New York City Schools.

Viteritti, J.P. 2003. Reading Zelman: The Triumph of Pluralism, and Its Effects on Liberty, Equality, and Choice. *Southern California Law Review* 76: 1105–1188.

Walsh, Kate. 2016. Are Textbooks Behind Teachers' Steep Learning Curve in the Classroom? Policy Institute. *The Brown Center Chalkboard*, January 19. http://www.brookings.edu/blogs/brown-center-chalkboard/posts/2016/01/19-textbooks-behind-teachers-learning-curve-classroom-walsh

Walz v. Tax Commission of the City of New York, 397 United States Reports 664 (Supreme Court of the United States 1970).

Weatherbe, Steve. 2011. Canadian Parents Battle Pro-Homosexual Public Schools. *National Catholic Register*, August 12. http://www.ncregister.com/daily-news/canadian-parents-battle-pro-homosexual-public-schools/

Weigle, Marcia A., and Jim Butterfield. 1992. Civil Society in Reforming Communist Regimes: The Logic of Emergence. *Comparative Politics* 25(1): 1–23. doi:10.2307/422094.

Weinberg, Lawrence D. 2007. *Religious Charter Schools: Legalities and Practicalities (PB)*. Charlotte, NC: Information Age Publishing.

West, Martin. 2012. Education and Global Competitiveness. In *Rethinking Competitiveness*, ed. K. Hassett, 68–94. Washington, DC: American Enterprise Institute Press.

West Virginia State Board of Education v. Barnette, 319 United States Reports 624 (Supreme Court of the United States 1943).

What Is Heteronormativity?|GEA—Gender and Education Association. http://www.genderandeducation.com/issues/what-is-heteronormativity/. Accessed 10 Oct 2015.

What Is Heteronormativity and How Is It Damaging? *About.com News & Issues.* http://civilliberty.about.com/od/gendersexuality/g/heteronormative.htm. Accessed 10 Oct 2015.

What Transgender Looks Like in Pop Culture. *US News & World Report.* http://www.usnews.com/news/articles/2014/06/06/laverne-cox-and-the-state-of-trans-representation-in-pop-culture. Accessed 10 Oct 2015.

Whitehurst, Grover. 2009, October. *Don't Forget Curriculum.* Brown Center Letters on Education. Washington, DC: Brookings.

Widmar v. Vincent, 454 US 263 United States Report (Supreme Court of the United States 1981).

Wiggins, Ovetta. 2016. After 10-Year Fight, Maryland Lawmakers Vote to Fund Private-School Scholarships. *The Washington Post*, March 29.

Wilson, Glen Y. 2000, August 1. Effects on Funding Equity of the Arizona Tax Credit Law. *Education Policy Analysis Archives* 8: 38. doi:10.14507/epaa.v8n38.2000.

———. 2002, March. *The Equity Impact of Arizona's Tax Credit Program: A Review of the First Three Years (1998–2000)*. Research Report. Tempe, AZ: Arizona State University. http://epsl.asu.edu/epru/documents/EPRU%202002-110/epru-0203-110.htm

Witt, Robert, and Jean Orvis. 2010. *A 21st Century Imperative: A Guide to Becoming a School of the Future.* NAIS Commission on Accreditation. Washington, DC: National Association of Independent Schools.

Witte, John. 2005. *Religion and the American Constitutional Experiment.* 2nd edn. Boulder, CO: Westview Press.

Witte, John Jr., and Joel A. Nichols. 2016. *Religion and the American Constitutional Experiment.* 4th edn. Oxford and New York: Oxford University Press.

Witters v. Washington Department of Services for the Blind, 474 United States Reports 481 (Supreme Court of the United States 1986).

Wolf, Patrick J. 2007. Civics Exam: Schools of Choice Boost Civic Values. *Education Next* 7(3): 67–72. http://www.eric.ed.gov/ERICWebPortal/detail?accno=EJ767503

Wolf, Patrick J., and Brian Kisida. 2010. School Governance and Information: Does Choice Lead to Better-Informed Parents? *American Politics Research* 38(5): 783–805.

Wolf, Patrick J., and Stephen Macedo. 2004. Educating Citizens: International Perspectives on Civic Values and School Choice. Brookings Institution Press. 1775 Massachusetts Avenue NW, Washington, DC 20036. Tel: 202-797-6000;

Fax: 202-797-6004; e-mail: webmaster@brookings.edu; Web site: http://www. brookings.edu/index/publications.htm, http://www.eric.ed.gov/ERICWeb Portal/detail?accno=ED493327

Wolf, Patrick J., and Thomas Stewart. 2011. The Evolution of Parental School Choice. In *Customized Schooling: Beyond Whole-School Reform*, ed. Frederick Hess, and Bruno V. Manno, 91–105. Cambridge, MA: Harvard Education Press.

Wolfe, Alan. 1997. Is Civil Society Obsolete?: Revisiting Predictions of the Decline of Civil Society in Whose Keeper? *The Brookings Institution*, Fall. http://www.brookings.edu/research/articles/1997/09/fall-civilsociety-wolfe

Wolman v. Walters 433 U.S. 229 (1977), 433 United States Reports 229 (Supreme Court of the United States 1977).

Wood, Peter. 2011. The Core Between the States. *The Chronicle of Higher Education*, May 23.

Wooldridge, Adrian. 1994. *Measuring the Mind: Education and Psychology in England, C. 1860–C. 1990*. Cambridge, UK: Cambridge University Press.

Wright-Carozza, Paolo. 2003. Subsidiarity as a Structural Principle of International Human Rights Law. *American Journal of International Law* 971(2003): 38–79.

Xiang, Yun, and Beth Tarasawa. 2015. Propensity Score Stratification Using Multilevel Models to Examine Charter School Achievement Effects. *The Journal of School Choice: International Research and Reform* 9(2): 179–196.

Youniss, James. 2000. How to Enrich Civic Education and Sustain Democracy. In *Making Civics Count: Citizenship Education for a New Generation*, ed. David Campbell, Meira Levinson, and Frederick Hess, 116–140. Cambridge: Harvard University Press.

Zelman v. Simmons-Harris, 536 United States Reports 639 (Supreme Court of the United States 2002).

Zorach v. Clauson, 343 United States Reports 306 (Supreme Court of the United States 1952).

INDEX

© The Author(s) 2017
A.R. Berner, *Pluralism and American Public Education*,
DOI 10.1057/978-1-137-50224-7

Made in the USA
Middletown, DE
09 December 2016